From the Durham Molesdales

Love to Nelle !

SOUTHERN LITERARY STUDIES
FRED HOBSON, EDITOR

LEE SMITH, ANNIE DILLARD,
and the HOLLINS GROUP

Lee Smith, Annie Dillard, and the Hollins Group

A Genesis of Writers

NANCY C. PARRISH

LOUISIANA STATE UNIVERSITY PRESS *Baton Rouge*

Designer: Barbara Neely Bourgoyne
Typeface: Cochin and Adobe Caslon
Typesetter: Wilsted & Taylor Publishing Services
Printer and binder: Thomson-Shore, Inc.

Library of Congress Cataloging-in-Publication Data:

Parrish, Nancy C., 1952–
    Lee Smith, Annie Dillard, and the Hollins Group : a genesis of
writers / Nancy C. Parrish.
        p.   cm. — (Southern literary studies)
    Includes bibliographical references (p.   ) and index.
    ISBN 0-8071-2243-2 (alk. paper)
    1. American literature—Virginia—Hollins—History and criticism.
    2. Women and literature—Virginia—Hollins—History—20th century.
    3. Women and literature—Southern States—History—20th century.
    4. American literature—Women authors—History and criticism.
    5. American literature—20th century—History and criticism.
    6. Smith, Lee—Criticism and interpretation.   7. Dillard,
    Annie—Criticism and interpretation.   8. Women—Southern States—
    Intellectual life.   9. Rubin, Louis Decimus, 1923– —Influence.
    10. Hollins (Va.)—Intellectual life.   11. Hollins College—History.
    I. Title   II. Series.
    PS267.H65P37   1998
    810.9'9287'09755792—dc21   97-32630
                                                                CIP

CONTENTS

PHOTOGRAPHS

All photos courtesy of Hollins College

PREFACE

The particular line of inquiry that drew me to this subject was the writing of Lee Smith, the contemporary Appalachian writer whose animated, humane fiction has been honored with two O. Henry Awards, the John Dos Passos Award for Fiction, the Robert Penn Warren Prize for Fiction, and the Lila Wallace Award. I first interviewed Smith in the summer of 1990, and during the course of our conversations was impressed by the extraordinary credit she gave to her classmates and mentors at Hollins College in Virginia as formative influences on her writing career. Curiosity about that fervent praise soon sent me to the Roanoke college to research Smith's collegiate records and writings in the archives, and there I discovered for myself the evidence of a remarkable writing environment that formed at Hollins College during the 1960s. So rich and complex was this evidence that it radically expanded the scope of my study. Resolving that I was only temporarily setting aside that book-length study of Smith, I began an investigation that led me not only through Smith's apprentice writing but, unexpectedly, into a cultural study of the creation of one particular writing community that has been exceptionally effective in nurturing women writers into successful publication.

More than a century of stereotyping has dismissed southern women's colleges such as Hollins as finishing schools with professors more mannerly than motivated and students more intent on weddings than on writings. The records at Hollins quickly disproved that conventional wisdom. A single class—the class of 1967—had included not only Lee Smith but Pulitzer Prize–winning writer Annie Dillard and literary scholars Anne Goodwyn Jones and Lucinda Hardwick MacKethan. In fact, I soon discovered that the contemporary literary scene—and the renaissance of southern literary studies in particular—has been significantly shaped by the cluster of writers who wrote, studied, and gamboled together at Hollins during the 1960s. Intriguing questions immediately arose: Were there particular social, political, and educational circumstances that gathered these writers? What ideas shaped their apprentice writing? To what extent is that apprentice work evident in the mature writing for which they are now known? How did tiny Hollins come to have on its English faculty Louis Rubin, a scholar who has been a most significant and sometimes enigmatic figure in southern literary studies? The sustained and exceptional success of this group of writers argued most powerfully for a close study of the environment they all credit so highly. To that end, I read student writing at Hollins from its earliest records in the mid-nineteenth century through the 1960s; investigated the pages of faculty minutes and alumnae magazines; surveyed individual and collective histories of women's colleges; and interviewed Hollins faculty and students to identify and explore those factors that seemed most helpful to the writers in the Hollins class of 1967.

I have intentionally brought many perspectives to bear on the material I have studied, and so brief comments concerning the structure are in order. The first chapter is intended to review how the higher education of women evolved in this country, particularly in a southern state such as Virginia. In particular, I examine how traditional, paternalistic attitudes about women and their roles shaped the nature and rate of the evolution of women's higher education. Paradoxically, the benign paternal impulses that established women's colleges would ultimately be undermined by the institutions they inspired. Hollins College is an excellent case study because its growth has been typical of that experienced by other private women's colleges; it is intriguing because its achievement has been so exceptional. The second chapter analyzes how and why the traditional ideas about women's higher education would come under siege during the 1960s. A strikingly new national phenomenon—writing programs inspired by the New Critical literary establishment—proved to be a significant factor in aiding undergraduates and alumnae in the successful publication of their writing. At Hollins, both writing program and guide to publication were embodied in the person of Louis D. Rubin, Jr., a tireless advocate for Hollins writers and, as time evolved, an influential figure in his own right in the area of southern literary studies.

The third chapter focuses on the issue in feminist theory of how a women's community operates. Is it, as many advocates suggest, primarily collaborative and cooperative or, as Elizabeth Fox-Genovese and others argue, less sentimental and far more competitive? By looking at the history of Hollins and the interaction of the Hollins Group in particular, we gain some insights into what has been a successful blend in one women's community. The final two chapters examine even more closely the early lives and apprentice work of Annie Dillard and Lee Smith. These chapters show the relative weight of feminist issues in the lives and writings of these women and attempt to show how their apprentice writing in a women's college community offers insights into some of their later published works. The afterword provides a final analysis of the evidence presented.

Many colleges can claim individual outstanding writers among their alumnae; Hollins can even boast of three Pulitzer Prize–winning writers. But perhaps more vital to the world of letters than a list of achievements is an understanding of what made high achievement possible for a group of women writers. In examining the history of Hollins, the influence of significant mentors in the 1960s, and the writers themselves in the class of 1967, we have a remarkable opportunity to learn how one women's writing community coalesced, evolved, succeeded, and persisted.

ACKNOWLEDGMENTS

In working on this book, I have acquired a mass of indebtedness that I can never hope to repay. To a great extent I owe the discovery of my topic to Lee Smith, whose books inspired my interest. Lee has given me an extraordinary amount of her time, has encouraged me with letters, and has paid me the honor that she first found herself in her teachers and peers at Hollins: the compliment of taking my work seriously. The words of Katie Cocker in *The Devil's Dream* seem to express Smith's own attitude: "No matter how big I get, I will always remember this moment. I will always try to be nice to the kids coming up in this business and treat them decent, not like Dawn Chapel did me. It's a great feeling to help another artist who's really struggling as a newcomer. And I know what it means to a new artist for someone else to just speak up for them a little bit." My interview with Smith led me to Hollins, where I discovered firsthand the generosity of the faculty. Though I was a stranger without an appointment, John Allen took me into his office and sketched a brief history of the time period in which I was interested. He sent me to Fishburn Library, where I met head librarian Richard Kirkwood, who quickly introduced me to the current archivist, Anna Kirkwood. To her I owe a great debt. She would patiently climb up and down the two stories to the archive storage to retrieve for me any information, no matter how small. She suggested sources that I couldn't have discovered on my own; she enlisted the help of other administrators on campus. Thanks also to Beth St. Cyr and Diane Graves for helping me to recheck sources in the archives, to Beth Harris and Denise Walker for securing permissions, and to Linda Steele, Denise Bryson, and the Hollins Information Office for their assistance in securing photographs. Richard H. W. Dillard took time from his sabbatical to come to campus and answer questions about his former students and colleagues. It was he who first told me about *Beanstalks;* and when I discovered that Fishburn Library had no copy of the magazine, he delved into his own records and sent me a photocopy for my use.

My research soon brought me again to Algonquin Books in Chapel Hill, where I met Louis D. Rubin, Jr. He was completely free with his time and open to all of my questions. He introduced me to Shannon Ravenel, editor at Algonquin and a Hollins graduate who has herself made important contributions to the growth and encouragement of new southern writers. Kind and helpful, too, were Bob Anthony, Alice Cotter, and Jeff Dix, the librarians in the North Carolina Collection, Wilson Library, at the University of North Carolina in Chapel Hill.

I have been particularly touched at how generous have been the Hollins graduates whom I have interviewed. Few people could have greater demands on their time. Annie Dillard, fresh back from a polar expedition and having just completed another book, not only answered my questions but helpfully criticized some of my strategy. She made her continued assistance only a phone call away. Lucinda Hardwick MacKethan, amid her papers, writings, and teaching at the University of North Carolina, took time at night to talk with me about my project. Jo Berson Buckley, Nancy Beckham Ferris, and Anne Goodwyn Jones were generous both with time and insights.

I am grateful, too, for the people who have given me the opportunity to test my ideas with conference papers. I presented early thoughts about Lee Smith's work at the Harvard Graduate Conference on American Studies and Its Sources, the Southern Modern Language Association/Southern American Studies Association Conference, the Tenth Annual Southern Writers' Symposium, and the Popular Culture Association of the South Conference. Peggy Whitman Prenshaw welcomed my work for review at *Southern Quarterly* and has kindly encouraged my continued efforts. Elizabeth Fox-Genovese graciously shared her time and advice to make certain issues about her work clear to me. Jerry Williamson of *Appalachian Journal* helped me through the refinements necessary for making my interview of Lee Smith a useful scholarly contribution. I am grateful to Louisiana State University Press and editor Gerry Anders for their help in publishing this book, and to copyeditor Nancy Riddiough.

I would give special thanks to the Commonwealth Center for the Study of American Culture at the College of William and Mary for the financial support they provided for my research and papers. The administration and English department at Lynchburg College were extraordinarily supportive of me. They financed my travel to the History of Education Conference in Boston, where I presented a paper on the history of Hollins; they also funded my presentation on the Hollins Group at the Modern Language Association Conference in New York. Bob Gross, Susan Donaldson, and Cam Walker read drafts of numerous papers and always gave me feedback that was useful. Bev Peterson and Sarah Bird Wright not only helped me with my work but guided me with advice on conferences and publishing.

Friends such as Kathleen Cahall and Loren Graham have believed in my success long before I could. More like family than friends have been Trisha, Don, Joshua, and Katie Hines; Christi Lewis; and Martha Moss. I take very special pleasure in thanking them.

I have been supported throughout this lengthy work by my family. I can only name them here because any full accounting of the meals, phone calls, and conversations they have offered on my behalf would require a book in its own right. They have my love, respect, and gratitude: my parents, Rebecca and Eddie Parrish Jr.; Glenna, Ed, Catherine, and Blanton Parrish; Sara and Ronnie Reed. Sally, Steve, Sarah, David, Rebecca, and Joseph Southall are especially dear for feeding me, cheering me, and giving me space to work. Eileen Ford has been a constant support to me; she knows her worth.

LEE SMITH, ANNIE DILLARD,
and the HOLLINS GROUP

INTRODUCTION

$\mathcal{D}$uring a 1990 interview, while attempting to describe her development as a writer, Lee Smith arrived at an intriguing image for what she considered to be a significant period in her literary growth. She observed, "There are these points in your life that are pivotal, and a lot depends on who you happen to run into at those points. . . . I went to Hollins. So it was like falling into a womb. It was very wonderful and supportive and there were all these other people who had the same passions that I had." The general intent of Smith's words seems fairly straightforward and clear: at Hollins she found support, kindred spirits, a turning point. And yet the image she chose for summarizing and incorporating her meaning is one that has, in contemporary politics and literary scholarship, become potent enough to invite greater attention. If we ever considered the womb to be a quiet incubation chamber peacefully nurturing a child, we were mistaken in fact and in metaphor. Far from being quiet, the womb has always been the site of dynamic, incredibly complex creative growth: the womb literally senses the direct impact of sounds, chemicals, and other physical sensations affecting a woman's body. Far from being complete like a loaf of baked bread, a newborn child has only begun the process that will bring her to maturity. Hardly settled, in fact, is even the most fundamental legal issue concerning the ownership of the womb: is it—as pro-choice advocates argue—the property of the woman or, rather—as anti-abortionists claim—the ward of the government? Not surprisingly, then, the metaphorical significance of the womb remains an equally contested matter: Is the womb a symbol of nurture or an indicator of regression? Is it bad form for scholars to be "essentialist" yet good criticism to validate the "blank page" of the womb as an alternative to the metaphorical penis, the pen?[1]

I pose these points as a way of suggesting that, by calling Hollins a womb, Smith has left us with a most thought-provoking metaphor that evokes not just the supportive intellectual climate of Hollins College in the 1960s but the historical controversies concerning the nature of women's higher education in this country. In a sense, women's higher education has always been a creative, contested cultural ground, what Victor Turner might term an ambiguous threshold where a person is caught "betwixt and between" the traditional positions assigned by custom and convention.[2] The evolution of the educational system for American women has indeed been a chronicle of women caught between professional aspirations and conventional social roles. What then becomes intriguing to study are the ways women have often found to successfully exploit the gaps created by the liminal state of their education system. One means for exploiting that gap and establishing high intellectual standards for women was found in the nineteenth-century cultural movement of professionalism. A phenomenon of the middle class, professionalism seemed to offer the opportunity for improving one's class status by establishing intelligence rather than family inheritance as the criterion for assessing social worth. Women's colleges clearly benefited from the notion that objective standards determined competence in American life. Seizing upon the opportunity to enter into nationally competitive accreditation, they successfully exploited the culture of professionalism in order to overcome cultural restrictions on women's higher education. This subversion of traditional class and gender distinctions created the possibility for shifting leadership training and responsibility to women themselves. As many scholars have observed, holding positions of authority in campus organizations is one of the historical opportunities of women's colleges and was an experience that, in all

    1. Nancy C. Parrish, "Interview: Lee Smith," *Appalachian Journal* 19 (1992): 400; Sandra Gilbert and Susan Gubar set up this metaphorical opposition in *The Madwoman in the Attic: The Woman Writer and the Nineteenth-Century Literary Imagination* (New Haven, 1979), 3–44.
    2. Victor W. Turner, *The Ritual Process: Structure and Anti-Structure* (Chicago, 1969), 95.

likelihood, would not come to their sisters who attended coordinate or coeducational colleges.

Interestingly, for financial and cultural reasons, northern women's colleges such as the Seven Sisters tended to capitalize more fully on that potential decades earlier than did their southern sisters. Paternalism in the formation of southern women's colleges had a distinctive shape, scholar Anne Goodwyn Jones (Hollins '67) argues: strictures concerning idealized white southern womanhood have been particularly enduring because that tradition was so crucial to the South's self-definition.[3] Consequently, the education of southern women such as those at Hollins has remained profoundly shaped by regional ideas about gender and economics. To highlight that regional difference in women's education, I use the case of Hollins for contrasting certain aspects of its development with those of the Seven Sisters colleges while showing their typicality among other nearby women's colleges. The case of Hollins shows both why that progress was slower in the South and how, in the middle of the twentieth century, one southern women's college suddenly proved able to develop a nationally competitive writing program that produced writers such as Lee Smith and Annie Dillard.

Hollins not only is representative of the staggered timetable in women's higher education, but it offers an instructive insight into how a successful and prolific group of writers established their literary roots. In the 1960s, Hollins was not simply a warm and protected place in which to mature, but a place in which fiercely competitive women tested themselves against their peers, their mentors, their culture, and their own prior self-definitions. For Smith and her peers, the years at Hollins were an active and complex gestation period for their themes and writing. And it does not belabor the metaphor to observe a further parallel: that the writing environment at Hollins proved so fertile that Hollins women have, in impressive numbers, been empowered to make striking contributions to the contemporary literary world. My research has persuaded me of how precisely this last point completes the analogy. Hollins-as-womb was a creative starting point: out of this boisterous and challenging writing environment has emerged a long line of women who have molded writing careers by their own visions and made striking contributions to the contemporary literary world, all while maintaining the critical and congenial

3. Anne Goodwyn Jones, *Tomorrow Is Another Day: The Woman Writer in the South, 1859–1936* (Baton Rouge, 1981), 4.

ties formed while at Hollins. Because such a high level of achievement in writing careers was disproportionate to any traditional expectations for a small Southern women's college, Hollins makes a compelling claim on our intellectual interests.

The assembling of a talented group of women was not entirely coinciden-tal. The writing program at Hollins was clearly given its initial strength by Louis D. Rubin, Jr., who has subsequently become a prominent scholar and editor in the field of southern literary studies. In essence, Rubin brought na-tional recognition to Hollins' writing program: he brokered the terms of how the program was funded and designed; he actively sought young writers; he energetically sought publication of his own work as well as the work of others; and he offered or oversaw the instruction of all creative writing students. The design of the program attracted dedicated faculty members and an exciting program of visiting writers. Rubin's personal commitment to his students and his ability to learn from them proved to be of great importance to the young women. Lee Smith, Annie Dillard, Lucinda Hardwick MacKethan, and others credit Rubin as vital in encouraging them to go on with their writ-ing. Rubin not only supported the students but actively fostered their profes-sional growth by bringing them in close and constant contact with successful professional writers and publishers.

In a sense, the Hollins writing program of the 1960s was a test of the extent to which male mentors can transcend paternalism and foster the achievement and autonomy of female students. Central in changing the traditional model of familial relations on the campus were the women in the class of 1967, the women of what I have called the Hollins Group. These writers essentially re-defined the familial atmosphere they found at Hollins, adjusting their roles from daughters in a tightly knit family to supportive sisters in a highly com-petitive academic community. They were talented, ambitious young women, who were able to seize upon the educational opportunities of the college at a moment when Hollins, and the writing program in particular, aspired to na-tional academic excellence. Focusing especially on the figures Lucinda Hard-wick MacKethan and Anne Goodwyn Jones, I describe the nature and evoke the liminal state of this community by documenting the women's experiences together, excerpting their published writing produced during those years, and analyzing the nature of the community formation that resulted from these activities. These women forged a collective identity by joining to face common obstacles and developed a strong sense of individual identity through competition with each other. Hollins was a place where these women explored their ideas, tested their writing, and established some significant relationships that would evolve as their adult writing developed. Later, as professional writers, these women have continued to offer one another criticism and support. Certainly, reading each other's writing and accepting each other's work for publication suggests a womblike security; but, in fact, these women often felt intensely competitive with each other. This apparent need for both competition and cooperation as spurs to creativity suggests that women's communities may not be—and perhaps should not be—the entirely blissful havens sometimes romanticized in feminist literature.

Finally, I single out for close study the early years and apprentice writing of the two best-known members of the Hollins Group, Annie Doak Dillard and Lee Smith. Though these women have taken different directions in their writing careers, their apprentice work shares a common theme: the struggle of each of these women to define herself in her own terms. Both the Doak and Smith families wanted their rebellious daughters to obtain educations at southern women's colleges, partly to restrain their individualistic natures. Both young women were hostile to the constraints imposed by the college over their lives. Yet both women, despite their impatience with constraint, lived up to expectations: Doak married even before graduation, and Smith turned down a fellowship in order to marry and raise a family. Hence, we see the contradictory character of this southern women's college: it heightened and disciplined the two writers' intellectual ambitions, while it channeled them into conventional roles. In the modest counterculture that was the Hollins writing program, these women found an intellectual alternative to the social pressures on young women at a southern college. It was a place where they could be temporarily free from the demand for conformity, identify the issues that concerned them, and search for their voices. Dillard experimented both with liminal subject matter and an unsettled persona; Smith worked with multiple narrators and more overtly feminist subject matter. The instruction, competition, and collaboration of their writing community worked powerfully to nurture them as part of a new generation of talented and independent women writers.

As Lee Smith has observed, there are points in a person's life that are pivotal; and yet women have not always enjoyed a historical record of positive self-defining moments in the lives of women. Without such histories, women lack the alternative models that could be most useful in helping them with their own self-definitions. The particular contribution of this research is that it documents the circumstances that contributed to the positive self-definition of an important group of women writers. The case of Hollins College shows that successful women's writing communities are rarely the product of mere chance; rather, they represent the product of enlightened cultural forces combined with individuals of inspired talent. It is an equation we must learn if we are to continue to strengthen and expand American literature and culture. It is time we gained a more complex understanding of what a womb-like writing community for women might be.

1

SOUTHERN STEPSISTERS
The Higher Education of Women at Hollins College

*H*ollins College is a small private institution for women, nestled in the foothills of the Blue Ridge Mountains in western Virginia. Its brick academic buildings and dormitories, mellowed with age and use, cluster around a small central quad framed by tall shade trees; an old farmhouse and silo are backdrops for the athletic fields. Tucked between an interstate highway on one side and a strip of gasoline stations and restaurants on the other, the campus is a tiny oasis easily overlooked by the casual traveler. Even a brief tour of the school would confirm that its enrollment is small. In fact, the entire student body of the college still numbers fewer members than many urban high schools. Little in a cursory tour of the school would readily reveal the influence that its alumnae have exerted in the contemporary world of American writing and publication. During the 1960s, Hollins placed an astonishing number of its English graduates in influential positions in the nation's publishing industry. New young editors from Hollins included Shannon Ravenel and Beverly Holmes at Houghton Mifflin, Ellen Hainline at Harper & Row, Lynn Tuach at *Reader's Digest,* Mimi Ridenhour at *Vogue,* Pam Fish at Random House, Suzanne Trazoff at Bantam, Laura Johnson at Bobbs-Merrill, Peggy MacDonnell Treadwell at *Redbook,* Carol Kinsey at *Seventeen,* Kathy Hershey at Louisiana State University Press, Frances Shin-

Hollins College campus, spring

nick at *Southern Engineering*, and Betty Kelly at Holt, Rinehart and Winston. Anna Sevier published a novel, master's graduate Sylvia Wilkinson published two, and Katie Letcher Lyle's poems appeared in several small collections. For the size of the school, the English program was prodigious: an average of nearly one-eighth of the entire student body were English majors. In one year, 1967, the percentage was even larger: of the 182-member senior class, 35 were English majors, one of whom had already been published professionally and another of whom had a professional book contract in hand. The first of these two women, Annie Doak Dillard, would win the Pulitzer Prize within seven years; the second, Lee Smith, would garner, among other awards, two O. Henry Awards and the Robert Penn Warren Award. Such a high level of achievement in a small private women's college within such a short span of years was all the more remarkable because, though a community of women writers had been strong and tenacious throughout the institution's history, the Hollins record of success in publishing and writing had been irregular at best.

What conditions had changed to foster this achievement? The answers to this question lie in intriguing cultural and intellectual influences that, over time, laid the groundwork for these women to become the highly successful and influential editors, publishers, reporters, scholars, and writers that they are. Most important has been the evolution of, and responses to, women's higher education in this country. Like most women's colleges, Hollins had always been an institution torn between familial ideals about women's domestic roles and high intellectual standards derived from professional aspirations. In this sense and in the broad context of women's higher education in this country, Hollins' history was more representative than remarkable. But what we learn in focusing on the specific case history of Hollins is the *way* in which the foundation for intellectual opportunity was established for an insistent group of young women in the class of 1967 who asserted themselves as self-confident thinkers and writers: we can learn specifically how change was brought about. At heart, the history of Hollins shows how the success of women's colleges derived from a paradoxical fact: that the high academic standards of women's colleges ultimately worked to undermine the paternalistic cultural restrictions that initially defined the schools.

From colonial times, the education of women in the South had never received the support that it had in the Northeast. There, some initial support for women's education had been based on the Puritan opinion that a sufficient level of education was necessary, even for women, so they could study the Bible as part of their self-examination for sinfulness. But no southern Anne Hutchinson made powerful and disturbing proclamations of the "inner light," asserting that God could indeed inspire the minds of women and men alike. More typical was the opinion in both the North and the South of pragmatists who supported women's higher education as a necessary means for instructing young citizens, the prospective franchised males of the republic. As historian Barbara Solomon notes, little changed in the "dialectic between women's demands for education and the opposition they encountered [until] . . . education became institutionalized at many levels."[1] Still, these early institutions of learning for women reflected regional perspectives on gender.

The northeastern women's schools have drawn special attention from historians, as though they in some way set the standard for all academies; but, in fact, academies and seminaries proliferated in various incarnations all around the country. Far from being the standard for academies, the northeastern schools reflected the unique Puritan legacy of a high literacy

---

1. Barbara Solomon, *In the Company of Educated Women: A History of Women and Higher Education in America* (New Haven, 1985), 14.

rate among women. Susan Coultrap-McQuin records that by the mid-eighteenth century half of all white women in the American colonies were literate; but that statistic is actually misleading since included in that percentage were New England women, who were nearly universally literate. Furthermore, support for the northeastern seminaries was strengthened because the almost universal literacy of New Englanders necessitated a movement toward public schools and an "expanding demand for low-paid, female teachers." Matthew Vassar would later claim that the crucial need his college filled was "to make women better teachers." The support and high requirements of the institutions to train them were far more justified in the North than in the South.[2]

Little changed in the academy system until the mid-nineteenth century when, as Burton Bledstein argues, the middle class in America seemed to develop a self-definition based on "three characteristics: acquired ability, social prestige, and a lifestyle approaching an individual's aspirations." This was, Bledstein concludes, a "culture of professionalism." This new definition of class seemed fluid and therefore promising to a young person—particularly to young men. It seemed to offer a young man the opportunity—through an assertion of will and desire—to surmount his limited financial resources and the absence of an effective apprenticeship system in order to raise his class distinction. In practice, this professionalization of American life included a structuring of professions that encouraged one to pursue the goals of "earning a good living, elevating both the moral and intellectual tone of society, and emulating the status of those above one on the social ladder." In essence, argues Bledstein, professionalization "embodied a more radical idea of democracy than even the Jacksonian had dared to dream. The culture of professionalism emancipated the active ego of a sovereign person as he performed organized activities within comprehensive spaces." Through one's profession, one could effectively reinvent oneself.[3]

Professions offered middle-class Americans an orderly system of access to occupations ranging from medical doctor to funeral director. In the happiest circumstance, an individual could advance himself by progressing

2. Susan Coultrap-McQuin, *Doing Literary Business: American Women Writers in the Nineteenth Century* (Chapel Hill, 1990), 22; Elizabeth Fox-Genovese, *Within the Plantation Household: Black and White Women of the Old South* (Chapel Hill, 1988), 46; Solomon, *Company of Educated Women*, 48.

3. Burton J. Bledstein, *The Culture of Professionalism: The Middle Class and the Development of Higher Education in America* (New York, 1976), 5, 80, 87.

through recognizable levels of achievement; in its more negative expressions, professionalism enforced rituals that "bred public attitudes of submission and passivity." The American university, the institution that eventually dominated the process by which individuals received their professional credentials, drew on the model of the German university. Administrators such as Harvard's Charles Eliot sought to establish the university as "the accepted authority of an elite of merit," a select group of men who "valued limitation, order and consistency." It was no coincidence, argues Bledstein, that women's colleges also finally emerged as a phenomenon requiring specialized analysis and design. Ultimately, the requirements of professionalism would invigorate both the academic and fiscal growth of women's colleges.[4]

The educators who designed professionalized higher education for women viewed the purposes of women's education as distinct from those of men. Such a view was, as historian Jill Conway observes, contradictory: "On the one hand, . . . [in the] women's sphere of competence, . . . many aspects of housekeeping and child-rearing were given new professional shape and required new forms of preparation. . . . On the other hand, the evangelical culture which fostered the founding of colleges and linked future social perfection to better education and moral understanding combined with the secular forces of the movement for women's rights, and each in its way held utopian expectations for the kind of society that would come into being if the moral and intellectual abilities related to women's nurturing and service roles could be deployed as a check on the acquisitiveness and competitiveness of American business culture."[5] Although the education of women was seen as an extension of their traditional "nurturing and service roles," the methods were similar enough to those employed in the male universities that similar benefits accrued. Bledstein concludes, "By screening students upon entrance, formalizing courses of study, publishing textbooks, standardizing examinations, and awarding degrees, higher educators convinced the public that objective principles rather than subjective partisanship determined competence in American life. Intelligence prevailed over family inheritance"—and, eventually, gender—"as a requisite for accomplishment in society." The door to professional life had begun to open for women.[6]

One may note intriguing and telling regional differences in women's

---

4. Ibid., 104, 323.

5. Jill Conway, *The Female Experience in Eighteenth- and Nineteenth-Century America: A Guide to the History of American Women* (New York, 1982), 89.

6. Bledstein, *Culture of Professionalism*, 10.

higher education. Until well into the nineteenth century, the South had done little to encourage a high level of literacy for women; and in a region that lacked a common school system, there seemed little utilitarian motivation to entertain the thought. Inevitably, then, female seminaries and colleges of the South developed more slowly than their counterparts in the North. By the mid-nineteenth century this conservative impulse was reinforced by the widely felt anxiety among southerners that the rapid industrialization in the North was damaging the fabric of American society. Why should southern women go to school if their true positions in life were to perform the duties of a housewife and mother? The implications of such an education threatened all the traditional paternalistic concepts that defined a lady's nature and role. And, if the apocryphal tale is true, Bryn Mawr's second president, M. Carey Thomas, did little to alleviate such fears in commenting that "only our failures only marry."[7] The female college, as an expression of the cult of professionalism, threatened the traditional notions of both class and gender that existed in the South: if intellectual merit were used as a criterion, women could, by entering professions traditionally closed to them, begin defining themselves.

Given the depth of the regional and national controversy over women's education, a women's academy established in the nineteenth century—which was Hollins' initial incarnation—was especially significant as a socially credible form of women's higher education. Unfortunately, widely varying standards would later haunt many academies and seminaries in their attempts to become women's colleges. Though they met the regularized guidelines of accrediting agencies, only with difficulty did female seminaries overcome the public's skepticism that they were simply "finishing schools" dedicated to the four cardinal virtues of "True Womanhood": piety, purity, submissiveness, and domesticity.[8] That skepticism persists to the present day.

For years southerners resisted the "female college" movement that had arisen in part, argues historian Thomas Woody, "as a criticism of the female seminary."[9] The southern seminaries—among which Hollins then num-

7. Quoted in Solomon, *Company of Educated Women,* 84.

8. Barbara Welter, "The Cult of True Womanhood: 1820–1860," *American Quarterly* 18 (1966): 152.

9. Thomas Woody, *A History of Women's Education in the United States,* 2 vols. (New York, 1929), 2:138. Georgia Female Seminary claimed for itself a collegiate curriculum even before women's colleges were established at Oxford and Cambridge, but Helen Lefkowitz Horowitz,

bered—discovered that the newly formed women's colleges, particularly those in the Northeast, were accorded a higher status and were articulating a different standard that, in effect, attracted the best students from the pool of seminary applicants. Northeastern schools were able to establish a formidable ideal for southern ones, because schools such as the Seven Sisters had begun with much greater advantages. Of the Seven Sisters, only Mount Holyoke began as a seminary; it gained classification as a college in 1888. The others—Vassar (est. 1865), Smith (1875), Wellesley (1875), Radcliffe (1879), Bryn Mawr (1880), and Barnard (1889)—actually began their institutional lives as colleges and so did not have to deal with altering an already-formed public perception about academy status. They still struggled to establish standards that the public would respect and come to expect: Wellesley and Mount Holyoke maintained preparatory departments for several years until they could be guaranteed a sufficient pool of qualified applicants. But philosophical and financial support were forthcoming.

In Virginia, women's colleges also lacked the strengthening challenge that the Sisters met vis-à-vis their brother colleges. In the North, men's colleges kept the Seven Sisters at their gates, separate and almost equal, the proximity creating both a spur to competition and resentment at exclusion. Radcliffe and Barnard formed literally at the gates of Harvard and Columbia, colleges that refused to entertain the possibility of admitting women students. Despite their intransigence in that regard, both Harvard and Columbia allowed their professors (all male) to teach some of the seminars at the women's colleges. Amherst College faculty planned for Smith College yet kept the college at a discreet distance in nearby Northampton. The original plan for Bryn Mawr would have placed it at the gates of Johns Hopkins had not a Haverford trustee—who was also a Bryn Mawr trustee—resisted the possible competition for Haverford. For their part, the Seven Sisters shrewdly wanted to

---

in *Alma Mater: Design and Experience in the Women's Colleges from Their Nineteenth-Century Beginnings to the 1930s* (New York, 1984), doubts the strength of that claim. Research concerning southern women's colleges, however, is appallingly scarce. The current histories of southern women's colleges are, with some notable exceptions, labors of love by alumnae or resident professors rather than the products of more rigorous scholarly research. The analysis cannot progress much further until the individual and corporate histories have developed to a degree comparable to those by Helen Horowitz, Mabel Newcomer, and Barbara Solomon. I set the cases of the Virginia schools—and Hollins in particular—against the broad outlines of their research and conclusions.

share the bouquet that proximity to a famous university afforded. As Helen Horowitz notes, Radcliffe located where it did in Cambridge because "in the eyes of literary Boston and Cambridge, only Harvard really mattered."[10] Proximity offered as well the hope of shared resources, which was the case at Radcliffe.

This self-conscious physical placement, by contrast, was not the case in Virginia, where a different paradigm was at work. The location of Hollins was typical for a Virginia women's school and suggested something about the way white southerners envisioned higher education for women. The image of the southern belle as aloof, aristocratic, and untouchable seems the best metaphor for the placement of women's colleges such as Hollins, Mary Baldwin, Sweet Briar, and Randolph-Macon that survived into the twentieth century. Those schools that began as seminaries were established without thought of becoming colleges; therefore, physical placement was tied more directly to local need. However, even the later women's colleges in Virginia— with only one exception—were located without any intention of proximity to an established men's college. The University of Virginia, a state-supported all-male university in search of a coordinate female institution, chose Mary Washington College, a college more than a hundred miles away from Charlottesville. The founders of Randolph-Macon Women's College also placed that school more than a hundred miles distant from its all-male predecessor and counterpart in Ashland, Virginia. Sweet Briar, Mary Baldwin, and Hollins were miles distant even from the nearest coeducational college. Only Westhampton College of the University of Richmond developed in any way as a women's coordinate college physically proximate to an established college. Though logical justifications can explain these choices in location, it remains striking that such reasoning came to bear with such regular results in these Virginia schools. Virginia's closest parallel to the postbellum women's colleges of the North—the Methodist-related Randolph-Macon Women's College—even resisted corporate funding for years, a stance indicative of the strength of denominational resistance to the challenge of secular authority that professionalization implied. Hollins, caught up in the problems of the postbellum South and isolated from larger challenges, became a provincial school dominated by a single proprietary family, who sought to run the school as a family business. Because all social and intellectual life was cen-

10. Horowitz, *Alma Mater*, 96.

tered on a campus dominated by paternalistic social values, physical isolation readily operated as a force to maintain a traditional familial atmosphere on the campus well into the 1960s.

Hollins and other Virginia women's seminaries that were tentatively seeking to professionalize found themselves on increasingly unequal footing with a developing pool of northern women's colleges that benefited from the regional phenomena of increased wealth, endowments, and patronage; more general acceptance of women's education; and the development of strong preparatory schools. A comparison of statistics from Massachusetts and Virginia for the higher instruction of women for 1888–1889 emphasizes the financial disparity. Massachusetts had nine schools, with 1,754 women engaged in collegiate study. Resources available to these students included a total of 284 instructors on the various faculties, approximately 75,000 volumes in their libraries, and more than 4.5 million dollars in tuition, physical facilities, and financial support. By contrast, Virginia had nineteen schools, with 1,402 women engaged in collegiate study. These schools had 188 instructors on faculty, approximately 10,500 volumes in their libraries, and $725,000 in tuition, physical facilities, and financial support.[11] In sum, women's colleges in Virginia were smaller, poorer, and more slightly staffed than their counterparts in Massachusetts.

Charles Lewis Cocke, the first principal and considered the founder of Hollins College, subscribed to regionalist economic policies that reinforced the southern social flavor of his school, effectively targeting an exclusively southern pool of applicants. In fact, the passion that perhaps most effectively damned Cocke's fiscal efforts in three crucial areas was his loyalty to the South. On the eve of Civil War, Cocke saw his school as a distinctively regional institution, serving a constituency in the slaveholding states, and he conducted his funding efforts accordingly. When he learned in 1861 of Matthew Vassar's endowment of a women's college in the North, he took clear pride in stating he had never turned to northerners to ask for money. Recruiting advertisements for the school went only as far north as the *Baltimore Baptist*. Eventually, to Cocke's self-limiting regional funding and recruitment efforts was added the weakness of the postbellum southern economy. By northern standards, the southern economy was pitifully weak, and that

11. A. D. Mayo, *Southern Women in the Recent Educational Movement in the South* (1892; reprint, Baton Rouge, 1978), table 6.

weakness quickly translated into weak schools—wherever such schools could be found. Educators such as Cocke, who sought the South as their only constituency, reasoned that regional pride and nostalgia for the Lost Cause would move southern families to send their daughters to southern women's schools. But Cocke's school enrollment did not recover to prewar numbers for decades, and ultimately his regionalist stance isolated him from the larger developments that transformed higher education for women. One indicator of the degree of disparity between the North and the South in terms of financial support is found in the United States Bureau of Education records for 1888–1889. The combined income of nineteen institutions for women's higher education in Virginia (one of which was Hollins, 160 students) was $64,481. During the same time period, Smith College (437 students) had an income of $68,225; Mount Holyoke (306 students), $69,765; Wellesley (685 students), $204,250; Vassar (311 students), $142,930; and Bryn Mawr (116 students), $52,000.[12] Southern women's seminaries like Hollins watched with growing envy as women's colleges such as the Seven Sisters, drawing upon the industrial wealth of the North, outdistanced them in financial resources and intellectual status by the end of the nineteenth century.

Toward the latter part of the nineteenth century, Hollins did begin benefiting from the trend that found increasing numbers of women seeking higher education. The Civil War had created a drop in enrollment; but by 1881, numbers had climbed to 115; to 209 in 1890; and to 236 in 1900.[13] Through a distinctive financial arrangement, the familial structure became incorporated into the legal framework of the institution itself: because the school had not always been self-supporting, Charles Lewis Cocke and his family literally *owned* Hollins by the time of his death in 1901. With the Cocke family as sole owners, the institution was easily afforded the possibility of being run as a business enterprise. The Cockes, however, lacked the inclination or perhaps the entrepreneurial skill to parlay this acquisition into a lucrative venture, and the familial fabric of the institution began to strain as Hollins came to recognize the pressing need to attain professional accreditation in order to compete with other colleges. Despite a rise in enrollment, the family-run school entered the twentieth century squarely confronted by the stark realization that it could not raise an endowment precisely because it was a proprietary institution.

12. Ibid.

13. Frances J. Niederer, *Hollins College: An Illustrated History* (Charlottesville, 1973), 30.

To achieve recognition and funding comparable to women's colleges such as the Seven Sisters, southern seminaries had to enter the professionalizing process of accreditation. In the case of Hollins, institutional change—from academy to seminary to women's college—meant the additional struggle of overcoming the limitations of being a family enterprise. The institutional fabric of Hollins had become obsolete. As a proprietary institution, the school could not raise an endowment and hence relied chiefly on tuition to pay its costs. Unlike its neighboring women's colleges, Hollins developed without the strong denominational ties that provided some dependable, organized source of financing for the school. Hence, Hollins could not pay the salaries to attract a first-rate faculty nor afford the library sufficient for thorough study. In these circumstances, accreditation was nearly impossible, and the school lagged well behind full-fledged women's colleges.

Again, Hollins was not exceptional among southern women's colleges. By 1916, of all the women's schools in the South, the Southern Association of College Women had certified only seven southern women's colleges as "standard": Agnes Scott in Decatur, Georgia; Converse in Spartanburg, South Carolina; Florida State College for Women in Tallahassee; Goucher in Baltimore; Sophie Newcomb in New Orleans; Randolph-Macon in Lynchburg, Virginia; and Westhampton College in Richmond. Sweet Briar and Hollins were both designated as "approximate colleges," which, according to historian Thomas Woody, "offered 'four years of work which might justly entitle especially good students to graduate standing in first class institutions.' The distinctions drawn between the 'standard' and the 'approximate' colleges were based on the fact that the latter had (a) preparatory departments, (b) more 'special-study pupils,' (c) 'poorer library and laboratory equipment,' and (d) did 'not pay as good salaries' nor 'secure as many professors distinguished for creative and research work.'" Woody concludes, "The cause of the poorer library, laboratory and salaries, mentioned above, was poverty. Compared with those which were rated as 'standard,' the 'approximate' colleges were poor; compared with colleges for women in the North, all Southern colleges for women were poor."[14] Without endowments, no matter how fine a Hollins education might be, the degree would not seem competitive with those from other colleges.

In 1925 the Cocke family offered to turn over the title to the college if a "fund of $650,000 [could be raised] . . . to assure the perpetuation of the col-

14. Woody, *History of Women's Education*, 2:222, 188.

lege"; but the task of fundraising proved quite difficult, especially in the weakened depression economy after the 1929 crash. However, not all Hollins supporters were persuaded that the slow response to a matching fund was tied to the national economy. In a scathing article in the April 1930 *South Atlantic Quarterly,* Hollins alumna Eudora Ramsay Richardson offered an angry interpretation of the situation. Richardson, who worked with the Southern Women's Educational Alliance and the National American Woman's Suffrage Association, wrote that in the new movement to gain membership in the American Association of University Women, southern women's colleges suffered because of regional bias. Despite their longevity and because of "lack of financial support, only one of these historic institutions—Wesleyan College—is sending out alumnae eligible to membership in the American Association of University Women."[15] She continued, "The fault lies not with the institutions but with a public which, despite all its prating of the cultural advantages possible only through the education of women, has not adequately supported its women's colleges. . . . For the most part women have been accepted in men's universities as step-sisters for whom life is rendered as intolerable as possible, or there have been made between women's colleges and men's, marriage arrangements that hark back to the day when the wife relinquished not only name but property rights and penal liberty as well." Large endowments were primarily given by men, she argued, and men did not support women's institutions. Southern women's colleges and southern women professors were, she concluded, "step-sisters" in the nation's educational process. Two years later the AAUW did finally approve Hollins' accreditation, even shortening the waiting time at the request of President Mary E. Wooley of Mount Holyoke College and President Marion Edwards Park of Bryn Mawr—but only after the Cocke family had succeeded in turning over ownership of Hollins to a board of trustees. Soon after the deed was transferred and accreditation acquired, then-principal Matty Cocke tendered notice of her desire to retire.[16]

The accreditation of Hollins and the selection of alumna Bessie Carter Randolph as president of Hollins in the 1930s promised a new progressive

15. Marguerite Capen Hearsey, "Hollins College: Unleveling Education," *Junior League Magazine,* March 1930, p. 39; Eudora Ramsay Richardson, "The Case of the Women's College in the South," *South Atlantic Quarterly* 29 (1930): 126.

16. Richardson, "Women's College," 127; Dorothy Scovil Vickery, *Hollins College, 1842–1942: An Historical Sketch* (Roanoke, 1942), 72.

Hollins College Main Building, ca. 1940

age for the college and reflected another stage of growth in southern women's colleges. The early part of Randolph's tenure was marked by her strenuous efforts to gain further accreditation for Hollins, a necessary move. Randolph's efforts met with success when Hollins was finally recognized by the American Association of Universities. National association with other women's colleges, however, prompted comparison as well; and during these early years of Hollins' accreditation, the Seven Sisters remained a difficult frame of reference for southern women's colleges. From 1930 to 1939, *Who's Who* listed 103 graduates of Seven Sisters colleges as high achievers while only 84 were listed from the forty-eight non–Seven Sisters women's colleges combined. Yet despite this clear difference in performance, private women's colleges in the South persistently attempted to associate themselves with the Seven Sisters rather than with comparable regional women's colleges. For example, Agnes Scott drew primarily from the pool of students in the Southeast, as did Hollins. Although the Agnes Scott *Bulletin* for 1955 did not make any academic comparisons, in its financial analysis the college compared its $12 million in total assets with those of the Seven Sisters—even with those of Smith ($33 million), Vassar ($34 million), and Wellesley ($41 million). That same publication included a map of peer private women's colleges: only Sweet Briar and Randolph-Macon are noted as the natural equals in Virginia—but all Seven Sisters are listed, despite the marked financial disparity.[17]

One of the dramatic effects of World War II was to create a prosperous American economy and to raise expectations that college was a generally accessible opportunity. The education industry experienced sharp growth, even in the South, and southern women's colleges finally became fully able to exploit financial potential in order to support the intellectual and professional ideals that they already held for themselves. In the 1950s Hollins president John Rutherford Everett succeeded in combining heightened intellectual standards and ambitious capital projects with successful fundraising. Like President Randolph, Everett had earned his Ph.D. at Columbia University; unlike Randolph, Everett was able to electrify the small college and begin a fierce campaign to make it actively competitive with other colleges. His goals were specific and practical. First, he determined that the school of 329 needed to double in size to be competitive and strong; by his last year (1959), enrollment was 640. Through a combination of Ford Foundation awards, alumnae contributions, loans, and duPont money, Everett secured funding for buildings and personnel and, simultaneously, made Hollins less tuition-sensitive and less subject to direct patron control. A new library opened in 1955. The endowment increased from $400,000 in 1950 to $3 million in 1960, largely due to gifts of Jessie Ball duPont. During his decade as president, Everett doubled faculty salaries, making the starting salary higher than that of any other college in the region. Everett then reduced the teaching load and nearly doubled the size of the faculty itself, from 39 in 1950 to 63 in 1960—all while securing travel and research money as well.[18]

The allocation of funding under Everett also represented a clear effort to redirect the school away from traditional southern ties and to make it nationally competitive. Change in the student body was a complex matter. In 1950,

17. Mary J. Oates and Susan Williamson, "Women's Colleges and Women Achievers," *Signs* 3 (1978): 799; *Who's Who in America, 1974–1975* (Chicago, 1974); James Ross McCain, "The Growth of Agnes Scott College, 1889–1955," *Agnes Scott College Bulletin* (April 1955): 3.

18. "Trustees Hear Report on College Progress," *Hollins Herald* (October 1955): 1; John A. Logan, Jr., *Hollins: An Act of Faith for 125 Years* (New York, 1968), 17–18.

70 percent of Hollins students were from south of the Potomac. At this time, faculty member Louis Rubin has observed, Hollins was "still very much a traditional, Southern institution in the old style—and charmingly so"; and yet all-female colleges such as Hollins were becoming rare. By 1957, though women were attending college in increasing numbers, only 13 percent of the colleges open to women were now for women only. All small private colleges had relatively high tuitions, but southern women's colleges still had the additional strain of battling a restrictive image of being finishing schools for southern ladies. In many respects, they did fulfill that function. Meals remained formal affairs where students dressed for dinner and faculty members presided. In the 1950s, "when a freshman enrolled at Hollins, she filled out an information card with a place for listing, among other things, the date and place of her debut!" But the increased funding and competitive staffing of the college brought about by the postwar economic boom and by President Everett's administrative decisions were beginning to attract a new range in student applicants. By 1959 only 56 percent of Hollins students were from south of the Potomac, and the old standards were starting to give way.[19]

By 1960 the financial and academic supports seemed in place at women's colleges, and women could feel poised to aspire to reach the heights of their intellectual potential. The paternalistic model of social structure, however, was still integral to the historical fabric of these institutions and still exerted strong influence. For the writers in the Hollins class of 1967, humor and mockery became means for undermining the cultural barriers, but even those women had little real idea of how long-held were the values they questioned. To entertain her classmates in the fall of 1963, freshman Lee Smith composed a parody about this institution, which would celebrate its 125th birthday the year they graduated. She called the piece "Genesis": "In the beginning, Charles Lewis Cocke created Hollins College. And the front quad was without form and void, and the Spirit moved upon the face of the duck pond. . . . And the Hollins girls were set under hard taskmasters, who afflicted them. And lo, one cometh forth to lead them out of their bondage. . . . And she led them into the Promised Land, a land flowing with liquor and honeys. And

19. Louis D. Rubin, Jr., "Hollins College: An Account of 25 Years in the Life of a School," 37, 25, 26 ([1967]; in Fishburn Archives, Hollins College); Solomon, *Company of Educated Women*, 44.

their fame waxed great in all the land." This brief excerpt shows Smith puck-ishly eulogizing Charles Lewis Cocke, founder of Hollins College, as a be-nevolent patriarch magically bringing forth a college out of the formless void of a front quad. His talents in financing were formidable, went the story: "And Charles Lewis Cocke said, 'Let there be money!' and lo, there were Donations." His benevolent vision of the future also included carnal pleasure that the narrator clearly savors: "And Charles Lewis Cocke blessed the stu-dents, saying, 'Be fruitful, and multiply, and fill the rooms in the three great dormitories for future years, and let Hollins girls multiply in all the earth.' And It was *so* Good." But even life in Eden was not without its particular evils: "And lo, in the dining room there was iced water and piped music, and lamb patties and mushroom omelettes; and It was Awful." From bondage and hard taskmasters the women are led to a Promised Land that sounds sus-piciously like a fraternity party, where the narrator discreetly closes her story, assuring the reader that the fame of these women "waxed great in all the land." Albeit humorously and unconsciously, Smith had captured an essen-tial legacy to the class of 1967: the historical challenges of paternalism.[20]

One can begin to trace the evolution of paternalism in women's colleges by recalling that Hollins began, as had many southern schools for women, as a small academy whose principal mission was to educate young girls to be charming wives and competent mothers. As was true with other neighboring women's academies that finally became Mary Baldwin College and Sweet Briar College, the academy that eventually became Hollins College under-went a series of false starts by earlier founders who were later forgotten in the shadow of a dominating personality who powerfully shaped the direction of the school's growth. Initially, an ambitious entrepreneur had built a resort hotel in the 1820s next to the healing waters of Botetourt Springs, confident that the area would become a popular spa. The hotel, though advantageously located near the railroad and turnpike, closed in 1839, to be replaced by an academy that was even more short-lived. Edward William Johnston moved Liberty Female Academy from what is now Bedford, Virginia, and renamed it in this new location for the newly chartered county of Roanoke. By 1842, however, the Roanoke Academy was so burdened by debt that the property was posted for sale.

20. Lee Smith, "Genesis," in *Beanstalks*, ed. Jo Berson et al. (Roanoke, 1964), 17.

Hollins commemorates 1842 as the year of its founding, for in that year the Reverend Joshua Bradley "came down from New York State for the stated purpose of improving education in Virginia" for young boys and girls. By 1845, however, Bradley concluded that he was, "at his age of life, totally unqualified to manage Virginia youths, especially the more high-spirited," and moved to Missouri.[21] The trustees then hired a math instructor and manager of the dining hall at Richmond College to direct the finances, instruction, and running of the school. Unintentionally, this hiring of Charles Lewis Cocke in 1846 not only established a permanent educational institution at the springs but also decided the philosophy of education that would shape the growth of the school for more than a century.[22]

Paternalism was a completely unsurprising force shaping women's educational institutions such as Hollins. Gerda Lerner has argued that male hegemony has traditionally expressed itself in a monopoly of the cultural definition and in the educational deprivation of women.[23] Charles Lewis Cocke's tenure as principal of the school reflected a certain conflict between those two impulses. With regard to the first issue—the social definition of women—Cocke molded the behavioral standards of his school around the firm belief that the parents of his students wanted to have inculcated in their daughters the graces and values of antebellum southern society. The finest institutional reflection of those values, he reasoned, was to structure the school as a family with himself as the father. Though not the god Lee Smith portrayed in her parody, Cocke directed with a strong hand and restricted the freedom of the young women quite systematically. He denied them social autonomy (no visitors without proper letters of introduction); intellectual autonomy (no books or periodicals without approval); and economic autonomy (no purchases without cash from the principal). He stated that they could not receive the attentions of young men and even forbade them to receive guests approved by their parents when he deemed the parents' judgment to be mistaken—both points on which Cocke's school was more restrictive than the other women's schools in the region.

Such restrictions on the behavior of women were not unique to the South.

21. Anne N. Montgomery, "Hollins College: A School with More Than a Century of Tradition," *Iron Worker* (winter 1954–55): 2; Niederer, *Illustrated History*, 9.

22. The Baptist school Richmond College, in Richmond, Virginia, was later renamed the University of Richmond.

23. Gerda Lerner, *The Creation of Patriarchy* (New York, 1986), 219.

But the particular image that inspired the regulations in southern schools such as Cocke's was the image of the southern lady, the symbolic centerpiece of the South's definition of itself, incorporating anxieties about honor, order, and slavery. Historian Anne Firor Scott observes that the image of the lady was a potent one, reflective of a culture whose "need to maintain the slave system contributed to the insistence upon perfect, though submissive, women."[24] Hence, the southern lady was to be a "paragon of virtue . . . [who, oddly enough,] was thought to need the direction and control of some man." Critic Joan Schulz, however, traces the subjugation in the image more directly to a paternalistic concept of family: "In an exaggeratedly masculinist society, such as the South has been, the term *father* becomes a synecdoche for the family and for one's place in the community and society." Southern women are forced to become submissive and to live out the traditional expectations of a wife and mother. "In all this," concludes Schulz, "they are not unlike other women in the United States, except that the demands and expectations are more exaggerated in the South because it is such an extravagantly patriarchal society." By creating a familial atmosphere at Hollins, Cocke was drawing upon this southern sensibility that a lady was to be trained to submit to the order of men. His rules for social behavior ensured that the young women in his care never left the constraints of a domestic space.[25]

Cocke's paternalism was not without a gentle, almost whimsical character. In a moment of blissful insight into student spirit, he created Tinker Day, a "wild card" school holiday announced annually by Cocke on the day of his choosing, when the entire college would go traipsing up Tinker Mountain for a day of picnicking and skits, a tradition that continues to the present day. "The presence of Mr. and Mrs. Cocke with their nine children and various grandchildren gave a familial atmosphere to the school" that was a comfort for many of the girls who could not afford to travel home during the course of their studies. This atmosphere was "encouraged by the fact that most faculty members were married and lived on campus with their children

24. Anne Firor Scott, *The Southern Lady: From Pedestal to Politics, 1830–1930* (Chicago, 1970), 17. Anne Goodwyn Jones and others have made the observation that Sarah Grimké explicitly linked slavery and the image of the southern lady; these critics also note that the feminist revival of the 1960s discovered its close relationship with protests against southern racism.

25. Ibid., 6; Joan Schulz, "Orphaning as Resistance," in *The Female Tradition in Southern Literature,* ed. Carol S. Manning (Urbana, 1993), 91–93.

as well."[26] Cocke's school—small, intimate, paternalistic—was representative of women's academies in its echoing of the family structure. As Schulz suggests, however, the exaggeration of the cultural requirement to train women to be ladies had a distinctively southern cast to it.

Though Cocke clearly tried to promote a certain cultural definition of women, he never solidified his educational philosophy in a way that established the educational deprivation that Lerner decries. Before he was twenty, Charles Cocke wrote to a female relative of the calling he felt: "[I propose] to devote my life to the higher education of women in the South, which I consider one of our greatest needs."[27] The direct motivation for that statement is unknown, but Cocke's career reflected a well intentioned but uncertain sense of mission to advance women's education. His ideas ranged from a belief that young women needed advanced, rigid mental training to a fear that education would lead women to usurp the proper places of men. Until his death in 1901, Cocke's journals and public speeches were profoundly unsettled records of his personal ambivalence as to whether the purpose of higher education for women was to make them ladies and wives or, indeed, to equip them for employment outside the home.

Though Cocke strictly limited the freedom of young women to decide their behavior, every major change he made in the school at Botetourt Springs strengthened the academic and intellectual standards for the women. In 1851, Cocke judged that the coordinate status of the school forced upon the Female Department a "necessary confinement . . . altogether incompatible with comfort and health," and so abolished the *Male* Department, which had *double* the enrollment of the Female Department.[28] Subsequent to this choice, Cocke worked methodically to develop a demanding program of instruction. Although many young women pursued studies at the school, "full graduate" diplomas were awarded only rarely, and the requirements for such were rigorous. Hollins president John Logan observed that at a time when higher education for women was often perceived as unnecessary, undesirable, even "defeminizing," Cocke "never tolerate[d] a watered-down course of

26. Donna Marie Packard, "Conservative Progress in the Higher Education of Southern Women: Hollins Institute, 1855–1901" (B. A. thesis, Princeton University, 1979), 86, 85.

27. Quoted in William R. L. Smith, *Charles Lewis Cocke: Founder of Hollins College* (Boston, 1921), 27.

28. Niederer, *Illustrated History,* 10.

study; [t]here was never in Mr. Cocke's day anything of the 'finishing school' about Hollins."[29] Alumna Virginia Strickler Milburne, in recalling her years at Hollins (1884–1886), remembered the instruction as "unbelievably serious": "to most of us older ones, the curriculum was the thing. And how proud we were of Hollins' high standards! We willingly worked hard for our parchments."[30] Cocke's intellectual standards had proved not only challenging but exhilarating to the young women.

By 1857 Cocke seemed to have arrived at some definite conclusions: "The plan and policy of the school recognizes the principle that in the present state of society in our country, young women require the same thorough and rigid mental training as that afforded to young men." The advent of war confirmed for Cocke the overwhelmingly practical justifications for educating women even to a point of self-sufficiency. Not everyone in the South shared such a pragmatic view, as Elizabeth Fox-Genovese has observed: "Teaching a Sunday-school class might be viewed as a social responsibility; teaching a favorite slave to read might even be tolerated; but earning a salary for regular teaching was viewed as an unfortunate necessity for widows or, even worse, wives who had fallen victim to their husbands' inadequacies. It was not a fit occupation for a lady." Nevertheless, after the war, Cocke wrote that all thoughtful southern parents must naturally be concerned about such practical matters for their daughters. Doubtless aware of the numerous women left widowed or forever single by the devastation of southern males in the Civil War, Cocke recognized that southern women should now be prepared for employment.[31]

Still, in 1898, near the end of his life, seventy-eight-year-old Cocke seemed to reach another—and unsettling—insight about the issue of equal competition of women with men, and his conclusion was unequivocal: "What a prospect, what an absurdity, what a violation of divine provision and

29. Logan, *Hollins*, 9, 10. In his history of Hollins, Louis Rubin argues to the contrary that "during the last several decades of the Nineteenth Century . . . Hollins became in effect the leading 'finishing school' from throughout the South" and "not really a full-fledged college"; Rubin, "Hollins College," 17. No evidence seems to corroborate this assessment, and so I have allowed President Logan's statement to stand as the primary judgment. Rubin may be correct in a broad sense in that few colleges in the South at the end of the nineteenth century were "full-fledged colleges" in the twentieth-century sense of the concept.

30. Niederer, *Illustrated History*, 29.

31. Vickery, *Historical Sketch*, 13; Fox-Genovese, *Plantation Household*, 46; Charles Lewis Cocke, "Education of Girls" ([n.d.]; personal papers in Fishburn Archives, Hollins College).

command!"[32] The sentiment Cocke articulated was precisely the same ideological notion of a limited women's sphere that had been evident since the earliest discussions of higher education for women: women should not aspire to usurp the places God has assigned to men. Cocke still held to the conventional philosophy that women's schools were essentially women's asylums. Despite such misgivings, the effect of Cocke's career was to create an educational institution that challenged women with strong intellectual standards. These cultural fissures or cracks in the institutional order were crucial, for in succeeding decades, paradoxically, the high intellectual standards that Cocke espoused undermined the paternalistic values that he considered so vital to women's higher education.

Cocke's death in 1901 was so momentous an event that it seemed to mark the end of an era at Hollins. To the contrary, however, the school was well able to carry on in his paternalist spirit because Cocke had designated his forty-five-year-old daughter Matty Cocke as his successor. "Miss Matty," as she preferred to be called, embodied the tensions of her father's educational philosophy. She was a lady, a charismatic leader, and a woman completely willing to allow her nephews, Joseph Turner and M. Estes Cocke, to handle the fiscal and academic leadership of the school during her thirty-two-year tenure. This style of management made sense to Miss Cocke. She had been reared on the grounds and in the academic buildings of Hollins and had, in fact, earned her highest academic degree there: a bachelor's. Understandably, she attempted to maintain the cohesion of the Hollins "family." Miss Cocke had no aspirations to be like Mary-Cooke Branch Munford, who was then spearheading the ultimately unsuccessful drive to open the University of Virginia to women students. It would have made no difference to Miss Cocke to know that, in 1902, state universities were closed to women only in Virginia, Georgia, Louisiana, and North Carolina; or that four state-supported colleges in Virginia—the University of Virginia, the College of William and Mary, Virginia Polytechnic Institute, and Virginia Military Institute—denied admission to women. In fact, Miss Cocke, ever the lady, sought no battles. She "especially did no fund-raising" because it seemed to her to be in poor taste, and that omission would haunt the college's development for years to come. Fortunately for Miss Cocke, as William Chafe has observed, going to college itself by the 1920s was becoming "an act of conformity rather than

32. Charles Lewis Cocke, "Fifty-second Address to Graduating Class," *Semi-Annual* (June 1898): 55.

deviance, and the atmosphere of special purpose [impelling women toward women's rights] began to evaporate." Women students in the 1920s were more likely to form social bonds than career aspirations; thus, maintaining a genteel atmosphere at Hollins seemed still a reasonable, even desirable, course for Miss Cocke to follow.[33]

Miss Cocke's personal reticence coincided with larger cultural reservations concerning the rapid advancement of women. The national women's movement had received deadly blows in "scientific" arguments from the resurrection by Dr. Edward Clarke and A. L. Smith of warnings that women's bodies were closed energy systems suffering physical abnormality when "overeducated."[34] In a voice that was geographically closer to Miss Cocke's school, this national concern about overeducation was reinforced by Sweet Briar Women's College president John McBryde in his 1907 address to the Richmond Education Association. In speaking of the intellectual goals of Vassar, Smith, Wellesley, and Bryn Mawr, McBryde observed, "I cannot help feeling that in all these institutions there has been from the very start an unfortunate tendency to compare woman's intellect with man's, and to insist too strongly on the development of woman's mind along exactly the same line with man's." Such an education "unsexed" a woman. In particular, McBryde thought that it would be more sensible for Virginia women's colleges to teach practical courses in cooking, dairying, and poultry raising: "Education which fills a woman's soul with foolish notions of a glorious independence apart from man and apart from home is . . . pernicious. . . . It can never be too strongly emphasized or too often repeated that home is the center of woman's influence and the source of her power, and the instruction in every subject of study should be directed with that important fact in view." In concluding his remarks, McBryde explicated his view of the final end of women's higher education:

> What, then, finally is the type of college woman that we should seek to send forth from our Southern colleges? I think we need to revert more to the ideal of womanhood in the Old South before the Civil War, which remains in nearly all respects the finest type that the modern world has seen.

33. Elizabeth Cady Stanton, Susan B. Anthony, and Matilda Joslyn Gage, *History of Woman Suffrage*, 6 vols. (Rochester, N.Y., 1881–1922), 4:966; Logan, *Hollins*, 14; William Chafe, *The American Woman: Her Changing Social, Economic, and Political Roles, 1920–1970* (New York, 1972), 92.

34. See Rosalind Rosenberg, *Beyond Separate Spheres: Intellectual Roots of Modern Feminism* (New Haven, 1982), xvi; and Woody, *History of Women's Education*, 2:205.

Among our young women of to-day we miss that exquisite grace, that refinement, rare tact, wonderful directing power, calm dignity, and absolute self-possession which characterized the women of the Old South. Our social code is too lax, our manners too free, and our young women are not sufficiently subjected to discipline and restraint to check this growing spirit of restiveness. We need in our college courses for women, to make a careful, loving investigation of the social and economic life of the Old South.

McBryde was Miss Cocke's neighbor both in geography and in sentiment. Miss Cocke sought to continue at Hollins the paternalistic, family-oriented ideals by which she had been reared and rightly understood that southern parents still wanted their daughters to acquire the grace and deference of the antebellum southern lady. She conducted her administration accordingly.[35]

Despite Hollins' high academic standards, the traditional paternalist images of southern womanhood persisted as part of the heritage of the institution. The wartime centennial celebration of 1942 was a study in contrasts. The Centennial Ball had an Old South theme complete with white-coated waiters singing spirituals on the steps. The companion event, however, was an address by Hollins president Randolph broadcast over a CBS coast-to-coast radio hookup. Professional aspirations struggled with nostalgia.[36]

Randolph was a jewel in Hollins' crown, one of the first Hollins graduates to earn a Ph.D. from Columbia University. Yet Randolph was on the defensive with regard to women's higher education, even at Hollins' centenary celebration. Keenly sensitive to the power of wartime discourse and to continuing suspicions that women's higher education was an unwarranted luxury in times of national crisis, Randolph mounted her own tactical offensive:

Although the higher education of women is one of the most recent and delicate—and costly—of all democratic experiments for the further liberation of the human spirit it is not an ornamental luxury—as the totalitarian philosophers would make us believe—but a basic necessity in a modern, democratic world.

. . . Every generation of democratic life in this country and in all other countries must have trained college and university women to help form that spearhead of primary thinkers who must work out in bold and convincing form the lines of attack in an advancing civilization.

35. John M. McBryde, Jr., "Womanly Education for Women," *Sewanee Review* 15 (1907): 479, 472, 482–83.

36. *Centennial Celebration of Hollins* (Roanoke, 1949), 20.

Randolph astutely cast her argument for women's higher education as the natural extension of the battle waged by democracy against the evil forces of totalitarianism. In doing so, she recapitulated a strategy recorded often in the annals of women's higher education: reworking the rhetoric of one ideology in order to subvert the power of another. Her language seemed defensive, calculated to mute any suggestion that women's higher education might be a luxury in time of war and to preempt the issue altogether by explaining the importance of women's higher education to American democracy faced with the threat of totalitarianism. She was not mistaken in taking this view: the national percentage of women with a bachelor's or first professional degree would fall from 41 percent in 1940 to 24 percent in 1950.[37]

As Hollins struggled toward financial and academic parity with other women's colleges, President Randolph oversaw great and successful efforts to strengthen the cultural and academic standards within the limitations she found at Hollins. She attracted to the campus prominent speakers such as Reinhold Niebuhr, Donald Davidson, Virginius Dabney, Robert Frost, and David Daiches. A prominent speaker at the centennial celebration was alumna Katherine Tupper Marshall, former editor of the *Spinster,* former president of the Euepian Literary Society, and wife of army chief of staff General George C. Marshall. Despite these efforts to strengthen the intellectual program of the college, the financial disparities still proved crucial. Faculty salaries were inadequate, and the building program had stopped altogether. Even publication of the 1942 centennial record was delayed by war until 1949. Hollins was simply unable to financially sustain its expanding academic ambitions, a circumstance that created a certain sense of intellectual limitation at the college. Randolph's eloquent efforts to raise the academic caliber of the school and her seventeen years in office were, reflected President John Logan, "in many respects a study in frustration, embracing as they did years of depression and global war and its aftermath." These years showed the evidence of strain upon and declining support for women's institutions of higher learning. So long as the economic and social systems depended on the assignment of most women in the South to domestic roles, the

37. Ibid., 16–17; Patricia Albjerg Graham, "Expansion and Exclusion: A History of Women in American Higher Education," *Signs* 3 (1978): 766. Barbara Solomon, *Company of Educated Women,* 189, notes that, in effect, "the operation of the GI bill reduced female access to higher education."

presidents of women's colleges were still required to make cogent responses to the nature and necessity of women's education.[38]

Those responses remained polite and diplomatic in the 1950s, even though women began attending college and moving into the work force in greater numbers. As we have seen, President Everett capitalized on post–World War II affluence, energetically seeking to raise finances and academic standards at the college during the 1950s. Still, even Everett continued the paternalistic definition of women's education as auxiliary to men's. On one occasion he wrote, "A woman must be prepared to move with her husband, and she must be wise enough to raise the children properly. The complexity of this modern world will not allow feminine ignorance to live with masculine learning." An uneducated woman "will wake up to find that she has no part in her husband's life because she is not only ignorant, she is also intellectually undisciplined and possessed of limited horizons and poor judgment." He continued that women should realize they exert great control through consumer spending and "are the great transmitters of culture." The persistence of a benign paternalism was not remarkable during a decade that valued a "feminine ideal—as opposed to the feminist one"—including as its central "constellation of virtues: youth, appearance, acquiescence, and domesticity." What was changing about this paternalism at Hollins during the 1950s was that it was becoming undermined by the growing national competitiveness of the college.[39]

Perhaps the single most crucial change during President Everett's tenure concerned the treatment and composition of the faculty. The competitive power of Hollins during the 1960s was due, in part, to the fact that Hollins had acquired a faculty who were knowledgeable not only about their subject matter but about the proper forms that made a college fit the national pattern of professionalism. At the beginning of Everett's tenure, only F. Lamar Janney and Mary Vincent Long were teaching in the English department. Joining them during the Everett decade were John A. Allen, John Rees Moore, Stuart H. L. Degginger, Jesse Zeldin, and Louis D. Rubin, Jr. Rubin proved exceptionally adept at incorporating the professional theories of New Criticism into a successful writing program at the school. Everett instituted de-

38. *Centennial*, 25; Logan, *Hollins*, 17.

39. John R. Everett, "Neglecting the Wife Can Prove Dangerous," *Hollins Herald* (October 1951): 1; Everett, "Nation Cannot Flourish with Uneducated Women," ibid. (July 1957): 1–2; Graham, "Expansion and Exclusion," 770.

mocratized general faculty meetings at the college; and as a result, the faculty initiated and implemented several bold curriculum changes. Several of these changes proved timely and crucial for the Hollins Group in the 1960s because they radically strengthened the writing program at Hollins within a relatively short time. If Hollins needed any further justification to focus on its writing program, it came in 1958 when alumna Mary Wells Knight Ashworth, another product of the strong student culture of the 1920s, won the 1958 Pulitzer Prize for *First in Peace,* a biography of George Washington. The college community was ecstatic.

The vitality of change during the Everett decade infused the faculty as a whole. It is initially startling to discover that during President Everett's tenure, faculty hiring was almost exclusively male. But recruitment of a largely male faculty was typical of women's colleges in the 1950s, primarily because the university system and GI Bill support had favored male Ph.D.'s. Everett desired to raise the academic standards at Hollins, and he viewed a Ph.D. faculty as necessary to that goal. Everett's argument for increased faculty salaries revealed that he saw this professional development in gendered terms, noting that "most all of the men" eligible for positions would be just completing military service. For Hollins, this was the first decade in the twentieth century when the Hollins faculty was not predominantly female: Everett essentially reversed the composition of the faculty from a 1950 female-to-male ratio of 4 to 1 to a 1960 ratio of 3 to 4, a ratio that has continued to the present day. By 1957, 70 percent of all courses were taught by Ph.D.'s. Although tenured faculty were not required to publish regularly in order to keep their jobs, more faculty began publishing—and publication itself is one of the professionalizing forms by which a faculty distinguishes itself as elite. Everett sought out and encouraged faculty members with an open-door policy that allowed him to work with them on an individual basis. Louis Rubin recalls an incident of that personal interest that occurred in 1958. Although faculty salaries were good, summer vacations still caused financial stress for the younger faculty members. A trustee of the college, Mrs. Jessie Ball duPont, sent $40,000 to the administration, and Everett immediately designated the money for faculty pay supplements during the summer. That action convinced the faculty that the trustees and administration genuinely cared about their welfare and, hence, engendered a fierce loyalty among the faculty.[40]

40. Everett, "How Attract Faculty at Present Salaries?" *Hollins Herald* (May 1954): 1; "College Doing Well Everett Tells Board at Annual Congress," ibid. (July 1957): 2.

By the time Everett left Hollins in 1960 to accept the position of chancellor of the City University of New York, he had created impressive institutional growth enabling Hollins to attract a strong faculty and student body. Gender expectations rooted in a patriarchal system remained at odds with the meritocratic ideal of liberal education, and John Logan, the Yale Ph.D. who followed Everett as president during the 1960s, continued to espouse such paternalistic social standards for women. His typical rhetoric essentially restated the justification of single-sex institutions for women as public spaces that allow women an exceptional opportunity to be leaders: "A woman's college continues to be the only place which offers positions of real leadership to girls, and more important, which offers them the opportunity to develop their identity as rational beings devoted to the life of the mind, free of the rituals of courtship which inevitably invade, and sometimes dominate, coeducational institutions. The mobility of today's college students insures that they can lead a full social life, if they choose it." Yet even in this instance, Logan was still quick to assure his readers that Hollins still retained "a civilized aura of good breeding," a phrase whose subtext a careful reader could recognize as drawing upon the traditional definition of a southern lady. When the Hollins Group arrived on the campus, the paternalistic social definition of women was still in force and struggling to persist. What aided the women of the Hollins Group in undermining that paternalist ethos were the professional aspirations encouraged by the nationally competitive writing program.[41]

In the period 1960–1967, under Logan's guidance, Hollins would mark a significant rise in academic standards, national recognition, and claims on the pool of applicants. The improved finances of Hollins and the expansive social consciousness of the 1960s enlarged the diversity of class backgrounds represented by women at Hollins. College board scores rose steadily, and enrollment doubled the population of the college to more than 950 students. Greater percentages of women stayed at Hollins to complete their degrees, and so eventually larger applicant pools competed for fewer positions. The college's writing program skyrocketed to national prominence when its writer-in-residence won the Pulitzer Prize. With some justification, Logan was able to observe, "Hollins was by no means either large or wealthy in 1960, but it had developed the resources to hold its own among the better women's colleges, although in comparison to the Seven Sisters it was performing pro-

41. Logan, *Hollins*, 22–23.

34 *Lee Smith, Annie Dillard, and the Hollins Group*

diges [*sic*] on a shoestring." High academic standards had allowed the college to enter into a new level of competitive power.[42]

The committed Ph.D. faculty, the new, more rigorous admissions standards, and the changes in curricular requirements were institutional changes designed to encourage individual achievement. What the Hollins Group discovered upon their arrival at Hollins in 1963 was, then, a campus that, infused by the financial gains and faculty hirings of the 1950s, was quite capable of competing for a large pool of applicants and of training those applicants in the rituals and methods of a profession. To a great degree, the invigorated sense of professionalism and confident self-comparison with other women's colleges encouraged a freshened competitiveness among the young women at Hollins during the 1960s. This individualistic competitiveness was tempered by a warm sense of mutual support that drew upon the contemporary women's movement and even more strongly upon a lingering familial atmosphere that shaped the social environment of the community. The nature of that familial atmosphere ultimately changed because the Hollins women in the 1960s displaced the paternalistic model of community with a more sisterly one. In doing so, they had finally capitalized on a foundation that had been forming in the *student* culture for nearly five decades.

As noted above, women's colleges have traditionally offered leadership opportunities and sororial affiliations for young women: experiences in which women look to each other for guidance and support. One important step in that direction, interestingly, occurred during the administration of Matty Cocke. Matty Cocke's unwillingness to take a strong leadership role in the administration of Hollins, judged historian Frances Niederer, proved deadly for institutional growth but healthy for allowing more student initiative. This weakness in administrative leadership allowed a sense of sisterhood to begin actively and publicly operating in the college. Except for a few curriculum changes and the incorporation under the name Hollins College in 1911, contemporary records of the time speak most vividly about the student activities and writing. Students began initiating their own calls for action on the campus. In 1917, students made the request that food rations be curtailed in order to help the war effort. In the 1920s, Hollins was "one of the very few Southern colleges cooperating in the National Student Forum, [seen by some as, in part,] a rebellion of youth against war." In 1922, the students raised most

42. Ibid., 20, 18.

of the money to pay for a theater that they wanted for college productions. In 1928, they held their first mock elections; notably, Smith received 205 votes; Hoover, 156; and Will Rogers, 1.[43]

Perhaps the most remarkable declaration was voiced by Hollins students near the end of Miss Cocke's tenure there. Greek sororities had been chartered at Hollins at the turn of the century and had enjoyed substantial membership during the years that followed. However, in 1929, in a startling move "initiated, developed, and consummated by the students themselves," Hollins women decided to abolish Greek societies on their campus. Although the Greek sororities had existed on the campus for twenty-five years, the students had decided that they were "undemocratic," divisive of the student body, and distracting from studies. This eviction of the sororities should not suggest that Hollins students lacked supportive rituals. To the contrary, May Day festivities, daisy chains on Class Day, Senior Bonfires, and Tinker Day continue to the present time. But sororities have not returned. Arguably, students at an expensive women's school would be of the same social class and so would see no need for further social distinctions. Yet sororities were well accepted at other women's colleges. The stated motivations for this decision suggest that these Hollins students were strong, principled women, serious about their academic goals and interested in an inclusive student body. Ready to make their own principled decisions about the structure of the community in which they lived, they made egalitarian sisterhood central to that definition.[44]

It is intriguing to compare this student decision with a situation that historian Helen Horowitz observed in one of the Seven Sisters colleges. During roughly these same years, Smith College had implemented a cottage residence policy that reflected a different structuring of student culture: "Educate women in college but keep them symbolically at home. Erect a central college building for instruction and surround it with cottages where the students live in familial settings. Keep them in daily contact with men as president and faculty. Build no chapel or library to encourage them to enter into the life of the town. Place students under family government as members of the town and prevent the great harm of the seminary—the creation of a sepa-

43. Niederer, *Illustrated History*, 57, 60; "Smith Wins Hollins Straw Vote," *Hollins Student Life*, October 20, 1928, p. 1.

44. Hearsey, "Unleveling Education," 40; Vickery, *Historical Sketch*, 57; Rubin, "Hollins College," 108.

rate women's culture with its dangerous emotional attachments, its visionary schemes, and its strong-minded stance to the world." Horowitz concludes, "Smith's residence policy allowed students to sort themselves out economically and socially: cliques embedded themselves in residential groups, giving spatial form to distinctions within the student body. In addition, college societies with their highly competitive process of selection further intensified divisions." Given this scenario at Smith, the vote against sororities at Hollins makes an intriguing statement in favor of an inclusive and cohesive women's community.[45]

By the 1930s the Great Depression virtually ensured that conservatism must mark the tenor of activity in a small southern women's college. Hollins did not differ from other small colleges in feeling the strain of inadequate finances; what was different, however, was the emotional legacy of a family that figured most powerfully in sustaining the college during this period. One example may best illustrate the point. The turn of the century had seen an astonishing number of women's clubs forming in relation to the reform and suffrage movements, representing direct, active participation by women in national public affairs. Hollins did not charter an alumnae association until 1925. The association's initial raison d'être, however, was not financial support but the more personal reason of maintaining the qualities they had known at Hollins: the nurturing of close emotional ties that students felt with the college, the recognition that women desired to bond together in public organizations, and the realization that associations of women could have a tangible impact on public institutions. In a time when the national financial picture was grim, the Cockes no longer headed the school, and the movement toward full accreditation and national competitiveness had begun, the sisterly ties remained.

During the Randolph era when financing of the college proved difficult, student writing at Hollins sometimes took on a tone of greater assertiveness. One writer, concerned that the narrowed academic life might extend to the student culture, wrote an editorial in the student newspaper, the *Hollins Columns,* warning that learning had become too passive. "Are we like frogs?" asked the editor. "How often do we sit in class with our mouths open, hoping that a bit of knowledge will fly in and miraculously stick?" Yet amid these

45. Horowitz, *Alma Mater,* 75, 155.

wartime concerns about the institution, research concerning Hollins alumnae was indicating that the strong student culture of the 1920s and 1930s was being evidenced in statistically measurable changes and achievements among Hollins graduates. In her study of Hollins graduates in the interim between world wars, Sarah Simpson noted that about 41 percent were "in the teaching profession" and 69 percent were married. Further, Simpson observed, 55 percent of Hollins graduates had "studied after college," and of that group, 28 percent had received advanced degrees. Such statistics indicated that career women from Hollins were beginning to create a new lifestyle. "Already this war is making changes in our lives," Simpson judged, "and no one can predict the extent or the ultimate effect on society." Hollins graduates of recent years were now showing recognizable similarities to the qualities of the "New Woman" that characterized Sisters' graduates earlier in the century.[46]

Following World War II, the student culture grew more openly assertive. One of the great student coups of 1956 was the successful campaign to abolish some of the stringent curfew rules governing trips to visit boyfriends in Lexington, Charlottesville, and Blacksburg. A more emphatic statement of student self-definition occurred in 1958 following fierce controversies over the jurisdiction of the Honor Court and over compulsory attendance at class or chapel. An unsigned editorial in the school newspaper stated: "We no longer want to be *made* anything—cultured, civic, or Christian. We want the *opportunity to become*—to become of our own choosing that which we wish to be. We appreciate and welcome guidance, but we wholeheartedly deplore any kind of requirement which interferes with our own rights as maturing individuals." This young woman's statement suggests a greater assertiveness and militancy in which students now more frequently articulated for themselves their own self-definitions and views of what their education should be. The 1958 editorial bespeaks a professionalized college community rather than a familial one: talents, rights and capabilities are innate to the student, not bestowed by any paternal or institutional largess. If, as Nancy Miller suggests, being a *feminist* is "to articulate a self-consciousness about women's identity both as inherited cultural fact and as process of social construction" and "to protest against the available fiction of female becoming," then this young woman was a feminist before the name became useful to define a movement

46. "A Lily Pond," *Hollins Columns*, March 23, 1948, p. 2; *Centennial*, 31–32, 35.

in the 1960s. The student editorial had demanded the final requirement of a college that claimed to respect the intellectual integrity of women: that the rights of the student be respected.[47]

By the 1960s, collegiate women were far from passive in describing what they perceived should be the nature of their education. An incident at Hollins in the fall of 1964 illustrates the point. A new curriculum had been designed, and when the editors of the *Hollins Columns* felt not enough care was taken to involve the student body, they protested until changes were made. Students no longer hesitated to force the faculty and administration to account for themselves. This pattern of assertion operated among the women at individual levels as well. One student whose record disqualified her for an independent senior project persuaded Louis Rubin to allow her to pursue a project anyway. Her paper on Proust's idea of reality was "better than almost any master's thesis" Rubin had ever seen. Such incidents exemplified the intellectual intensity of Hollins women during the 1960s and attested to the fact that faculty-student and student-student relationships were more collaborative than paternalistic.[48]

By the time the Hollins Group arrived in 1963, a strong student culture had become so well established that Hollins women had become accustomed to stating their own ideas of what their education should be. They wrote about it in signed articles in the school newspaper; they had "heated discussions" in the college coffeehouse. With this strengthened control over their education came a familial atmosphere at Hollins that was progressively more sisterly: peer criticism, support, and ideas were weighty and worthy features of the college community. Hollins women in the 1960s impressed President Logan as being particularly responsible in the exercise of their rights: "Other students across the country are militantly demanding rights and privileges which Hollins girls have been responsibly exercising for some time." His description of the campus atmosphere became a theme repeated by both faculty and students at Hollins during the 1960s: "Hollins people—faculty, students, parents, and alumnae—feel a great possessiveness about it, an intense sort of caring about what it is, and what it is to become. It is a profoundly intellectual community, without engendering that sense of anxiety and unease

47. Niederer, *Illustrated History*, 147; "We Want the Opportunity to Become . . . ," *Hollins Columns*, March 20, 1958, p. 2; Nancy Miller quoted in Carolyn G. Heilbrun, *Writing a Woman's Life* (New York, 1988), 18.

48. Rubin, *"Hollins College,"* 102, 110.

one feels on so many campuses nowadays. It has a saving sense of humor." Intellectual intensity heightened and disciplined the Hollins Group's intellectual ambitions; a sisterly writing community offered an alternative to the conventional social roles traditionally espoused by the college.[49]

As has been widely observed, changing social mores and demographic features of the postwar "baby boom" generation contributed to a national trend of strong student cultures during the 1960s. By the mid-1960s, Dillard, Smith, and Jones regularly attacked the administration for infringing on student autonomy. In one single article in the student newspaper, Jones attacked President Logan for being ineffective in dealing with the student legislature, restrictive in having a dress code, and lazy in responding to requests for unlimited curfews. Both Smith and Jones argued in print that the students at Hollins had to escape the "well-bred, wealthy girls" image and work for diversity in the student body and excellence in their academic experience. The administration, argued Jones, needed to engage in a dialogue with the students.[50]

"Dialogue" was Jones's polite way of telling the administration that women at Hollins would no longer be defined entirely by paternalistic social standards. Hollins was becoming a community with a heightened respect for women's self-definitions, even in the face of a long tradition of paternalistic behavioral standards. As Jill Conway has demonstrated, "It is not access to educational facilities which is the significant variable in tracing the 'liberation' of women's minds. What really matters is whether women's consciousness of themselves as intellects is altered."[51] The paternalistic ethos had infused itself into the small community of Hollins in a complex manner. Cocke had constructed the college as a southern elite family; and though in subsequent years the "daughters" felt strong support for their intellectual efforts, they met real restrictions on their personal autonomy. The community could not have escaped its paternalistic origins had not the definition of the "fam-

49. Cindy Hardwick, "The View from Senior House," *Hollins College Bulletin* (November 1966): 39; Logan, *Hollins*, 21.

50. Anne Goodwyn Jones, "Legislation Was Squelched," *Hollins Columns*, April 12, 1966, p. 2; Jones, "Appeal for Debate Is Due," ibid., April 26, 1966, p. 2. See also Lee Smith, "Moral Conformity: Poor Conception," ibid., October 4, 1966, p. 2, and Annie Dillard, "SGA Lacks Real Powers," ibid., September 29, 1966, p. 2.

51. Jill Conway, "Perspectives on the History of Women's Education in the U.S.," *History of Education Quarterly* 14 (1974), 9.

ily" been shifted from a paternalistic to a more sisterly orientation. That is, the Hollins of the 1960s became a remarkable place because it integrated an emphasis on academic achievement with a high value placed on cooperation and community among women—and did so with few marks of its paternalistic past. Those changes in student culture had much to do with writing.

Many Hollins women from the decade of the 1960s would later describe the community of writers there as a "womb of support," to use Lee Smith's term. This writing community not only brought them consciously into the writing life but nourished and fostered their professional growth as well. It is tempting to explain this extraordinary community of support among the Hollins Group solely in terms of the women's movement that exploded into public consciousness during their freshman year with the publication of *The Feminine Mystique,* and the cultural shift signaled by that movement did indeed have a complicated bearing on the Hollins Group. But at Hollins, the idea of a sisterhood was neither new nor consciously radical. If one were to identify what was novel about Hollins in the 1960s, it would be the timing of its development; that is, that by 1961 a changed familial sentiment and a newly infused academic professionalism were both in full force at Hollins and that the student culture exploited every opportunity to explore their own voices. To state that Hollins in the 1960s became an expanded public space for women writers is to draw attention to the nature, strength, and historical particularities of the institution where that public space evolved. Hollins could have slept as a finishing school, but the tensions in the college kept arguing for alternative definitions of women and kept moving the school toward intellectual challenge, toward the "opportunity to become of our own choosing that which we wish to be."

Lee Smith's "Genesis" proved to be an extraordinarily apt symbol of the confluence of historical influences at Hollins during the 1960s. The parody survives only because Smith was able to include it in *Beanstalks,* a literary magazine written, published, and marketed by a small group of determined freshmen whose writing had been rejected by the established literary magazine on campus. Smith ends her wry tale with the climactic action of a contemporary Exodus: "Hollins girls were set under hard taskmasters, who afflicted them" until one of their number "led them into the Promised Land." No longer content to be "made" anything, Hollins women were prepared, in the terms of Lee Smith's parody, alternately to lead and follow each other out of bondage to the old assumptions. Competitive and supportive, Hollins women in the 1960s made their way into a promised land of self-definition and self-confidence as writers, making Smith's funny, complicated parody a true parable of Hollins women—finding their way by discovering their own voices. Smith proved to be perceptive beyond her own grasp when discussing, among the many subjects of her freshman writing, the genesis of Hollins College.

2

A LEGACY OF WOMEN'S WRITING
The Guidance of Louis Decimus Rubin, Jr.

*H*istorically, writing has provided one of the important means by which women have often privately defined themselves in opposition to societal expectations. A diary or journal offered a protected space for confidences, speculations, even heresies. It seems only logical, then, that public writing opportunities—such as those provided at women's colleges—have figured as vital expansions of the intellectual forum for women. Among their peers, women found an early audience. Sara Evans and Nancy Cott have observed that female academies and seminaries were significant precisely because they "emphasized the primacy of gender, . . . increased women's awareness of themselves as a group. In these schools women not only discovered themselves as intelligent but also experienced an intense community of women suffused with the ideas of women's difference and special mission."[1] Here women had the opportunity to explore definitions of themselves. The writing tradition at Hollins reflects how that more public definition evolved. Further, it gives us insight into how contemporary writing programs find their roots in the New Critical impulse to professionalize the teaching of creative writing.

---

1. Sara M. Evans, *Born for Liberty: A History of Women in America* (New York, 1989), 65. See also Nancy F. Cott, *The Bonds of Womanhood: "Woman's Sphere" in New England, 1780–1835* (New Haven, 1977).

Early writing societies at Hollins were little different from other literary clubs of the period. At both men's and women's colleges, these organizations constituted voluntary associations in which young people could develop their intellectual interests and test their literary and debating skills, independently of the authorities who set the formal curriculum and governed their social lives. Such societies gave room for modern ideas and for youthful autonomy. In 1855, the Valley Union Institute (Hollins) formed such a society and, by preceding nearby Augusta Academy (Mary Baldwin) by nearly four decades, proved itself something of a progressive leader in this area of the country. The formation of a literary society actually reflected the nature of the literary marketplace of the nineteenth century, in which women had gained a powerful social voice. When extended into the context of a paternal institution such as Cocke's seminary, however, women's writing also became a bond for the student community. The young women wrote for their peers, and in that writing they found the opportunity to understand themselves more nearly on their own terms, not just on the terms of the authority that presided over them.

Hollins' commitment to women's writing became publicly manifested in 1855 in the establishment of the Euzelian (Love of Wisdom) Society, an organization that developed along lines similar to other conventional literary societies of the time. The Euzelians were fascinated by the authors and issues that they read and debated but were even more energetic in pursuing their own writing. Antebellum Euzelians, undaunted by technological limitations, published their monthly, the *Rising Star,* on foolscap. Charles Lewis Cocke encouraged these young writers to continue their interest in that craft: "I urge you to cultivate a taste not only for literature, but for *making literature.* The literature of a country determines its institutions, its social conditions, and its destiny. It is really its inner life whence its external manifestations spring."[2] These remarks still argue the point of women's power for gentle suasion, but Cocke's assertion of women's clear ability to "make literature" really affirms a more direct action. This point becomes especially significant when one compares the case at the Augusta Academy in nearby Staunton, where young women were allowed to study literature only under strict supervision and where even "standard" novels were under lock and key during school hours. At Hollins, women were actively encouraged to *create* literature.

---

2. Vickery, *Historical Sketch,* 16. Vickery gives the remark as addressed to the graduating class in 1891; William Smith, in *Founder,* 115, gives the date as 1862.

Once initiated, a women's writing society persisted at Hollins even though specific organized groups sometimes had limited lives. The exigencies of the Civil War forced the disbanding of the Euzelian club in 1862, but by 1873 the group had reorganized and in January of 1878 began publication of the *Album*, which included serious reviews of published works, humorous articles, and chatty columns. In 1874 the Euepian (Pure Diction) Society was formed and combined with the Euzelians in publishing the *Annual* and then the *Semi-Annual*. Soon the societies emphasized even more specifically the aspect of reading from original compositions. Their meetings were places where Hollins women could publicly debate historical matters ("Was Cromwell Justified in Beheading Charles I?") or topics of general interest ("Are Women Given More to Revenge than Men?"). Because of these publications the young women found new models by watching their peers lead organizations and pose arguments. As separate, public female spheres, these societies afforded the possibility for developing women's culture at the college "by the extension, rather than by the rejection, of the female sphere."[3]

The January 1878 volume of the *Euzelian Album*—eight pages long—had two "editresses" and reflected contemporary taste in magazines. Amid the more formal pieces in these magazines were articles that indicated a warm women's community at the school. A wistful commentary on examinations ended: "Sad silence reigns in the halls which a short while ago were filled with the sound of happy laughter and bright voices. Do your best, girls!" A later article in 1878 included a seemingly odd bit of trivia: a note on the amount of money George Eliot recently made on a piece of her writing. Nothing further is made of the note, but it does remain as a pointed observation about a woman succeeding handsomely at the profession of writing, as were American "literary domestics" such as Augusta Evans Wilson, Mary Virginia Terhune, Maria McIntosh, and Harriet Beecher Stowe. Comments on campus life came to occur more frequently amid the serious essays and lighthearted poetry. The *Album* of October 1879 included a commentary on the transgression of accepted taste in hairstyles in the community: "To our sight there is nothing sadder than a sane woman with her hair banged. A lunatic might be excused for such an erratic style of hair dressing," but not, the writer implies, a Hollins girl. The pages fairly breathe with the energy of

---

3. Vickery, *Historical Sketch*, 27; Niederer, *Illustrated History*, 16; Estelle Freedman, "Separatism as Strategy: Female Institution Building and American Feminism, 1870–1930," *Feminist Studies* 5 (1979): 518.

women expanding their sphere of endeavor by running publications, experimenting with public assertions of their opinions and ideas, and writing for a supportive community of women readers.[4]

At Hollins, the literary societies contributed tangibly and intellectually to the women's community. They donated what became the nucleus of the school library and began presenting gold medals for scholarship and essays. The editorial on the new hairstyle of bangs spoke to a community sense of fashion, but an article entitled "Woman" in the November 1879 *Album* thoughtfully addressed the philosophical aspect of the women's community at Hollins. The unsigned author wrote:

> [Woman's] intellect long reposed in a living tomb [when others denied her intelligence]; but the slumber of ages is broken, and she nobly comes forth to fulfill her mission, and plead the cause of justice and humanity. Already her literary productions have delighted the hearts of thousands; and, they are characterized by a depth and purity of thought rarely found in the writings of man.
>
> May our little paper . . . go forth on its mission to encourage and inspire the minds of our little band, and unite them in their efforts to promote the welfare of their sex in one sacred "bond of union."

The literary societies pursued precisely that mission: to encourage a sense of freedom and support within a women's community by providing a publication in which women could express their social and political views. By 1884 Hollins women not only discussed "Does American Society Deny to Women, as Such, Any Rights?" but also considered the proposition, "Has the Present System of Education in America a Tendency to Unfit Women for the Home Life?" They "saw themselves as being on an academic level with their college brothers" and debated gender issues with passion and directness.[5]

As a final note on the nineteenth-century student culture, it must be observed that the liveliness of this postbellum writing and discussion occurred within a limited context. Southern families had, after all, sent their daughters to Hollins so they would become ladies. Although the high-spirited motto of the yearbook *Spinster* was "Where singleness is bliss, 't is folly to be wives," the *Semi-Annual* still entitled the 1899 list of upcoming weddings as

4. "Locals," *Euzelian Album* (January 1878): 6; see Mary Kelley, *Private Woman, Public Stage: Literary Domesticity in Nineteenth-Century America* (New York, 1984), viii; "Banged Hair," *Album* (October 1879): 11.

5. "Woman," *Album* (November 1879): 8; Niederer, *Illustrated History*, 29; Packard, "Conservative Progress," 100.

"The Ultimate End of All." Interestingly—and perhaps logically so—the young women of Hollins Institute ended the century sharing with Cocke the tension between conventional expectations of women's roles and a keen appreciation of women's intellect. As Nancy Cott observes in writing about nineteenth-century women's education, "The orientation toward gender in their education fostered women's consciousness of themselves as a group united in purpose, duties, and interests. From the sense among women that they shared a collective destiny, it was but another step (though a steep one) to sense that they might shape that destiny with their own minds and hands." In the case of Hollins, that step was gained by small but steady increments of change within the student culture.[6]

Early in the twentieth century, the ground rules for literature were undergoing significant changes as the study of American literature became institutionalized in the college system. In 1909 speakers at the Modern Language Association convention were worrying "how to bring literary study more in line with 'the ideal of masculine culture.'" Hollins women did indeed begin a series of celebrations of men's writings: 1909 saw a large celebration of the centenary of Poe; 1912 included a festival in honor of Dickens; the grandest celebration by far was the 1916 celebration of the tercentenary of Shakespeare's death. On the other hand, the student culture at Hollins was strengthened by the network of support for student writing within the college community. Two new student publications, *Hollins Student Life* and the *Magazine,* took over when the Euzelian and Euepian Literary Societies faded. In 1928, *Hollins Student Life* ran advertisements for the essay contest on interracial cooperation. By the same year the new literary magazine *Cargoes* had begun winning awards in Virginia college magazine competitions. State magazines had begun to remark upon the writing success of Hollins' alumnae, such as Mrs. E. M. Gilmer ("Dorothy Dix") of New Orleans, one of the most popular writers of the day. The cumulative effect of these activities and publications was to have the students experience a writing life vitally integrated both with their studies and with the political world around them, even at a time when the modernist professionalization of literature was implicitly denying women any authority over determining what was "worthy and 'best'" in American writing.[7]

6. Packard, "Conservative Progress," 103; Cott, *Bonds of Womanhood,* 125.

7. Elizabeth Ammons, *Conflicting Stories: American Women Writers at the Turn into the Twentieth Century* (New York, 1991), 16; Niederer, *Illustrated History,* 90; Ammons, *Conflicting Stories,* 15.

Louis D. Rubin, Jr., in his office at Hollins College

At Hollins in the early 1950s, a creative writing program had been designed, and even that was radically changed and expanded in 1957. By 1960 the creative writing program became the first humanities program in the college to offer a master's degree. Central to this new program was the creation of one-year appointments for a writer-in-residence, an addition that was to have powerful and shaping effects on the writing program at Hollins. In 1957, Louis D. Rubin, Jr., arrived at Hollins. The college administration was making a concerted effort to become nationally competitive, and he had the energy and insight to seize opportunities and direct that effort on behalf of the community of writers. Rubin's scholarly development and the evolution of the professionalized writing program had an important bearing on writers at Hollins, and so both bear a closer examination.

Praised as a "legend" by writer Eudora Welty and excoriated for his paternalistic grip on the southern critical establishment by Jefferson Humphries, Louis D. Rubin, Jr., has undeniably had a formative influence on the shape of southern literary studies. In 1963, however, the greater part of his career lay still ahead of him; to his students at Hollins, Louis Rubin was simply a fine teacher who took them and their writing quite seriously. At Hollins, his passion and vision for the writing program led him to take personal responsibility for each English major in the department; and that personal interaction between Rubin and his students helped change his thinking about women writers, inspired cordial mentor-student relationships, and established bonds of respect and affection that have continued as a community of support ever since. Though sometimes criticized for his authoritarian ways, Rubin has been consistently credited by faculty members and college records with the phenomenal strengthening of the writing program. His role in developing an environment for writers demonstrates the degree to which Hollins women had forced traditional paternalism to become paternalism-by-negotiation, a new type of interpersonal relationship acknowledging a central place for women's voices and women's stories.

Louis Rubin advised his students to write about the life experiences they had known; his own scholarship has reflected that theoretical perspective. Rubin's literary interests had their beginnings in a childhood spent in Charleston, South Carolina, where, according to his own accounts, Rubin first gained his interest in southern history. For Rubin, "place" was really the nexus for a community made cohesive by bonds of commitment and aspiration, and the South after the world wars was still a place to which one "'belonged' . . . and [in which one] did not merely reside." Similarly, Hollins came to be a very special place for Rubin—not just a college but a cause to which one belonged. Hence, both in his scholarly and teaching careers, Rubin celebrated the ties of affection and—according to his critics—nostalgia. Such a sentimental view when applied to literary studies has proven exclusive and restrictive, suggest critics Joan Schulz and Jefferson Humphries, who fault Rubin for overlooking the writings of people who existed outside the literary community as he conceived it.[8] But Rubin lacked such a critique until late in his career, and so his early-developed sense of belonging to the South—of *"place* as a community"—remained an unchallenged assumption in nearly all of his scholarly work.[9]

8. Schulz, "Orphaning as Resistance," 91. See also Jefferson Humphries, "Introduction: On the Inevitability of Theory in Southern Literary Study," in *Southern Literature and Literary Theory* (Athens, Ga., 1990), vii–xviii.

9. Louis D. Rubin, Jr., "The Way It Was with Southern Literary Study: A Reminiscence," *Mississippi Quarterly*, 43 (1990): 149; Louis D. Rubin, Jr., *The American South: Portrait of a Culture* (Baton Rouge, 1980), 7; Rubin, "Hollins College," 9. Interestingly, in *The Curious Death of the Novel: Essays in American Literature* (Baton Rouge, 1967), v–vi, Rubin does discuss "the difference of a Jew in a Christian society" as one of the examples of "the writer's relationship

Rubin earned his master of arts degree from Johns Hopkins in 1949 and then stayed for four more years as an instructor and an editor for the *Hopkins Review*. Teaching creative writing proved to be an unanticipated delight and intellectual stimulation for him. One of his first students in creative writing was John Barth, and among his early colleagues were poet Julia Randall Sawyer, whom he would later hire to teach in the English department at Hollins, and writer Russell Baker. Although he was pleased with his teaching assignments, it was as editor of the *Hopkins Review* that Rubin began to pursue what would become his best-known scholarly interest, his critical study of southern literature. He and coeditor Robert Jacobs began devoting increasingly greater space to the study of southern writers, culminating in a collection of twenty-nine essays in 1953. The title of the collection, *Southern Renascence: The Literature of the Modern South,* was suggested by Agrarian poet and critic Allen Tate. It was the editing of these *Southern Renascence* essays that effectively marked the beginning of Rubin's shaping influence on southern literary studies and foreshadowed his association with the writings of the Agrarians, the primary body of work he would illuminate and promote effectively in the years to come.[10]

While at Johns Hopkins, Rubin also energetically pursued doctoral studies with southern historian C. Vann Woodward in history but felt that he met with open hostility from the English department over the idea that "there really *was* something that might be called a Southern literature." In fact, he clashed so bitterly with one member of the English department on this point that he eventually formed a committee of George Poulet (director), Leo Spitzer, George Boas, Elliott Coleman, and C. Vann Woodward to supervise his dissertation, "The Weather of His Youth: A Study of the Form of Autobiographical Fiction in the Work of Thomas Wolfe." Owing to this conflict, the doctoral degree he earned in 1954 was in the field of Aesthetics of Literature rather than English, creating a situation that Rubin believed haunted his job search for several years. George Boas eventually helped him secure a job at the University of Pennsylvania as the executive secretary of the American

---

with and alienation from his society" but does not draw a personal connection with that experience. The original version of the chapter "The Experience of Difference: Southerners and Jews" appeared in the *Southern Review* as a review entitled "Southerners and Jews."

10. *Hopkins Review* 6 (1953): table of contents. Rubin and Jacobs both wrote essays for this symposium, as did Agrarians Donald Davidson and Andrew Nelson Lytle; Rubin, "Southern Literary Study," 152.

Studies Association, and there, under the direction of Robert Spiller, Rubin administered the Carnegie grant that was intended to establish regional chapters of the association throughout the country. In this capacity, Rubin was also able to maintain his commitment to the idea that the Agrarians were central to southern studies by applying for—and securing—the Rockefeller grant that funded the official reunion of the Agrarians at Vanderbilt in 1956.[11]

Rubin quickly tired of being what he described as "a visiting academic Rotarian."[12] Rubin had continued writing features for the *Richmond Times-Dispatch* and the *Baltimore Sun,* and so when he received an offer from his friend James J. Kilpatrick to become an associate editor of the *Richmond News-Leader,* he accepted the position with the full intention of making journalism his life's work. He soon discovered, though, that he missed the academic life and began applying for teaching positions. President Everett of Hollins, consolidating his plan to establish a nationally competitive college, hired Rubin. In doing so, Everett gained for Hollins a proven scholar, an inspiring teacher, and a man who, as events unfolded, did in fact establish a nationally acclaimed writing program. In rapid succession Rubin had published *The Lasting South; No Place on Earth: James Branch Cabell, Ellen Glasgow, and Richmond-in-Virginia;* and *Teach the Freeman: The Correspondence of R. B. Hayes and the Slater Fund for Negro Education, 1881–1893.* The English department head, Mary V. Long, retired, and Rubin became chair of the English department, a position he was to hold until 1967, when he went to teach at the University of North Carolina in Chapel Hill.

Despite some initial reservations about the academic goals of Hollins, Rubin came to the college with a seemingly indefatigable passion for writing, teaching, and publication. In 1967 Rubin praised President Logan, Everett's successor, for being "willing to take a chance with a new idea, to support those who wanted to try out new projects." In reality the projects reveal the energy and ambition of Rubin during his decade at Hollins: "The establishment of an English Department news-letter for present and former students; a national literary magazine, *The Hollins Critic;* a week-long festival marking the birth of the Irish poet William Butler Yeats; an annual poetry contest for women high school students east of the Mississippi; supplements to the budget of the campus literary magazine, *Cargoes,* in order to print the entire texts

11. Rubin, "Southern Literary Study, " 151, 154.
12. Ibid., 154.

of several student novels; book publication of a group of student term papers on the French novelist Marcel Proust; an undergraduate scholarly journal, *The Hollins Symposium;* an annual contest for Southeastern college and university newspapers." Faculty members also credit Rubin with finally securing in 1961 a long-desired chapter of Phi Beta Kappa. No one, of course, can accomplish such results without the support of students, colleagues, and administrators; but the overwhelming consensus in the Hollins College community of that time was that Rubin was the originator and primary driving force behind each of these achievements. During his decade at Hollins, Rubin edited or wrote six books and numerous articles while maintaining a full schedule of teaching, advising, and faculty meetings. With each publication he always gave generous credit not only to his colleagues but to his students. For example, in *The Faraway Country* (1963) Rubin thanks not only John Aldridge but his students Katherine Letcher, Shannon Ravenel, Elizabeth Seydel, and Anna Sevier.[13]

The crucial institutional structure that Rubin established at Hollins, however, was the writing program. The concept of collegiate writing programs in this country shared the same impulse that motivated the formation of American literary studies earlier in the century: the desire to establish one's field of interest as a professional field that required apprentice work and academic training as prerequisites to a career. Michael O'Brien has observed that "the New Criticism was . . . the intellectual equivalent of professionalization for the student of literature." Critic Bruce Bawer explains this connection by observing that at the beginning of this century, "professors of poetry did not teach the writing of poetry, and they almost never taught the work of living writers. . . . [This practice] did not change noticeably, in America, until mid-century, when a substantial number of universities began to offer courses and workshops in writing." The writing programs were, he argues, "in a roundabout way . . . a consequence of modernism—an unfortunate, unforeseen by-product of the modernist precept that poetry should be avant-garde and should *epater le bourgeoisie,* of T. S. Eliot's pronouncement that poetry must be difficult, of Ezra Pound's deliberate composition of poetry for an audience not of ordinary literate people but of poets. During the

13. Rubin, "Hollins College," 69–70. Ravenel was for years editor of Houghton Mifflin's annual *Best American Short Stories.* She is now editor of Algonquin Books' *New Stories from the South: The Year's Best.*

modern period, such attitudes as these, on the parts of poets, effectively alien-
ated them from the general public; no longer 'the unacknowledged legislators
of the world,' they became Talmudic scholars of a sort, communing with
themselves and with one another in language that was often deliberately private, uninviting, exclusionary." Deprived of a general audience, Bawer concludes, poetry had "retreated to the only place that would have it—the university." In essence, the writing programs began as preserves for protecting
and extending the influence of modernist literary theory. Through this network system, a particular brand of literary criticism—New Criticism—was
quickly propagated. William Stafford remembers with awe the instruction
he received from powerful New Critics such as John Crowe Ransom and
Robert Penn Warren. On one occasion, wrote Stafford, John Crowe Ransom
mistakenly analyzed two of Stafford's poem as one poem: "That afternoon
the new criticism welded my poems brilliantly together, and I was too grati-
fied, and too timid, to pull them apart." Such was the authoritative power of
the New Critics.[14]

Bawer observes that the university creative writing program has ultimately become "a venue in which, all too frequently, the quality of the verse
that a contemporary poet has written seems a far less reliable index of his relative importance than the grants and fellowships he has received, the writing
colonies he has attended, the universities at which he has studied, taught, or
given readings and the number of books he has published."[15] At a practical
level, the establishment of writing programs underwrote writers' incomes
and legitimated writing as an academic study leading to professional careers
as creative writing teachers if not self-supporting writers. Graduates from the
Iowa program, for instance, were deemed certified writers whose work should
be accepted for publication and who would be the best leaders of other writing programs such as those at Stanford. Gradually such programs gained in
popularity because they were such strong, self-sustaining educational systems. Certain programs, such as Iowa's, seemed to dominate the network.
Louis Rubin, as a product and a proponent of New Critical theory, understood how to bring these standards of professionalization to Hollins. Draw-

14. Michael O'Brien, *The Idea of the American South, 1920–1941* (Baltimore, 1979), 224;
Bruce Bawer, "Poetry and the University" in *Poetry After Modernism*, ed. Robert McDowell
(Brownsville, Ore., 1991), 59, 62; William Stafford, *Writing the Australian Crawl: Views on the
Writer's Vocation* (Ann Arbor, 1978), 158.

15. Bawer, "Poetry and the University," 56.

ing on his experience in the writing program at Johns Hopkins, Rubin used his considerable administrative, entrepreneurial, and pedagogical skills to create a similar program that allowed Hollins to become a powerful if not an iconoclastic writing center in the 1960s.

The means by which Rubin created a nationally recognized writing program at Hollins were initially tied to institutional changes at the school. He wished to admit a small number of graduate students—no more than two or three—from a pool of male and female applicants. The graduate students would have independent study courses, but central to Rubin's concept was the notion that graduate students and undergraduates would be equal members in the advanced writing seminars. Part of the reason for this design arose from Rubin's belief that the Hollins women seldom experienced men taking them seriously as intellects. He decided "that having a few young men on campus [in the graduate program] who thought that writing was the most important thing in the world would be a hell of a good thing for some of those girls to see—particularly the Southern girls [who felt torn between a profession and marriage]." Not everyone in the English department liked the idea of the graduate program in creative writing, and some argued "that a small liberal arts college could not sustain a major writing program, . . . that writers do not make good literature teachers, and . . . that creative writing has only a peripheral place in the college curriculum."[16] But Rubin was convinced of its importance, Everett wanted Hollins to start breaking new ground, and a graduate program in creative writing was a move in that direction.

A second institutional change integral, in Rubin's thinking, to the success of a writing program and to the attraction of good students was a central feature of other professional writing programs: the funding for a professional writer who could live for a year on the campus and work closely with the creative writing students. The first appointee was novelist and critic John W. Aldridge. However, it was the second writer-in-residence who brought the stroke of luck that launched Hollins' national reputation as a literary center. William Golding, a writer relatively unknown to the American reading public at the time, readily accepted Rubin's offer of the position of writer-in-residence. Although it had been in print for seven years, *Lord of the Flies* received little critical notice in America until after the 1959 paperback version

16. Rubin, personal interview, May 7, 1991; Renee Crist, "Writers' Reunion," *Hollins* (January 9, 1987): 9.

was issued. Just as Golding arrived on campus at Hollins, *Lord of the Flies* became wildly popular in American universities and schools and among the wider reading public. Suddenly Hollins gained notice in national publications such as the *New York Times Book Review.* The July 1963 *Esquire* listed Hollins in its Directory of the American Literary Establishment. Annie Doak (Dillard) and other young women began applying to Hollins, they said, primarily because of the writing program. Golding certainly spread Hollins' fame: he visited thirty campuses during his year there, prompting *Time*'s comment that he was "a rarely resident writer-in-residence at Virginia's Hollins College."[17] The celebrity Golding's presence gave Hollins' writing program a national recognition that it had never heretofore enjoyed.

The recognition created by Golding's residence and the savvy guidance of Louis Rubin helped establish the strength of the writing program, allowing it to attract a succession of important writers. When Rubin taught at the Bread Loaf Writers' Conference in 1962, he met poet Howard Nemerov and hired him from Bennington College for a year's residence at Hollins. The 1963–1964 list of speakers, including Iowa program writer Flannery O'Connor, attracted great attention. On this matter of a writer-in-residence Rubin had proved to be astute: good writers-in-residence attracted other good and interested younger writers to his program. The institutional structures of the program were in place to attract talented young writers, but creating a challenging, supportive environment was vital to sustaining these writers. It was largely due to Rubin's efforts, then, that the Hollins Group found a cooperative, competitive writing environment at their small campus that was richly filled with models, mentors, and opportunities for writing and self-discovery. It is worth taking some time to examine these elements in detail and in order of occurrence to see how Hollins may have appeared at the time to the Hollins Group during the years they were developing their craft.

The freshman year in college is an impressionable time for any young person, and an astute young writer would be testing the air to see what literary winds prevailed. Rubin's promotion of the writing program ensured that the women of the Hollins Group could quickly find extensive evidence of successful publication by alumnae of the writing program. When they arrived on

---

17. *Time* magazine noted that *Lord of the Flies* had first been published in America in 1955 and had sold only 2,383 copies before going out of print; the 1959 edition, however, had quickly sold 65,000 copies (June 22, 1962, p. 64).

campus, the first issue they read of the school newspaper announced that *Porphyry*, a first novel by alumna and former Rubin pupil Anna Sevier and originally published in its entirety in the college literary magazine *Cargoes*, had been accepted for publication by Atheneum. In spring of their freshman year, Katie Letcher Lyle, a former student of John Allen and Louis Rubin, had ten poems accepted for a forthcoming volume of poetry. Sylvia Wilkinson, whose novel *Moss on the North Side* had recently appeared in *Cargoes*, won a $1,000 Saxton Fellowship to complete the book for publication by Harper & Row. The incoming freshmen could not help but see the standards established by young women who, though only a few years older than themselves, were winning contracts with major presses.[18]

The women of the Hollins Group also met and worked with an array of professional writers who had succeeded in the literary mainstream of New Critical or Agrarian writing. In 1963 the English department, rather than having a single writer-in-residence, was sponsoring a series of writers who could each stay for a few days on campus, give a public reading, and work individually with writing students. Flannery O'Connor began the series in October; Pulitzer Prize winner Karl Shapiro visited in November; Eudora Welty visited in December; Pulitzer Prize winner Robert Penn Warren read in January; Andrew Lytle visited in February; in March, Peter Taylor, Richard Wilbur, and George Garrett worked with the Literary Festival. The year ended with the April visit of Library of Congress poetry consultant and former Hollins writer-in-residence Howard Nemerov. The students viewed it as an exceptional opportunity to work with any one of these writers; having access to so many was extraordinary.

Freshmen writers soon learned as well to recognize the pattern of regular publishing by the English department faculty members. On a routine and daily basis, students had the model of Rubin himself as an active writer and publishing scholar. Faculty member John Allen observed that Rubin spent about fifteen hours per week on his own writing—in addition to his teaching and other activities. During their freshman year, in the space of a few months

18. "Anna Sevier Publishes Novel She Wrote Here," *Hollins Columns*, September 17, 1963, p. 4.; "Katie Letcher Lyle to Present Concert," ibid., April 9, 1964, p. 1. Lyle (Hollins '59), president of Grapheon and associate editor of *Cargoes*, had read her original compositions at a Hollins literary festival that had featured writers Randall Jarrell and James Dickey; Wilkinson studied as an undergraduate with Jarrell at the Woman's College of the University of North Carolina. Her first novel had been her M. A. thesis for Hollins in 1963.

he had published in the *Kenyon Review* "The Self Recaptured," an article on autobiography in works of fiction; *The Faraway Country*, an argument for the formative influence of landscape in twentieth-century southern writing; and, in the *Journal of Southern History*, the article "The Difficulties of Being a Southern Writer Today; or, Getting Out from Under Faulkner," a discussion of how "New Southern writers must write about their own experiences in their own way." Later, writers of the Hollins Group would also find these subjects to be of interest. For his colleagues in the English department, Rubin was a generous collaborator who characteristically requested their writing for books he edited. The other members of the department became increasingly productive in their writing as exposure to Rubin lengthened. John Allen, observed Richard H. W. Dillard, began to produce more and finer poetry "after Rubin turned him on to himself as a poet."[19]

An influential female role model for the students was English faculty member Julia Randall Sawyer. Sawyer, a friend of Rubin's from the Johns Hopkins years, was the only female member of the English department at this time, and therefore a uniquely significant figure for her students. Sawyer and Rubin were close friends who readily disagreed over points in literature yet dedicated books to each other.[20] Rubin even sometimes acted as an unpaid literary agent for her. As we shall see in later chapters, Sawyer was particularly important for Lucinda Hardwick (MacKethan), Annie Doak (Dillard), Anne Goodwyn Jones, and—to a lesser degree—for Lee Smith. Sawyer, a prolific poet, was passionate about literature, and her romantic nature intrigued the young writers, partly because she articulated the struggle they felt in perceiving themselves as writers. Once when a student interviewer asked if she considered herself to be a poet, Sawyer replied, "No. We spend most of our lives trying to identify what we are. Writing it down is a good way of finding it out." Sawyer's students would later follow that philosophy, seeking self-definition through their writing.[21]

19. John Allen, personal interview, January 17, 1991; "Louis Rubin's New Article Discusses Dilemma of Today's Southern Writers," *Hollins Columns*, January 9, 1964, p. 2; Richard H. W. Dillard, personal interview, March 5, 1992.

20. Rubin's dedication for *The Writer in the South: Studies in a Literary Community* (Athens, Ga., 1972) was "To Julia Randall—'Thou art not of the fashion of these times, / Where none will sweat but for promotion.'"

21. *Calliope's Comments* (the Hollins English Department newsletter) (May 1, 1965): 11; Kay Kendall, "Julia Sawyer and John Allen Will Give Poetry Reading Sponsored by Grapheon," *Hollins Columns*, April 16, 1964, p. 1.

Another professional area in which Louis Rubin exerted his influence was in seeking numerous avenues for seeing the work of Hollins faculty and students into print. January 1964 marked the first publication of the *Hollins Critic*, Rubin's idea for a small, bimonthly journal of criticism and writing aimed at a general informed audience. A more personal form of support for publication came in March 1964, when Rubin bought a printing press, which the *Hollins Columns* instantly dubbed Rubin's "Tinker Toy."[22] Rubin, John Allen, and John Moore undertook the physical work of running the press and made a first formal printing consisting of thirty numbered copies of *4 Poems by Julia Randall.* The second printing consisted of three poems by creative writing students for the May Day 1964 celebrations. John Allen's *Pismire Agonistes and Other Poems* constituted the third publication, a limited edition of approximately forty-five copies. In January of 1966, Tinker Press also published *The Duel and Other Poems,* a book of poems by student Margaret Ferguson.[23]

In addition to his own publication and that of his colleagues, Rubin worked equally hard on behalf of student involvement in all aspects of publishing. Anna Sevier was the first product of the Hollins seminars and was an advisee of Rubin. Despite some opposition within the department, it was Rubin who pressed to devote the entire 1962 issue of *Cargoes* to the publication of her senior project, and it was he who sent a copy of that issue to Hiram Haydn at Atheneum Publishers. Rubin wanted Sevier to enter the master's writing program at Hopkins, but her father refused to send her, wanting her to go instead to Katherine Gibbs in New York. In Rubin's opinion, Sevier had not been given the opportunity she deserved.[24] In some instances, as was true with Anna Sevier, Rubin acted as literary agent to publishers. In other cases, Rubin attempted direct publication, as when, impressed with student essays from his course on Proust, he persuaded the administration of the college to publish the collection of essays as a book. He also helped develop during 1963 the first Nancy Thorp Prize, a poetry contest for female students in high

22. The colophon, designed by Lewis O. Thompson, showed Tinker Mountain looming as a backdrop to Hollins College. Tinker Creek borders the campus—hence the name Tinker Press. The press was a 2,000-pound 1913 proof press with Caslon Old Style handset type: Owie Easton, "Mr. Rubin Acquires New Tinker Toy to Be Used in Connection with Hollins," *Hollins Columns,* March 19, 1964, p. 3. Later Rubin acquired an 8-by-12 Chandler & Press job press.
23. *Calliope's Comments* (May 20, 1966): 6, 9. Margaret Ferguson Gibson later published several volumes of poetry and won both the Lamont and Melville Cane Prizes for poetry.
24. Rubin, personal interview, May 7, 1991.

schools east of the Mississippi. Notably, the winner was selected by the English faculty and by advanced creative writing students. Here, as in other instances, Rubin credited the seriousness of the students and helped support a critical women's writing community by taking into account their criticisms in the judging of the contest.

A final example of Rubin's support for student publication was the establishment of the *Hollins Symposium*, a lithographed scholarly journal publishing the best student papers from different courses. An editorial committee of students selected the *Symposium* essays from among papers submitted through various departments at Hollins. In her senior year, Annie Doak Dillard's essay on Emily Dickinson would appear in the *Symposium*. The mere establishment of such a journal attested to the thoughtfulness with which the students' writing and criticism were considered. With their own editorial board, Hollins women writers were able to make their own critical judgments concerning the writing of their peers without pressure from the institution that created the board.

Rubin's climactic years of teaching at Hollins—marked by energetic teaching and work on behalf of student publication—intertwined with the collegiate careers of the Hollins Group. Beginning with their freshman year, the English department faculty engaged these women's minds in class and shared life with them outside of class. Rubin did not single-handedly foster a sense of community and support at Hollins, but he did promote many activities that broke down barriers isolating class from campus life. Students saw Louis Rubin, Julia Sawyer, and Richard Dillard perform in Faculty Follies dressed in swimsuits or in bird outfits or with the faculty band—the Hollins Hambones—in madcap concerts to benefit scholarship funds. A review of a benefit concert for *Cargoes* captures some of the good cheer that existed between Rubin and the student body. "If you missed the concert," wrote Therry Steinhardt,

> you missed, for example, hearing Dr. Ralph Steinhardt and Dr. Louis Rubin play Schubert. (Schubert lost.) The Glenn Gould of the Constant Temperature Bath blended his melodious ivory-tickling with the efforts of the distinguished Herr Rubin upon the amplified harmonica. In all fairness, we must state that Rubin got the better of the concerto, i.e., he finished first. His cadenza was received with cries of Encore! Bravo! and Gesundheit!
>
> . . . As for the Hambones! . . . [All] joined Loos Rubin for a vocal duet that ended the evening on a suitably low note. (C-flat, I believe.)

Louis Rubin as chair of the Hollins English department
Photo by Kathy Thornton

This personal interaction of faculty members with students was important to the community life, judged Rubin: "The teacher-student relationship at Hollins is the finest I have ever known. It is personal, and yet it is quite digni-fied; it is founded on mutual respect. Occasionally it can be abused, but very rarely; faculty members remain faculty members, students remains students, and each respects the other's status." That personal engagement with students produced an energy and a loyalty that extended far beyond the years spent at Hollins.[25]

The freshman year was, admittedly, an exceptional year of literary events

25. Therry Steinhardt, "Cargoes Benefit: 'An Evening Unique,'" *Hollins Columns*, January 13, 1966, p. 3; Rubin, "Hollins College," 110–11.

and high enthusiasm greeting the Hollins Group, one that their sophomore year did not match in sheer volume.[26] What proved most notable for the Hollins Group during this year was Louis Rubin's absence. Rubin was on leave in Europe and in North Carolina on an American Council of Learned Societies Fellowship to conduct a critical study of the form of the novel. His letters back to the college provide yet another perspective on the way Rubin interacted with students while on campus. In November of 1964, Rubin wrote an open letter to the editor of the *Hollins Columns* from Salerno, Italy. The letter was a humorous report on family news that ended by noting "that we miss you all."[27] The gentle humor of the correspondence—and of its reception—testifies to the warm esteem in which Rubin and the Hollins community held each other. After his return from Italy, Rubin accepted a second-semester appointment at the University of North Carolina and Duke Co-operative Program in the Humanities, where he aggressively pursued his scholarly interests. He also assumed general editorship of the new Louisiana State University Southern Literary Studies Series.

The final two years at Hollins of the class of 1967 continued to involve the students in a rich literary ferment.[28] From the schedule of literary events, sev-

26. The only major institutional change on the literary scene was *Hollins Columns'* cosponsorship of a national awards competition for college newspapers. Irish writer Benedict Kiely was writer-in-residence, and visiting writers included Allen Tate, Rubin's former pupil John Barth, Fred Chappell, Russell Baker, Mary Lee Settle, and Randall Jarrell. Speaking at the literary festival in March were playwright-in-residence Arnold Weinstein, Daniel Hoffman, and Reed Whittemore. Weinstein's new play, "The Party," was given as a special performance.

27. "Rubins Ravage Ravello, L.D.R. Looks for Pencil," *Hollins Columns*, November 5, 1964, p. 4.

28. Their junior year (1965–1966) found William Jay Smith, poetry critic for *Harper's* and faculty member at Williams College, as writer-in-residence. A Rhodes scholar, Smith had already won the *Poetry Magazine* Prize in 1954, the National Book Award for Poetry in 1962, and a Ford Foundation grant to interest poets in writing for the theater. At Hollins, Smith worked with the advanced creative writing class, taught a seminar on the French symbolists, and hosted the premier of his play *The Straw-Market*. Visiting writers to the college included George Garrett and David Slavitt. At that time Garrett had won a Sewanee Review Fellowship in poetry, the Grand Prix de Rome, and a Ford Fellowship in drama; Slavitt had been a regular contributor to the *Yale Review*, the *New Republic*, the *Kenyon Review*, and the *Sewanee Review*. The annual literary festival in March featured John Hawkes and Charles Eaton. At this time Hawkes was assistant professor of English at Brown University and recipient of a Guggenheim grant, a National Institute of Arts and Letters Award, and a Ford Foundation Fellowship for study with a professional theater company. Eaton, a protégé of Robert Frost's at the Bread Loaf Writers'

eral emerged as remarkable. Eudora Welty returned to the campus to receive the Hollins Medal in honor of her work in fiction. Richard Dillard and his wife/former student Annie Doak Dillard published poetry in *The Girl in the Black Raincoat* poetry anthology.[29] The senior year for the Hollins Group was also Rubin's last year at Hollins: in the fall of 1967 he left to take a position at the University of North Carolina at Chapel Hill. His departure prompted numerous farewell exchanges in the college paper. In several public letters, he explained that his "research interests in the field of Southern literary studies will best be served by moving to a large university such as Chapel Hill." The editors of the paper published a tribute to Rubin, crediting him for the work he had done to establish Hollins as a strong college and closing with remarks that again suggest the close faculty-student relationships felt on the campus:

> As is the case with all good teachers and advisors, he has greatly influenced and inspired his students. It is perhaps in these personal relationships with his students for the last 10 years that all his efforts are most meaningful and lasting. Actually, we can't wait until 1:15 tomorrow when Louie D., cigar in mouth, will point out the spelling mistakes, the bumping headlines, the 50¢ words where a 10¢ word would have been better, and all the other imperfections which characterize the *Columns* . . . .

Conference, was a runner-up in the National Book Award contest in 1957. Perhaps the event that touched closest to the hearts of the students, however, was the publication of Julia Randall Sawyer's first major book of poetry, *The Puritan Carpenter.* Advance praises were written by prominent critics—Allen Tate, Howard Nemerov, and George Garrett—and are implicit evidence of the network of influence and goodwill that Rubin had established for Hollins writers. The friendly ties, however, did not make any less sincere Tate's judgment that Sawyer's book "will take its place as one of the few distinguished volumes of the 1960's. The range and subtlety of her sensitivity, her large literary cultivation, her mastery of verse techniques, and not least her intelligence, rank her with the best poets of our time." The students were pleased and impressed at the success of their favorite female teacher.

During the senior year of the Hollins Group, the young women routinely found successful writers—and promising Hollins alumnae—as elements of their literary environment. Colin Wilson was writer-in-residence; Howard Nemerov and James J. Kilpatrick were featured speakers on campus. Sylvia Wilkinson's novel was finally published, not by Harper & Row but by Houghton Mifflin, where Shannon Ravenel (Hollins '60) was editor.

29. The spring issue of *Southern Poetry Review* included two poems by Richard Dillard and two by Julia Randall Sawyer. Richard Dillard published his first book, *The Day I Stopped Dreaming About Barbara Steele and Other Poems* and also joined with Louis Rubin in securing a contract with Macmillan for a textbook.

At any rate, we knew we're not the only ones, by a long shot, who want to thank him for all he's done and been, nor the only ones who wish him success and happiness at Chapel Hill.

In the next issue, Rubin replied in kind, stating, "There is no other college quite like it. To have been part of it for ten years has been a privilege that I shall cherish for all my days."[30] An era had ended.

This review of Rubin's career through his years at Hollins establishes several specific characteristics of Rubin's academic character. He was a man who had a vision about literature that was, in part, translated into an academic community joined by affection and intellectual interest in the study of writing. His willingness to be humorous in the Faculty Follies and his gruff but warm personal rapport with the students testified to his affection for that community. His indefatigable efforts to publish his own work and that of his colleagues and students were evidence of the commitment to writing and publication that he believed the community should hold. As a mentor, he demonstrated for his students a viable career that balanced personal interest with high achievement.

Yet this portrait does not fully describe the complex cultural issue of having an authoritative male scholar teaching at a women's institution of higher learning during the 1960s. Because Louis Rubin has been such a powerful scholar in southern studies—in fact has sometimes been described by the suggestive epithet "The Father of Southern Literary Studies"—his opinions have had far-reaching influence and are subject to new scrutiny. Rubin has assuredly been a supporter of the Agrarians and a scholar schooled in New Critical theory, and these longstanding intellectual attachments are particular points on which he is criticized. Critic Michael O'Brien has argued that Rubin's anthologies created a restrictive canon because they followed too neatly Allen Tate's highly partisan definition of southern literature. Jefferson Humphries has faulted Rubin for being generation-bound, for failing to embrace new approaches to literary theory such as deconstruction, and for faltering in any support of avant-garde readings. The Agrarian and New Critical perspectives of the "Rubin generation," writes Humphries, led to a false "kind of global synthesis" that failed to look at "the complex ways in which

---

30. "Rubin Accepts New Post," *Hollins Columns,* March 14, 1967, p. 1; "Louis Rubin," ibid., March 14, 1967, p. 2; Louis Rubin, "Rubin Leaves Hollins with His Blessing," ibid., March 21, 1967, p. 6.

Rubin and his notorious amplified harmonica

the literary, the historical, and all the 'human sciences' that study both, are interrelated." By these lights, the New Criticism, with its preference for studying the literary work as a locus of objective meaning, was limited in scope.[31]

Revisionists have also criticized the Rubin generation's belief that the historical roots of southern fiction tension drew on the legacy of the Civil War to the exclusion of such issues as the revolution in race relations then occurring in the South. The older generation, Humphries argues, has "a rather sentimental and celebratory view of the past" that is only "a thinner, watered-down version of the nationalist, ideological organicism of the Old South."[32] Humphries' assessments—sketched only briefly here—demonstrate the best and worst of what literary history-as-hindsight has to offer. On one hand, Humphries criticizes the fact that southern critical standards were formed

31. Michael O'Brien, *Rethinking the South: Essays in Intellectual History* (Baltimore, 1988), 167; Humphries, "Inevitability of Theory," vii–xviii.

32. Humphries, "Inevitability of Theory," xvi, xv.

around the theories of white male Agrarians, that they ignored the legacy of significant women and African-American writers, and that they drew such power from the New Critical literary establishment that they effectively discounted alternative literary theories. On the other hand, Humphries represents literary criticism as an unforgiving discipline, assessing only by contemporary insights and standards.

Revisionist scholars also assert that the Agrarian and New Critical theorists held such a stranglehold on international literary studies that for years it seemed scarcely possible to conceive of an alternative literary perspective. In southern letters, Allen Tate and the other Agrarian writers whom Rubin admired dominated the critical center of any significant study of southern literature, and feminist critics argue that these powerful scholars dictated a self-serving understanding of southern literary history.[33] Critic Carol Manning observes that as recently as 1979, Rubin's preface to *The Literary South* credited an all-male list of "my personal friends and most of the leading scholars in my field. For in general, the study of Southern literature has largely involved a community of scholars and gentlemen who are friends and fellow workers, and it has been a privilege to be part of this activity. I must also thank those students who have helped me in forming ideas and insights."[34] The difficulty with this perspective, argues Manning, is that this all-male critical community of scholars favored writers much like themselves: "The reputations of the scholars who have chiefly shaped our thinking about Southern literature—Allen Tate, Hugh Holman, Louis D. Rubin, Jr., Lewis P. Simpson, to name a few—rival the reputations of many of the artists about whom they write. We might safely say that the critical theory on the Southern Renaissance has itself become part of the Southern Renaissance." Susan Donaldson makes the case more pointedly: "Tate's version of the Southern literary profession may appear reassuringly unified and homogeneous—it is, after all, implicitly defined as white, male and critically detached—but the tidiness of that definition requires the dismissal of most women writers in the South" and of most African-American writers as well. Critic Jan Cooper

33. See Susan Donaldson, "Gender and the Profession of Letters in the South," in *Rewriting the South: History and Fiction*, ed. Lothar Honnighausen and Valeria Gennaro Lerda (Tubingen, Germany, 1993), 35.

34. Louis D. Rubin, Jr., ed., *The Literary South* (Baton Rouge, 1979), vi–vii. This observation about an all-male scholarly community was made by Carol S. Manning in her introduction to *The Female Tradition in Southern Literature*, 7.

concurs: "Holman, Rubin, and Tate (as well as other critics) agree that a profound change took place in Southern literature around 1920, a shift from two dimensional, sentimental, primarily rhetorical works to a literature of universal significance. These critics base such observations almost exclusively on the writing of white Southerners" and virtually ignore Zora Neale Hurston, Jean Toomer, Richard Wright, and Langston Hughes, who drew on the southern past but who "did not view the Southern mythic past in the same way as their white contemporaries."[35]

Rubin has admitted some limitations regarding African-American writers and, in particular, has cited an instance in 1960 when he had, as an editor, rejected an essay on Jean Toomer's *Cane* because "I did not even know that I *didn't* know" about black southern writers. In his preface to *The Writer in the South,* Rubin conceded that he could not contribute to the discussion of black southern writers because "the black Southern writer . . . obviously has been involved in a relationship to Southern society and Southern attitudes that is very different from that of the white Southern author, so that my generalizations and suppositions about the community relationship would require a whole new kind of approach and examination. I should like to do that some day." In fact, in 1974 he published with Blyden Jackson *Black Poetry in America: Two Essays in Historical Interpretation.*[36]

By admission, too, Rubin's view of southern literature was shaped by his personal experience of the South. Southern writing had provided, he wrote, "a way of defining myself, of understanding who and what I was," and his identity was that of a white male in a segregated, male-dominated region. Rubin was certainly aware of some paradoxes of southern life. He wrote, "To be a Southerner today is still to be heir to a complex set of attitudes and affinities, assumptions and instincts, that are the product of history acting upon geography, even though much of the history is now forgotten and the geography modified." Certainly his personal view was shaped by his life in and affection for the South. Revisionists do make some valid critiques of the way in which the historical canon developed in the South, but there is a dan-

---

35. Carol S. Manning, "The Real Beginning of the Southern Renaissance," in *Female Tradition in Southern Literature,* ed. Manning, 37; Donaldson, "Gender and the Profession of Letters," 36; Jan Cooper, "Zora Neale Hurston Was Always a Southerner Too," ibid., 61.

36. Louis D. Rubin, column, *Chapel Hill Weekly,* April 16, 1972, p. 2; Rubin, *Writer in the South,* xiv; Louis D. Rubin, Jr., and Blyden Jackson, eds., *Black Poetry in America: Two Essays in Historical Interpretation* (Baton Rouge, 1974).

ger in oversimplifying Rubin's case by ignoring instances in which he has gone against the grain of the critical establishment by championing Thomas Wolfe and other writers detested by the New Critics and by promoting women's writing. [37]

Given Rubin's literary orientation, what can be made of the rest of his record concerning the treatment and potential of women writers, and how did his literary perspectives influence his thinking prior to Hollins? The picture is complex, even in his early scholarly work concerning the Agrarian writers. Good intentions seemed undermined by critical assumptions. The goal of *Southern Renascence,* wrote Rubin and Jacobs, was to advocate "[n]o single critical outlook, no one critical approach; and essays were accepted from 'persons of varying tastes and interests. . . . Nor have the editors intended that the views embodied in the essays coincide with their own views. The editors hope that the volume provides the first reasonably thorough treatment of the literature of the modern South. They are aware that gaps exist in the presentation.'" Despite these stated goals that avowed openness, the volume undeniably reflected the critical values of the Agrarians. As Carol Manning has observed, "This orthodox view of the Southern Renaissance—as bounded by two wars, quarterbacked by the Fugitives/Agrarians at Nashville, and inspired by the South's attempt to move forward while looking backward—is neat and convenient, but it is hardly realistic. Like most definitions of literary movements, it provides content for literary journals and coherence for college literature courses, but the dating is arbitrary and the described canon constricted. What it slights in particular is the work of Blacks and women. Indeed, it is a decidedly white male-focused view of Southern literature." It should not pass without notice that essays about the women writers Ellen Glasgow, Katherine Anne Porter, Caroline Gordon, and Eudora Welty were included in *Southern Renascence.* One daring feature of this 1953 collection was the inclusion of an essay written by a black woman scholar, Irene Edmonds. To include an essay by an African-American woman in 1953 indicates that Rubin and Jacobs perhaps simply dismissed some contemporary racial and gender biases as being irrelevant to good scholarship.[38]

The entire scope of Louis Rubin's influence on southern literary studies is

---

37. Rubin, "Southern Literary Study," 149; Rubin, *American South,* 17.

38. Louis D. Rubin, Jr., and Robert D. Jacobs, eds., *Southern Renascence: The Literature of the Modern South* (Baltimore, 1953), v; Manning, "Southern Renaissance," 38.

beyond the interests of this study of Hollins writers in the 1960s, but one final note should be made concerning this issue of Rubin's editorial influence in southern studies. Despite the limits of Rubin's literary interests, his edited collections have included essays that revisionists cite as perceptive and useful. A most recent example of this mixed condemnation and praise occurs in *Female Pastoral: Women Writers Re-Visioning the American South* (1991). Here, Elizabeth Jane Harrison criticizes scholars such as Rubin and Malcolm Cowley who found "gender roles . . . not [to be] an important issue" in their work.[39] Then Harrison cites "*Gone with the Wind* and Others: Popular Fiction, 1920–1950," an article by Rubin's protégée Anne Goodwyn Jones included in Rubin's *The History of Southern Literature*.[40] Rubin has also supervised women writing dissertations on southern women writers of the nineteenth century. And at Hollins he encouraged his students to write about their own experiences of life. Whatever the limitations of Rubin's critical perspective, he consistently opened breaches that have allowed women's voices to be heard in the scholarly publications and collections he has edited.

In considering Rubin's influence at Hollins, one finds some evidence that Rubin may have originally held the conventional paternalistic attitude that a southern women's college might have standards less intellectually rigorous than those at colleges attended by men. In 1957, Rubin declined a job offer from the University of Texas to accept the position at Hollins "*even though* it was a women's college" [emphasis his]. At the end of his decade at Hollins, Rubin's understanding of women's education included certain paradoxes that suggest a paternalism of which he was unaware. Having declared that Hollins women aspired to high intellectual standards, he still acknowledged "that most of our students were not planning professional academic careers, that higher education for most of them was being undertaken for its own sake, and not for its immediate, practical vocational use." He judged that to be an advantage for them: "For, to return to my own field of competence, literature was not written in order for graduate students and college professors to analyze it; it was written for what it could embody of the truths of human experience, to please and enthrall even while it gave order and meaning to ev-

39. Elizabeth Jane Harrison, *Female Pastoral: Women Writers Re-Visioning the American South* (Knoxville, 1991), 141.

40. Ibid., 44. Rubin's *History of Southern Literature* (Baton Rouge, 1985) included not only Jones's "*Gone with the Wind* and Others: Popular Fiction, 1920–1950" (363–74), but also Hollins Group member Lucinda Hardwick MacKethan's "Plantation Fiction, 1865–1900" (209–18).

eryday existence. We professional scholars tend to lose sight of that elementary fact."[41] This idea that Hollins graduates would marry and primarily rely upon their degree as a cultural enhancement is an acknowledgment strikingly similar to traditional paternal views of women's higher education.

A different interpretation of this point was offered by Henry Taylor, a Hollins master's degree holder and Pulitzer Prize winner. Taylor, who entered the graduate writing program in 1965, noted about the program's apparent deemphasis on publishing, "There's a general philosophy among the teachers that what really matters is that you do the best writing you're capable of. Anything else is gravy. Instead of treating publication as the crowning achievement of a young writer's career, it's more like, 'Well, that's nice.'"[42] Rubin did not consider the Hollins program to be designed to turn out professional writers because, in a practical sense, the market could sustain only a few writers. From a realistic perspective, Rubin simply recognized the fact that in the late 1950s and early 1960s many women viewed marriage, rather than an academic career, as the sequel to their undergraduate education. Given this scenario, Hollins women were ideal liberal arts students engaged in intellectual work for its own sake.

Golding, whom Rubin hired as writer-in-residence in 1962, expressed a far stronger reservation about Hollins. After spending his year at the school, Golding gave a fairly cynical description of the student body at this "rich girls' college":

> Under the trees, along the cemented paths, go the drifts of girls, sympathetic and charming, giggling or absorbed, shy of the bearded foreigner behind his plate glass [in the library], but courteous to the helplessness of old age. Some of them are Northerners, but the most part Southern, and some are from the deep South. Like all women students, they are inveterate, comically obsessive note-takers, who hope by this method to avoid the sheer agony of having to think for themselves. Often they have an earnestness before the shrine of this unknown god Education, which seems at odds with their careful make-up and predatory scent. They will propose a scheme of studies which leaves them no time to eat in the middle of the day; but 40 per cent of them leave to get married before they reach the end of their studies.

41. Rubin, "Hollins College," 2, 5.

42. Henry Taylor quoted in Garrett Epps, "Learning to Write Can Be Fun," *New York Times Book Review*, August 7, 1988, p. 1.

They are intimidating, ingenuous, and delightful; and about the realities of life in the world at large they know absolutely nothing at all.[43]

Even though Golding had been in residence at Hollins for the greater part of one academic year, he clung to a patronizing view of the women students with whom he had worked. His assessment of the students suggests either that Hollins was indeed a finishing school for young southern ladies or, perhaps, that Golding, like many of his peers, discounted the intellectual capacities of women because he feared the "feminization" of literary studies.

Although Rubin had come to Hollins a few years earlier with a gender-inflected opinion, his experience with the women students and his own marriage to an academician forced him to revise that assessment. His thoughts on this point are worth quoting at length, as they reflect a specific instance in which the female college in the South undermined traditional notions of gender. After a decade of teaching at Hollins, Rubin concluded that the women students there were virtually unmatched in their intellectual intensity:

> I had thought, before I began teaching at Hollins College, that while women undergraduates would be good enough students, perhaps more organized and less erratic than young men of comparable age, they would mostly be lacking in the kind of intellectual intensity and whole-soul dedication to ideas and images, as opposed to "life," that the really first rate male student possessed. The fact that proportionally few women went on to graduate study, and fewer reached the level of the Ph.D., seemed to me to be a limitation, an indication that women students generally held themselves back, and conceived of intellectual pursuits as a kind of ornament, a social grace or talent as it were, to be followed when not occupied with more important things, with Real Life. I could not have been more mistaken! For my best students at Hollins College habitually brought to their work a driving dedication, an intensity fully as charged as that of any male undergraduate—or graduate student as well, for that matter.

Further, Rubin judged, faculty members "who came to Hollins with the preconceived notion that teaching women would involve a different and less intensive kind of teaching [only discovered] that what was required of them

43. William Golding, "The Glass Door," in *The Hot Gates and Other Occasional Pieces* (London, 1966), 141–42.

was if anything more demanding preparation, more direct and central engagement with the fundamental, qualitatively important aspects of the subject being taught." The significant fact that these reminiscences demonstrate is that two opinionated white male academicians came to the same women's college, and one of them, Louis Rubin, allowed the *students* to change his mind.[44]

Rubin was not only department chair, adviser, and newspaper adviser but also teacher to most of the Hollins Group. In creative writing courses, Rubin's method was to have each student bring her manuscript to him, and they would discuss the work over a series of conferences. When the two of them considered the manuscript to be sufficiently developed to garner useful criticism, it would be copied, distributed, read aloud in class, and discussed. Each student had a certain quota of writing per term. About his teaching Rubin has reflected that taking his students' work seriously was perhaps more significant than any critical observations he had made about their work.[45]

Rubin's influence on his student writers at Hollins seems tied to his southern literary perspectives in several essential ways. First, by bringing to campus so many writers whose work reflected the Agrarian view of southern literature, Rubin implicitly established that writing as one of the standards for his students. A second point—one partly contradictory to the first—was Rubin's insistence that "New Southern writers must write about their own experiences in their own way." Third, he taught the rigorous, New Critical engagement that a reader and writer must have with a text. The value of this rigor, he argued, was intrinsic: "You've got to come to terms with language and you've got to come to terms with yourself in a way you might not do" in other content courses. Rubin did not teach a course on southern literature at Hollins, and so the southern writers he treated were placed in the broader context of New Criticism that represented current international mainstream literary theory. His 1964 comments on the difficulty of studying writers such as Proust, Joyce, and Malraux seemed to reflect a certain humility about literary study: "For how many of us, no matter how interested, can pretend to know the modern novel? I can't, at any rate. I know some novelists and novels, I don't know others, and I must make do with what I know." At best, he concluded, literature should be a help in self-understanding: "[Proust, Joyce, and Malraux] aren't

44. Rubin, "Hollins College," 4, 5.
45. Rubin, personal interview.

'light reading.' But the reader who is willing to do what is required will find it worthwhile. She will find, too, that the territory isn't nearly so remote or far distant as she may have thought; in fact, she had been living in it herself all the time and didn't even know it." This unprepossessing approach to literary study—and even the attentiveness to the female pronoun in his writing—suggests that Rubin was a fairly receptive teacher.[46]

If the writing of students accurately reflects the instruction of the teacher, then self-understanding must have been a central theme of Rubin's. Dillard's *Pilgrim at Tinker Creek,* Smith's *Last Day the Dogbushes Bloomed,* Jones's *Tomorrow Is Another Day,* and MacKethan's *Dream of Arcady* all deal with issues of identity such as what it means to be a mystic, to be a southerner, or to be a woman. In their later work, Smith, Jones, and MacKethan became more pointedly feminist in their writing. The writing of his students, then, argues that Rubin taught that the essential purpose of literature and writing had to do with self-understanding and self-definition: these women felt free to write self-defining fiction and scholarly works closely related to their lives. What Rubin taught the women of the Hollins Group, wrote Annie Dillard, was "that writing is full of joys. He never filled us with a lot of romantic nonsense. He would tell us you didn't have to go off to Nepal to find things to write about—that you'd already had enough experiences by the age of five to write the great novel. We also learned a lot of moral things, such as the value of loyalty. He had good sense and a good heart." Students saw him as the champion of experimental writers such as his former student John Barth, though they thought that his primary scholarly interest was in Proust and Joyce. Two of the first graduate students in the Hollins writing program were John Hawkes's protégées. Rubin's interests in terms of literary theory seemed "cosmopolitan," observes Lucinda Hardwick MacKethan. In sum, the primary effect of Rubin's literary training on his teaching was that it fostered a perspective on writing that would be readily appealing to young writers: an emphasis on language and on the work of art as a source of intense experience and insight.[47]

The closest substantive comment about any of Rubin's southern literary

46. "Louis Rubin's New Article Discusses Dilemma of Today's Southern Writers," *Hollins Columns,* January 9, 1964, p. 2; Rubin, personal interview; *Calliope's Comments* (May 20, 1964): 5, 7.

47. Paul Duke, "A Southern Literary Giant," *University of Richmond Magazine,* 42 (1990): 19–20; Lucinda Hardwick MacKethan, telephone interview, September 16, 1991.

Lucinda Hardwick MacKethan with Louis D. Rubin, August 1988

theory in evidence at Hollins was Lee Smith's statement that she came to share with Louis Rubin an understanding of what southern writing means: "To me, it doesn't mean anything much in terms of theme. It just means the particulars of the novel; it really means setting and it has something to do often with voice, with colloquial voice, with conversational tone, with old-style storytelling, with things told at some length, not just straight to the point, so it has to do with narrative strategy, I guess." But even Smith was clearly persuaded that Rubin did not use his position to press his own literary views. She, in fact, has credited him for encouraging her to seek her own self-definition and to overcome the restrictive cultural assumptions about what she could do as a southern woman. Smith observes, "My ambition was to be a writer but I knew it would be hard since it was expected that a Southern girl be a lady and nothing more. Then, before I knew it, Louis had me working on a novel. I don't know what my life would be like today had he not persuaded me that I could do it." Smith and other members of the Hollins Group benefited by following Rubin's ideas about writing technique or writing from experience; it remains undocumented whether other students failed because they had ideas contrary to Rubin's. Still, when pressed to describe

Rubin's specific advice about writing, these women concur that he simply urged them to write about the things they observed in their own lives. Their observations seem consonant with Rubin's opinion that from a talented student, good writing is only evoked, not taught: "Given the talent, given the innate inclination, . . . it is possible for the right teacher to happen along and make the student heed the inclination and perfect the talent." His students agree that he urged them to write out of their own experience and to find their own voices. Since many of the women were southerners, he managed to encourage the continuing creation of southern letters by an assertive generation of southern women. In the minds of the Hollins Group, however, Rubin was not a southern literary scholar but a significant mentor who promoted a writing environment in which they could define themselves.[48]

Whatever the exact nature of Rubin's influence on these women, he was, MacKethan has observed, "not at all coddling and not at all patronizing. He set very high standards and he gave us to believe that there was no reason in the world why we wouldn't meet those standards." About his courses Rubin wrote, "It was, in short, the most difficult teaching I had ever hitherto encountered, this business of teaching the young women of Hollins College, and also the most stimulating. Never before had I felt quite so intensely the pressure of getting at the fundamentals of my subject matter, the need to analyze, to look closely and carefully, to deal with what really *mattered* about it. And when I could feel that I *was* doing that, could see the essential questions presenting themselves and see the answers unfolding as I talked and thought, there was a tremendous excitement to it, a sense of genuine accomplishment. *That* was teaching! *That* was why one taught!" As he saw it, "the 'prestige' in the dormitories became less and less a matter of a student's social prowess, and increasingly one of academic prowess . . . , a perceptible quickening in the intellectual curiosity of the student body, . . . and the chief cause lay in the students themselves." Hollins students wrote about "emphasizing the intellectual" and talked about it in class meetings. One of the English majors, he recalled, "did not come in with her examination this year after the allotted three hours. She showed up five hours later. She got so interested in the question, she explained, that she could not bear to stop writing when the exami-

48. Virginia Smith, "On Regionalism, Women's Writing, and Writing as a Woman: A Conversation with Lee Smith," *Southern Review* 24 (1990): 793; Duke, "Southern Literary Giant," 20; Rubin, *An Apple for My Teacher: Twelve Authors Tell About Teachers Who Made the Difference* (Chapel Hill, 1987), xi.

nation period was up. So she drew a line across the page to note what she had done during the prescribed time limit, and she kept on writing. She wrote more than a hundred pages." Such quickened intellectual energy spilled over into all aspects of college life and may have helped precipitate a dramatic drop in attrition. Whereas the class of 1956 had graduated only 76 women from the original freshman class of 179, the class of 1966 graduated 141 of its original 191 members.[49]

The point again illustrates that Louis Rubin felt challenged and instructed by his students. In volume after volume of his published work during this period, he notes that Hollins students "have helped me to arrive at whatever insight into the subject under discussion these lectures [on southern literature] may display." Judging from the records from that decade, one must conclude that his actions were often more interactive than coercive and his desired results more altruistic than self-serving. The evidence suggests that the women of the Hollins Group had the talent and energy to engage in a dialectic of sorts with the authority they found at Hollins and that Rubin's power was shaped and limited in subtle ways by the students. Among several instances cited by faculty member John Allen, one seems especially representative. Lee Smith was a high-spirited undergraduate who was constantly in trouble for breaking curfew, and she did not yield to disciplinary procedures readily. On one occasion, Allen and Louis Rubin ended up discussing "what would Lee *accept* as punishment." The women felt affection for Rubin because he protected them from institutional punishment, took their writing seriously, and insured their success in publication. Thus, Rubin's years at Hollins reflect a certain evolution in what were originally stereotyped, paternalistic ideas about women's education because he allowed his students to influence his opinions on that point. One essential difference between Rubin's and the traditional treatment of women at Hollins was that Rubin took action based upon the women's understanding of themselves and their goals.[50]

Although the Hollins women were united in the opinion that Rubin did not unduly press literary perspectives upon them or dominate them, no one contests the opinion that Rubin was a powerful force on the campus. Even by his own accounts, Rubin used the power that was offered to him at Hollins to

49. MacKethan, telephone interview; Rubin, "Hollins College," 5–7, 88–91, 110.

50. Rubin, *Writer in the South*, xv; John Allen, personal interview, January 17, 1991 [emphasis his]; Anne Goodwyn Jones, telephone interview, January 6, 1993.

guide the students as he thought best. He exerted an undeniable control over his colleagues by insisting on advising all of the English majors. By this means he developed a personal relationship with even the few English majors whom he did not personally teach and also extended the already powerful grip he maintained on the English program. He liked to advise all the English majors, he has stated, "because that was my one way of finding out what was going on." Rubin's personal interest in advising all students could be interpreted as ensuring that all students were treated uniformly. On the other hand, it could suggest that he was protecting the program against colleagues whom he perceived to be less qualified to advise women students; such an interpretation would argue that Rubin had sufficient faith only in his own vision. A more democratic arrangement would have distributed advisees among other English faculty members, and this decision not to share power aroused resentment among some of Rubin's colleagues. Former colleague John Allen has divided feelings about Rubin. Rubin was, states Allen, an "extraordinarily able publicizer, . . . entrepreneur . . . and literary agent." He was generous and "dedicated his life to put people into print who deserved it." Still, judges Allen, he was the "image of paternalism," a man with a "fatherly attitude to the students" who "kept his hand on everything [in the department]." Another former colleague, Richard H. W. Dillard, confirms Allen's assessment that the English program was "his ship." Dillard observes that Rubin was very much "'Daddy' to his students" and that they brought their problems to him. Dillard himself shared this image of Rubin as a stern father figure whose booming voice calling for Dillard would send the younger man into a nervous state. Though Rubin and Dillard liked and collaborated with each other, it remains unclear what Rubin thought of a first-year professor marrying one of his students and equally unclear to what extent Dillard himself viewed Rubin as a paternal authority figure. Dillard agrees that Rubin was able to overcome the "conservative inertia that gets into faculties" precisely because Rubin had a dominant personality and unbelievable energy—and because he acted immediately when he had an idea. The criticisms of Rubin may have validity; however, they may also reflect personal resentment about Rubin's dominance more than a concern that he was exercising undue influence over his advisees.[51]

51. Rubin, personal interview; Allen, personal interview; Richard Dillard, personal interview, March 5, 1991.

If Rubin's actions could be described as paternalistic, then it was a paternalism by negotiation, a philosophy that was significantly shaped by the women whom he taught. He consciously encouraged his students to find their own voices, actively sought the publication of their work, and defended them against the administration when they broke sexist college regulations. It was more the case that he wished to manipulate the system on behalf of the women he instructed than to manipulate the women themselves. Given the cultural constraints on women in the 1960s, Rubin's actions seem those of a mentor seeking to be a positive agent for supporting his students; and given the problems created by sexual dynamics in a women's college at that time, a "fatherly" attitude toward the students may have been perhaps the safer and more viable role option for a male mentor. By contrast, Richard Dillard's romantic involvement with sophomore Annie Doak certainly raised an alternative case of a man engaging a woman from a different, yet still unequal, power base.

An equally significant point is the fact that Rubin did not attempt the paternalistic practice of forcing female dependence at the cost of the women's community. He demonstrated his respect for student insight by promoting the custom of having student judges for literary contests and student control of editorial boards. He states his pedagogical view of such a community quite specifically:

> For my part, it seems to me that the student is going to have many, many years during which she will have to make her way largely on her own, in which she cannot expect to be part of a group sharing the same essential interests and welcoming her companionship, and in which her superiors will not personally concern themselves with her well-being. Let her, therefore, get all the personal help and individual attention that she can, all the self-confidence and respect for her own individuality that comes of being part of a small group, while she can still do so. The chances are that, having been thus educated in an atmosphere in which she counts for a great deal in her own right, and encouraged to approach knowledge on an individualistic basis, she will be better rather than worse equipped to fend for herself later on.

As a mentor, he hoped to encourage these women to be self-confident writers prepared to confront an unsupportive world.[52]

52. Rubin, "Hollins College," 114. As an academician married to Dr. Eva Redfield Rubin, political science professor and published scholar on U.S. constitutional law, Rubin wrote in 1972

Rubin sustained this personal interest and support by essentially setting up a network through which Hollins writers could keep in touch. Such an extended network could be construed as an extension of Rubin's personal influence; an alternative view would construe it as an extension of the sense of shared community that Rubin described as the personal spirit of the college. It certainly proved a boon to the women at a time when women's networks lacked the scope and strength of their male counterparts. To him, students at Hollins were one's friends: "They remain one's friends after they graduate. When they get married, their husbands frequently become one's friends." One institutional way Rubin developed of maintaining that network of affection and information was through *Calliope's Comments,* a periodical established to keep alumnae of the English program informed of the activities of the department and of the alumnae. The newsletter contained reviews,

---

that he found the disparity in treatment of academic women to be reprehensible: "As a man, I did not have to make such a choice [between academic career and family]. Society did not inform me, in effect, that if I wanted to live a normal family life, find a mate, have children, etc., I could not expect, therefore, to have a professional career. Society didn't give me an either/or ultimatum. It didn't tell me that if I wanted to utilize my brain and make use of the nineteen years or so of education I received, I would have to sublimate and deny my masculinity." Rubin made one further intriguing observation: "If anyone thinks that women have an equal chance in academic life, he had better think again. The cards are stacked against them in a fashion that is the more formidable because *it is largely unrealized by those doing the stacking*" [emphasis mine].

These last words raise the difficult issue of the degree to which a self-conscious male advocate of women is to be held accountable for unconscious biases. Such a matter would prove difficult for a well-intentioned male to confront in any area of endeavor; but for a prominent person in a field, the accountability is accentuated because a much wider sphere of power and influence is involved. If one evaluates in Rubin the historical tendency of paternalists to force female reliance upon a dominant father figure rather than to nurture self-reliance or faith in the power of women, then the publication successes and feminist writings of the Hollins Group argue that Rubin's paternalism was weak. Even the competition among the Hollins students related to a desire to please their professor did not prevent these women from creating their own autonomous and rebellious women's community.

In 1987, Rubin wrote a column for the *Chapel Hill Weekly* stating that in his years as a college professor, "I have seen not only my own wife but numerous other academic women pushed around, passed over, ignored, humiliated, at best tolerated, by supposedly unbiased scholars and administrators. I have taught and now teach numerous young women in my own field of scholarship. They are equally as talented and as gifted as their male counterparts." The conviction of these statements in the press suggests the support of women's scholarship that Rubin has maintained throughout his career.

book recommendations, and other comments to continue the intellectual stimulation encouraged at Hollins; it also reported the activities of former students and professors, thereby providing an effective network of information. A far smaller and more personal network was the one Rubin still maintains through correspondence: "I've been away from Hollins now for twenty-four years," Rubin said in 1991. "I'll bet you there's not a week goes by that I don't get at least three or four letters from former students, many of whom I've kept up with." Because of Rubin's ability to see writers into print, particularly after Rubin and former student Shannon Ravenel established Algonquin Books of Chapel Hill, the state of North Carolina has become an important center for Hollins alumnae.[53]

The special atmosphere at Hollins bred a continuing loyalty that has extended particularly throughout the marketplace of southern literature, in which Rubin has continued to lobby for more scholarly treatment of southern literature and for more attention to young writers. In 1967, he helped establish the *Southern Literary Journal,* which he edited for many years with C. Hugh Holman, and in 1968 helped establish the Society for the Study of Southern Literature. In 1982, he published "Southern Letters and the State of the Art," in which he decried the paucity of critical essays on writers such as Doris Betts, Hollins alumnae Sylvia Wilkinson and Lee Smith, James Seay, Pat Conroy, Nikki Giovanni, Reynolds Price, and others. "Each generation of writers . . . deserves a hearing," he observed, and "the overall condition of literature nowadays is a considerable mess." The "mess" Rubin described was the collapse of economic support for professional authorship occasioned by the mergers and rising costs of a trade publishing industry that now sought books that could compete for television and movie screen rights. As a result, the short story had virtually disappeared as commercial fiction, and university presses filled the breach as best they could. Unfortunately, continued Rubin, "for the most part nobody Up There [in the New York City publishing industry] cares about the kind of books that the Southerners write nowadays."[54]

Rubin's response to the situation took two directions. First, *Southern Literary Journal* began to commission evaluative essays on younger writers such as Sylvia Wilkinson and Lee Smith. Rubin continued, "We have already

53. Rubin, "Hollins College," 110; Rubin, personal interview.

54. Louis D. Rubin, Jr., "Southern Letters and the State of the Art," *Southern Literary Journal* 14 (1982): 3–7.

commissioned a half-dozen overall evaluative essays on younger writers for our fall 1982 issue, and thereafter we will actively seek out good criticism of the more recent writers wherever we can find it."[55] Rubin asked Hollins alumna Lucinda Hardwick MacKethan to write what was, in fact, the first critical article on Lee Smith's writing to appear in any scholarly journal, "Artists and Beauticians: Balance in Lee Smith's Fiction."

The second decision was equally pragmatic. The current disarray in the New York publishing profession, Rubin judged, had thrown upon the university and smaller presses the entire weight of discovering good young novelists; only smaller presses could still take the risk of small press runs. In 1982, with $50,000 in hand, Rubin and Ravenel founded Algonquin Books as "a fresh outlet for young writers who were finding it rough to crack the established New York publishing market." Algonquin, because it is a small press (publishing about twenty books per year), would work through five or six drafts of a manuscript with a writer.[56]

In all of his editorial and publishing efforts, Rubin consistently continued to promote the writing—and therefore extend the community—of Hollins women. He not only supervised the dissertations of Lucinda Hardwick MacKethan and Anne Goodwyn Jones but solicited their scholarship for journals or books he edited. Both MacKethan and Jones were included in Rubin's *History of Southern Literature.* Shannon Ravenel (Hollins '60) worked as editor at Algonquin Books. In the years since leaving Hollins, Rubin has also consistently promoted his women students as significant figures in southern literature. He has written that "in the past decade or so there has been a veritable explosion of important and interesting young Southern novelists in their forties, thirties and even twenties," and through them "we have been able to recognize and explore both continuity and change. . . . To understand Simms you need Faulkner, and you also need Walker Percy and Lee Smith. Again, *and vice-versa.* In short, the more that the study of Southern literature gets and stays involved with contemporary Southern writers and writing, the better off both will be."[57] In these and numerous other instances Rubin encouraged and maintained a network of Hollins writers and scholars.

55. Ibid., 5.
56. Duke, "Southern Literary Giant," 19, 20.
57. Rubin, "Southern Literary Study," 162.

Rubin's support of women writers has not been confined to the Hollins Group. A most recent instance is the case of writer Kaye Gibbons, who took a course with Rubin at the University of North Carolina. For a class assignment she turned in a thirty-page story written from experience and using her own voice—again an example of that female bildungsroman that Rubin seemed to encourage among his students. Rubin advised Gibbons to expand it into a novel; she completed *Ellen Foster* in six weeks and had it published by Rubin's Algonquin Books. The book won the Sue Kaufman Prize for First Fiction from the American Academy and Institute of Arts and Letters, honors from the Ernest Hemingway Foundation, and a prize from the American Library Association. Algonquin has also published the works of Hollins writer Jill McCorkle, who also felt lucky "having Lee Smith and Louis Rubin as teachers, encouraging me to go to Hollins, the Hollins program, my instructors and the people in my class. The most important thing I learned was that I could be a writer and also be myself."[58]

Finally though, even as director of the writing program, Rubin certainly did not create the talent and ambition of the women in the Hollins Group. Indeed, suggests Lucinda Hardwick MacKethan, "I think you can in some ways overplay Louis Rubin's role. I think he was central; I think it may not have happened if he hadn't been there. But it may have happened, too. It was a remarkable group of people." Yet for each of the women of the Hollins Group, Rubin was, and has remained, an immensely significant mentor. A brief anecdote captures a sense of the configuration of the writing community that was established among Rubin and his students at Hollins. In 1990, MacKethan published the critical work *Daughters of Time: Creating Woman's Voice in Southern Story,* a book that reflects the influence of the Hollins community in the 1960s. As a first order of business, in the acknowledgments she thanked Rubin, "who at Hollins College was the first person to encourage me to find my own voice [and] has continued to offer that encouragement for, heaven forbid, a quarter of a century." After crediting Rubin, though, MacKethan proceeded to present a powerful, thoughtful—and clearly feminist—interpretation of the struggles and "the process of self-creation that Southern women embarked upon when they began to speak." Quite naturally, Mac-

---

58. Robert Merritt, "Gibbons Miles Away from 'Ellen Foster,'" *Richmond Times-Dispatch,* May 7, 1991, sec. B, p. 5; Jill McCorkle, "Achievement, Tradition, Vision, 1842–1992," *Hollins* (October 1991) 54.

Kethan included in her book an analysis of *Fair and Tender Ladies* by her Hollins classmate Lee Smith: the student culture originating at Hollins had continued as a mature critical and personal network. The configuration was a Hollins legacy: an encouraging mentor, critical and supportive peers, and writers vitally concerned with women's voices and identities.[59]

59. MacKethan, telephone interview; MacKethan, *Daughters of Time: Creating Woman's Voice in Southern Story* (Athens, Ga., 1990), xii–xiii.

3

THE HOLLINS GROUP
"Anarchy and Arrogance Forever"

*I*n her 1990 study of southern women writers, *Daughters of Time: Creating Woman's Voice in Southern Story,* Lucinda Hardwick Mac-Kethan offers an evocative image of women who have struggled to discover their own voices through their writing. "My study," writes MacKethan, "concerns the possibilities for reversal, for empowerment, that Southern women seized upon when they moved beyond the role of daughter and into the role of storyteller. Central to my exploration of this direction are certain questions: what does the entity of Daughter entail? what 'veiled' strategies does a woman bring to the mission of voicing herself in male gardens? can she take possession of her own garden, a place where she is free to imagine, to design, to produce creations that bear her distinctive personality and purpose? how, ultimately, does she speak a story out of the condition of voicelessness?" The obstacles, strategies, and search for voice that MacKethan sketches in this metaphor are striking echoes of the change in status that southern women were accomplishing in the women's community at MacKethan's alma mater, Hollins. To use her terms, young women of good families had traditionally been sent to the protected haven of Hollins to become educated southern daughters dependent on male guidance and protection. For a woman to leave behind that dependence and become the writer of her own life story required risk, a "garden" of one's own, and support for experimentation. As Mac-Kethan observes, risk was a crucial obstacle because a woman who writes actually creates her own interpretations of life, and "the cost to the writer who uses her daughterhood [to write her own ideas] is the threat of losing her secure position within the family that has identified and sustained her primary sense of who she is." The women of the Hollins Group entered Hollins ready to take such risks and discovered among themselves a community of women who provided the space, challenge, and support necessary for their writing.[1]

The Hollins Group was certainly, in the conventional understanding of the term, a community: "a grouping of people who reside in a specific locality and who exercise some degree of local autonomy in organizing their social life in such a way that they can, from that locality base, satisfy the full range of their daily needs." But in replacing the paternal underpinnings of that community with sisterly supports, Hollins women created a foundation often demonstrating, in the 1970 phrase popularized by Robin Morgan, that sisterhood is powerful. The notion of sisterhood seems an accurate description of the affiliative power and exuberance of these women who felt freed from intellectual subordination and united in the common interest of writing. Such a sisterhood, argued Morgan, would naturally be a close, intense, supportive female community empowering women and forging solidarity. Morgan's radicalized definition of a women's community was based upon the belief that women would band together based on a "politics [growing] out of personal experiences," such as daughterhood, that were universally shared by women. The natural product of this theory would be the emergence of women's communities fundamentally different from those historically structured by men. Learning from their history of subordination, women would create groups that were nonhierarchical, collective, experimental; such groups would have the "potential of cutting across all class, race, age, economic, and geographical barriers—since women in every group must play essentially the same role. . . . Given the freedom to organize themselves, women would be supportive of each other rather than competitive with each other." Certain precedents exist for Morgan's theory. In fiction, Charlotte Perkins Gilman described such a feminist utopia in her 1915 novel *Herland;* real-life precedents were evident in women's reformist communities such as

1. MacKethan, *Daughters of Time,* 5, 11.

Hull House in the 1890s and, more recently, in the formation of the National Organization for Women in the 1960s.[2]

Elizabeth Fox-Genovese calls Morgan's analysis of a sisterly community into question. In her controversial book *Feminism Without Illusions,* Fox-Genovese essentially argues that not only have class and racial differences historically divided the sisterhood of women, but a certain egotism has as well. Briefly, Fox-Genovese argues that white, middle-class feminists have sentimentalized the notion of a women's community by denying that it is a place where intense individualism undermines community spirit. In doing so, many feminists have failed to consider economic, cultural, and social differences in asserting sisterhood as a universal possibility. Aside from the limitations of this exclusive community, she observes, the concept of sisterhood actually draws from the same familial metaphor that patriarchy does and yet ignores the implications of that metaphor: "Most feminists seek simultaneously to destroy the vestiges of families' control of women and to celebrate women's instinctive embodiment of the value of community that derived from their experience within families."[3] Ultimately, such feminists simply confirm the Enlightenment philosophy that the claims of the individual are prior to those of the community. Thus, even in its theoretical conception, the claim for an idyllic women's community undermines itself.

The women's community at Hollins during the 1960s offers itself as an actual case for reexamining how a women's community may be constituted and what it may accomplish. As women in college during the 1960s, the Hollins Group was in what Arnold van Gennep, Victor Turner, Richard Daly, and others describe as a liminal state. Marginalized as women, as writers, and as college students, their condition of being "betwixt and between" social roles offered them "an escape from the current structures of society . . . and occasion[ed] the development of a community and communion of equals, which Turner calls *communitas.*"[4] The Hollins Group, a relatively homogenous

2. Allan D. Edwards and Dorothy G. Jones, *Community and Community Development* (The Hague, 1976), 12. See Robin Morgan, ed., *Sisterhood Is Powerful: An Anthology of Writings from the Women's Liberation Movement* (New York, 1970); quotation is p. xx.

3. Elizabeth Fox-Genovese, *Feminism Without Illusions: A Critique of Individualism* (Chapel Hill, 1991), 7, 40.

4. Richard Daly, "Liminality and Fiction in Cooper, Hawthorne, Cather, and Fitzgerald" in *Victor Turner and the Construction of Cultural Criticism: Between Literature and Anthropology* ed. Kathleen M. Ashley (Bloomington, Ind., 1990), 71.

group of southern daughters, initially banded together as a counterculture defined by restrictions that confronted them; but even after outflanking and coopting the people and organizations that once limited them, they succeeded in retaining their sisterly community based on both support *and* competition. They did not consciously design "veiled strategies" for expressing themselves; the significant influences on them were neither exclusively females nor students. But the female student culture was absolutely essential to their success as a productive writing community that has maintained close, competitive, and intellectually profitable relationships not only during their college years but in their subsequent professional lives. The transgressive moments of their social lives—when they confronted and rejected traditional social expectations—translated into equivalently questioning subject matter or techniques in their writing. Ultimately, the experiences of the Hollins Group demonstrate a notion of community that was feminist, long-lived, and a synthesis of the philosophies of Morgan and Fox-Genovese.

"Writers tend to come in groups," observed Louis D. Rubin, Jr., chair of the English department during the 1960s: "One turns the other one on. . . . Each gets the other going." Such was clearly the case for a core group of women writers who came to Hollins in 1963: Lee Smith of Grundy, Virginia; Annie Doak (Dillard) of Pittsburgh, Pennsylvania; Cindy Hardwick (MacKethan) of Milwaukee, Wisconsin; Anne Goodwyn Jones of Chapel Hill, North Carolina; Jo Berson (Buckley) of Nashville, Tennessee; Anne Bradford (Warner) of Houston, Texas; and Nancy Beckham (Ferris) of Chapel Hill, North Carolina. As a group they were racially and economically homogeneous: white women from middle- to upper-class families who, though they had been accepted at other colleges such as Duke, Vanderbilt, and Wellesley, chose Hollins for the variety of reasons that influence any high school seniors—financial encouragement, acceptable academic requirements, family ties, and professional interest. High school senior Annie Doak had become interested in Hollins because a respected teacher of hers was an alumna of Hollins and had urged her to attend there; when she learned that William Golding had been a recent writer-in-residence, Doak was persuaded that Hollins was the place where she could pursue her writing. Like Doak, Lee Smith had attended a private girls school and known a Hollins alumna; she, too, based part of her decision to attend Hollins on its reputation as a writing center. Cindy Hardwick chose Hollins in hopes that it would advance her toward her goal of being a poet. Admittedly, not all of the Hol-

Lee Smith, Annie Dillard, and Colin Wilson, who was writer-in-residence at Hollins in 1966–1967.

lins Group initially aspired to writing careers, but the newly minted fame of the college made it clear to each of them that writing was a vital interest at Hollins.[5]

Another significant factor for the young women in choosing Hollins was its ambience as a southern women's college. Cindy Hardwick's case was

5. Rubin, personal interview. For clarity, I shall use the maiden name of a woman unless comments or analysis refer specifically to events after she left Hollins or married.

representative of the young women on this count. Although Hardwick's Kentucky-born parents had spent most of their adult lives in the North, they never wanted their children to consider themselves as northerners but as "exiles," and so naturally Hardwick looked south for her higher education. She also chose Hollins because family members knew and respected the school and because Hollins offered her a larger scholarship than did Duke or Vanderbilt. Lee Smith had been interested in attending Bryn Mawr, but her parents did not want her that far from home and strongly opposed her attending any northern college. Anne Goodwyn Jones had a full scholarship to Wellesley, but her parents did not want her securing her education far away and among "strange Yankees." Annie Doak's mother hoped that at Hollins her daughter would pursue her interest in writing while having her rough edges smoothed. In each of these cases, the parents of the young women urged Hollins as their preference because it promised to instill in the young women the cultural values of the South. To varying degrees the young women shared or rejected the reasoning of their parents, but all finally agreed upon Hollins as their choice.[6]

These factors for these women in choosing Hollins accurately reflected the divided nature of the college itself at this time: the writing program aspired to national competitiveness and reputation, and the campus atmosphere retained the respect for certain familial values that was the hallmark of southern women's colleges. By the 1960s, the cultural messages were mixed, and traditional feminine ideals competed with feminist aspirations. The customs of the campus remained conventional, quaint by today's standards, and were designed to mold the young women into proper young ladies. Students attended Coca Cola parties where dress was "casual"—a skirt and heels were acceptable; the college held student-faculty coffees every Friday afternoon; and twice-weekly chapel attendance was required of all students, even though Hollins was not a church-affiliated school. Founders Day perpetuated a certain homage to paternalism in that the entire senior class paraded to the cemetery to place flowers on the grave of Charles Lewis Cocke. Advertisements in the school newspaper echoed the stereotypical expectation that Hollins girls were seeking bachelors rather than bachelor's degrees: "3 ways to get your BACHELORS. Choose books, (they need so much study!) . . . bache-

6. MacKethan, telephone interview; Jones, telephone interview, January 6, 1991; Annie Dillard, letter to author, December 14, 1991.

lors themselves, (they can be fascinating!) . . . or fashion, (it's real fun!) We award degrees in the latter two with all the requirements for straight 'A's.'" Not all of the incoming freshmen were receptive to this conventional view of women's roles and education. Though students were required to dress formally for meals, they sometimes resisted by wearing raincoats over their night clothes or shorts in order to meet the requirement. Annie Doak Dillard recalls, "Someone our freshman year made a speech in which she said that the purpose of our liberal education was to make us interesting wives for our educated husbands. It was absurd at the time, and we laughed it off." It would be naive to suggest that the entering freshmen were completely serious and had no thought of fun or boyfriends, but Annie Doak's response makes clear that their ambitions included not only husbands but professional achievement as well.[7]

Even though the Hollins Group had come to a cloistered community, the political changes of the 1960s were making themselves felt. Betty Friedan's controversial book *The Feminine Mystique* was newly published and widely debated their freshman year. President Kennedy's assassination disrupted classes and social events. The civil rights movement made its influence felt as well. By spring of freshman year, Cindy Hardwick described in the school newspaper the poverty of Oldfields, a black community in the area that had originated as "a home for the personal servants of the first Hollins students"; it would be a topic and a political project to which Hardwick, Anne Goodwyn Jones, and Annie Doak Dillard would return several times. Dean Mary Phlegar Smith also challenged the entering freshmen to expand their worlds to include topical political concerns such as the nuclear test ban treaty, civil rights, and Vietnam: "Who last September would have believed that a partial nuclear test ban could be worked out and agreed to by our great country and Russia and scores of other nations as well? Who could have anticipated the course of the rising tide of demands for civil rights? Who would have thought that the protests of a religious group . . . the Buddhists in a far off country would cause serious concern to you and to me, who probably do not even know what a Buddhist believes?" The comments of Dean Smith and the student leaders were calculated to expand the students' concerns to include international affairs and local involvements, but these voices often proved inad-

7. Unless otherwise indicated, the following descriptions of Hollins in the fall of 1963 are taken from the September 17, 1963, issue of *Hollins Columns.* Annie Dillard, letter.

equate competition for the popular advertising and social messages that attempted to construct female identity at the small southern women's school.[8]

President John Logan praised individual achievement, encouraging the class of 1967 to pursue "imaginative scholarship" and to "take the full measure of yourself." He also commended the close affiliations made possible by the small, intimate campus: Hollins, Logan wrote, "has a beauty and warmth which will draw you to it more insistently with each passing year." Here, he affirmed, "You will form durable friendships . . . both among your classmates and the faculty, and you will take the measure of yourself." These customary remarks were to prove especially prophetic for the Hollins Group. Nevertheless, a small campus could also pose social restraints for young energetic women in the 1960s. In Annie Doak Dillard's mind, however, it proved to be a boon for them as writers: "What was heavenly about Hollins was that we lived in dorms, didn't have cars, ate in the dining room, lived tucked away in all sorts of natural splendor, and did our work." In fact, blithely unaware of potential social restraints upon them, the Hollins Group arrived prepared to capitalize on the best intellectual expectations that the college espoused.[9]

Into this unsettled world of perceptions about women in September 1963 entered one of the smallest freshman classes in Hollins's recent history. An unusually large number of upper-level students had returned to the college that fall, and so dormitory space—and hence admissions places—was at a premium for first-year students. Consequently, the school could afford a higher level of academic standard for entering students: verbal and math aptitude scores averaged 30 and 20 points higher than those of the preceding year, and 44 percent of the entering class had graduated with scholastic honors. What distinguished the women of the Hollins Group was that they "hit this campus full of arrogance and ability and full of themselves": they were women who wanted to write. The administration's freshman orientation persuaded these women that they were perhaps "the first really brainy class" that Hollins had ever had. Lucinda Hardwick MacKethan later observed, "We felt that we were very different. We felt that we were much better, much

8. Cindy Hardwick, "Oldfields Is Now Self-Sufficient Community with Church, School," *Hollins Columns*, April 9, 1964, p. 3; Mary Phlegar Smith, "Dean Smith Discusses Challenge of Scholarship," ibid., September 17, 1963, p. 1ff.

9. John A. Logan, Jr., "Logan Salutes Select Students," ibid., September 17, 1963, p. 1; Annie Dillard, letter.

smarter, much more intellectually aware. . . . I think we just took it for granted that we were better than they [students at rival institutions] were without really trying to find any basis. We were just quite sure there wasn't anybody better." The atmosphere and expectations at Hollins reassured the young women that they could compete with men in nearly every field of endeavor.[10]

Professor Richard H. W. Dillard concludes that clichés about women's education of the time were probably true: "It was a lot easier to be a bright, arrogant, chance-taking writer in a group without male students in 1963." The Hollins Group developed their conceptions of audience based almost entirely on the peer audience around them and so felt little pressure to make their writing cater to a male audience. Nancy Beckham and Anne Goodwyn Jones were aware of a feminist movement, but at the time the Hollins Group as a whole saw no particular necessity for participating in that movement. The experience of being at a women's college had the effect of eliminating apprehensions about gender discrimination, concludes MacKethan: "I don't think that any of us felt that competition with men was going to be a problem. I wasn't worried about it. Nobody made me think that I needed to worry about it, so I didn't. I think we all felt that when we got into situations where we'd be with men we would [hold our own]. We didn't talk about it. . . . We didn't talk much politics anyway. Hollins was not all that politically active a campus until our senior year [with concern about the Vietnam War]. . . . I think those of us who were in the creative writing program were so involved in doing that that we didn't pay a tremendous amount of attention to politics. I think we argued about it some but I don't think we were engaged in it quite as much as other people even on campus." They already felt that their female peers were as significant an audience as they could find, and the women in the writing seminars proved to be their most constant readers. Even the freshman room assignments seemed particularly designed to draw this group of women together. Nancy Head Beckham, Anne Bradford, Annie Doak, and Lee Smith shared the same floor of their freshman dormitory; in fact, Beckham, Bradford, and Smith shared the same phone extension. Jo Berson and Cindy Hardwick were in the same dormitory with each other. As though

---

10. Richard Dillard, personal interview. Dillard's comments here reflect what he heard concerning these women when he arrived at Hollins in the following year; MacKethan, telephone interview.

mere proximity in the dormitories were not enough, the first English course of their freshman year, Contemporary Poetry and Fiction, collected all of the Hollins Group but Anne Goodwyn Jones and Anne Bradford. The writing program option allowing students to take creative writing every semester of their academic careers virtually ensured that these young women would have to contend with each other as writers and critics for four years.[11]

Each member of the Hollins Group attributes tremendous importance to the fact that the English faculty emphatically and repeatedly assured them that they were exceptional writers. Had these young women not done so before, they quickly came to believe it: Annie Doak had her poetry accepted for the literary magazine during the first semester; Cindy Hardwick was featured at the spring Hollins Literary Festival during her freshman year, sharing the podium with Peter Taylor, Richard Wilbur, and George Garrett. The English faculty also provided them with challenging mentors such as Julia Randall Sawyer. The sole female English professor, Sawyer was a writing model for Annie Doak, Anne Goodwyn Jones, and Cindy Hardwick. Sawyer, according to MacKethan, embodied for them the ideal of "what every poet ought to be. Every word that came out of her mouth was poetry. You talk about a deadly serious person, literature was life and death to her. . . . It mattered as much as Vietnam or anything else." At the classes in Louis Rubin's basement, Sawyer and John Allen would fight fiercely over all writing—their own, that of other professionals, and that of the students. Though a somewhat formal person, Sawyer sometimes invited students to visit in her home or to work as assistants to her. Students remember her most for the dedication to writing that she inspired. MacKethan observes that Sawyer and the other English faculty "made us feel like we were this kind of experiment in intellectual intensity. We really did have this feeling right off the bat that we were extremely special. And we never had to lose it, thank goodness."[12]

Though MacKethan admired Sawyer, she expressed her most heartfelt appreciation to Rubin in the dedication of her book, *The Dream of Arcady: Time and Place in Southern Literature,* and in her acknowledgements for *Daughters of Time: Creating Woman's Voice in Southern Story.* MacKethan, like Lee Smith and others in the Hollins Group, considered Rubin to be "the first person to encourage me to find my own voice." The freshman class included

11. Richard Dillard, personal interview; MacKethan, telephone interview.

12. MacKethan, telephone interview.

Richard H. W. Dillard as professor of English at Hollins

an unusually large number of literary-minded students partly because, as English chair, Rubin read and screened the admissions essays. He was a personal and academic adviser to the English majors; he was their protector when they got into trouble with the social codes of the administration. Rubin's opinion of the talent of these women was unqualified: they "could write rings around other people. They wrote, they talked together. That was a perfect intellectual group." To the women of the Hollins Group, Rubin was a gruff but good-hearted professor who took their writing seriously.[13]

The third professor who was a significant influence on nearly all the women of the Hollins Group arrived on campus during their sophomore year. Richard H. W. Dillard, a native of Roanoke, had taken his doctoral de-

13. MacKethan, *Daughters of Time,* xii; Rubin, personal interview.

gree in nineteenth- and twentieth-century literature from the University of Virginia in 1964. Rubin assigned this "tremendous acquisition" of the English department to teach creative writing, sophomore English, and a course in the modern novel. In the next few years, Dillard established an energetic record of scholarship and creative writing, reviewing Blair Rouse's *Ellen Glasgow* for the *Mississippi Quarterly;* publishing an interview with Floyd Dell; collaborating with W. R. Robinson on two books; and completing a book of poetry entitled *The Day I Stopped Dreaming About Barbara Steele and Other Poems.* But perhaps more important to his students, Dillard quickly became a lively and well-loved professor on campus. He was often called the "Beatle Professor" for his upbeat spirit and taste for popular culture. He characterized himself a "'Mr. Chips of the new generation'" and seemed to have a talent for relating to the interests of his students.[14]

At the end of his first year of teaching, Dillard employed the forum of the English department newsletter to include in the list of his scholarly projects his upcoming wedding plans: "Also, I am writing the preface to a Harper & Row paperback edition of Oliver Goldsmith's *The Vicar of Wakefield* and *She Stoops to Conquer,* and I have, most importantly, acquired a bride-elect, Miss Annie Doak, a poet in her own right, to whom I shall happily be wed in June." Many of the students had crushes on the twenty-six-year-old Ph.D. and poet; and if, as Kronik suggests, a mentor is "by design a positive force, an agent of growth and well-being [who] easily incites attachments," Dillard certainly was that person for many of the young women. He was not just their professor; he was a friend. Surprisingly, the marriage seemed to do little to upset the emotional chemistry of the Hollins Group. No overt jealousies erupted over the marriage; and after the couple spent part of the summer in England, they returned to Hollins to set up housekeeping in a college community where Annie Dillard then had to face the anomalous position of being both student and faculty wife.[15]

Aside from the intellectual and personal interest of English faculty, the

14. His dissertation, "Pragmatic Realism: A Biography of Ellen Glasgow's Novels," provided material for at least one scholarly article published while Dillard was still a graduate student; "Wood Resigns, Dillard Joins English Dept.," *Hollins Columns,* April 16, 1964, p. 1ff.; *Calliope's Comments* (November 1, 1964): 5; Jo Berson, "Desonay, Weinstein, Dillard, and Bull Add to Hollins' Changing 64–65 Face," *Hollins Columns,* October 8, 1964, p. 3.

15. *Calliope's Comments* (May 1, 1965): 8–9; John W. Kronik, "On Men Mentoring Women: Then and Now," *Profession 90* (1990): 56.

Annie Doak Dillard as she appeared in the 1967 *Spinster*. The
photographs that follow in this chapter are all from that issue of
the *Spinster*.

first-year women could scarcely fail to recognize the good fortune they had in
working with an impressive line of writers-in-residence. Few undergraduate
writers at that time had enjoyed the experience of having a respected author
study one's writing in an individual conference session. Publishers such as
Hiram Hayden visited the campus, and quickly the freshmen became aware
of Hollins' strong ties with the publishing industry. Successful careers in
writing and publishing seemed not only a reasonable expectation for Hollins
women but a natural pattern. MacKethan considers it absolutely critical to

their growth that they wrote a great deal and saw much of it published on campus: "[We had] all the opportunity in the world to write and be published. That really made a difference, at least for me."[16] Naturally, then, the Hollins Group sought to participate actively in the campus publications or to create their own arenas of readers.

Community theorists observe that subcommunities that have been segregated for whatever reason find that "it may give them a chance to make a distinctive contribution to community life, for example through their distinctive music or food or political ideologies." Or, as Victor Turner has suggested, in the "gap between ordered worlds almost anything may happen. In this interim of 'liminality,' the possibility exists of standing aside not only from one's own social position but from all social positions and of formulating a potentially unlimited series of alternative social arrangements." In the 1960s, Hollins was a community that was in such a gap with the young women sharing a feeling of resistance, or at least reflecting the national mood of students demanding an end to academic and parietal restrictions to which other generations had been subjected. The Hollins Group found that the Hollins writing program was a gathering place for kindred spirits who would act upon, and write about, their criticism of campus life.[17] Two obstacles early in their college careers effectively allowed the women of the Hollins Group to bond together outside the traditional institutional and student social arrangements of the college. The older students, apparently less charmed than Rubin by the young freshmen, seemed to restrict the newcomers' publication in the literary magazine *Cargoes.* Only Annie Doak was able to get a single entry accepted for the winter issue. Angry and affronted, a small group of freshmen decided to publish their own magazine, *Beanstalks.* Because they were so intensely serious about writing, they viewed their rejection by the older creative writing students as unfair. The competition with the other creative writers proved to be a highly motivating force. In April, Lee Smith published a lead article in the *Hollins Columns* calculated to entice a potential audience for *Beanstalks:*

> Looming ominously upon the Hollins horticultural horizon is the new plant *beanstalks* . . .
> This amazing young sprout was carefully nurtured by eminent biologists,

16. MacKethan, telephone interview.

17. Edwards and Jones, *Community,* 19; Victor W. Turner, *Dramas, Fields, and Metaphors: Symbolic Action in Human Society* (Ithaca, 1974), 13–14.

Josephine "Jo" Read Berson

i.e., editors, Annie Doak, Jo Berson, Cindy Hardwick, and Lee Smith. Many freshmen have contributed to the magazine. Nancy Beckham, the business manager, and her jolly crew of ad-sellers have handled the financial end of *beanstalks.*

So please don't eat the beanstalks, read it! Find the talent lurking in the freshman class. . . .

. . . Don't forget that on May 1 you too may obtain your personal *beanstalk* to love, honor, and cherish until death do you part. Amen.[18]

18. Lee Smith, "Beanstalks to Be Published May 1," *Hollins Columns,* April 16, 1964, p. 1.

On May Day weekend of freshman year, five hundred copies of *Beanstalks* were placed on sale at twenty-five cents a copy. The supply sold out within a few days. The magazine contained poetry and fiction written entirely by the freshmen and was financed primarily through advertisements from local businesses—though one ad in Russian was contributed by Annie Doak's roommate, Anne "Megarex" Megaro. The cover design was by Annie Doak, who later would have other artwork of hers included in copies of *Cargoes*. The table of contents included nineteen works by the freshmen, including two poems by Cindy Hardwick; "Hedonist" by Anne Bradford; "Search" and "Question" by Jo Berson; "Euterpe on Campus" and "Weekend" by Annie Doak; and two short fiction pieces, "The Wading House" and "Genesis" by Lee Smith. *Beanstalks* is of interest to literary scholars because "The Wading House" is the initial version of what was to become Lee Smith's first published novel, *The Last Day the Dogbushes Bloomed.* At the time, however, *Beanstalks* was the opening salvo in the competition with the older students, a contest that led this small group eventually to take over every publication on campus. The publication of this literary magazine, as any organizing for common purpose can do, helped the Hollins Group to see themselves—if only for a time—as a cohesive, effective writing and publishing group.

This example of cooperation was important since, in general, the group members felt so competitive that, for much of their freshman year, they viewed each other as rivals.[19] None of the women characterized freshman relationships with each other as primarily social; until senior year, most of them had almost completely separate sets of friends with whom they socialized. The initial ties of the Hollins Group grew out of desire—even pressure—to write. Some of the pressure arose from the intense format of the creative writing course. The women read each other's work in class constantly; in fact, they had little time to show their work to other friends before it was shown in class. Each studied the reactions of her peers with intense interest. The Hollins Group also saw themselves automatically in competition with the creative writing courses that preceded them, feeling that the older writers were condescending to them without reason. *Beanstalks* marked a turning point because they willingly collaborated with each other in what amounted to a vow that they would never be shut out of publications again. Soon they became readers for the *Hollins Columns* and *Cargoes* and began accepting the

19. MacKethan, telephone interview; Richard Dillard, personal interview.

writing of other members of the Hollins Group. The collaboration/competition seemed to inspire them to advance in the various literary organizations on campus. On the heels of the publication of *Beanstalks,* Annie Doak quickly declared English as her major, one of only four freshmen to do so. By fall of sophomore year Lee Smith had declared, and Anne Bradford, Nancy Beckham, Jo Berson, and Cindy Hardwick followed suit before the end of the academic year. Their official writing careers had begun because they had created space in which to experiment with their ideas.

Richard Dillard's arrival at the beginning of their sophomore year indirectly inspired the second major experience that bonded the women of the Hollins Group. Usually, during the second year creative writing students acquired more caste in the program; or, as MacKethan notes, "When you got to be sophomores, you got to go and sit in Louis Rubin's basement and drink beer. We had been looking forward to that. Instead of that happening we were thrown with Richard H. W. Dillard, which we started out feeling very angry about." Because Rubin was on leave for the year and because the advanced creative writing course had a record enrollment of twenty-three students, the class was split, with the eleven sophomores being assigned to new faculty member Dillard; the juniors, seniors, and graduate students were assigned to John Allen, Julia Sawyer, and writer-in-residence Benedict Kiely. Again, through an act of exclusion these writers coalesced into a group with the common purpose of proving themselves as writers. Richard Dillard observes that the women "were mad [because they weren't] in with the 'big kids,'" and so "there was a kind of bonding that went on. We were the outcasts, the outsiders. We were the ones that had to sit in some other little house." Dillard, a young instructor himself, shared this feeling of exile and quickly won the affections of his students. The women, again pushed into a segregated subcommunity, forged a rebellious group identity. Their homemade poster articulated their sentiments about the entire experience: "Anarchy and Arrogance Forever."[20]

Richard H. W. Dillard's sophomore creative writing course was organized as a workshop that met on Wednesday nights in Benedict Kiely's campus apartment from 8 to 10 P.M. with a break in the middle of class. Students would read works aloud, then discuss the writing and thereby gain confidence in themselves as critics. Dillard describes his teaching style as unobtrusive: to

20. MacKethan, telephone interview; Richard Dillard, personal interview.

act as "master of ceremonies," "keep the fights from starting," and move discussion along. In essence, he was "encouraging and praising as much as anything else." The Hollins writing program had "none of that sort of hierarchical stuff," not like Iowa's "pecking order" in which students were ranked by faculty opinion. Each student felt her opinion equal in weight to those of both faculty and student readers in the room and came to take her work as seriously as that of anyone else. Dillard observed, "The idea that you wanted to be a writer wasn't something odd. It was, 'Oh yes. Now get to work.'" Hence "whatever . . . competitiveness they had was very much subsumed in the sense of camaraderie." Dillard's course description gives an insight into a women's community that functioned well with a tension between cooperation and competition. For example, Annie Doak carefully watched—and envied— Lee Smith's progress in the program, but that competitive spirit did not deter Doak from collaborating with Smith on projects such as the magazine *Beanstalks.* Here the women had the public space to write, challenge, and praise each other in an egalitarian environment in which well-argued comments of students held equal weight with those of the professor. As the chapters on Dillard and Smith will show, these women were at liberty to follow their personal interests and techniques in creative writing, and they took full advantage of the space. This intense focus on their own writing and the freedom to explore their own ideas would be one of the primary contributions of the Hollins writing seminars to the professional writing of these women.[21]

Dillard's creative writing seminar had an air of exuberance that was not confined to the classroom. In November of 1964, novelist Mary Lee Settle gave a reading on campus and then, reported Dillard, "had several misadventures with the sophomore creative writers which are worthy of note but too fantastic for detailed reporting." The seminar introduced innovation to the writing program as well. In January of 1965, Dillard and dramatist-in-residence Arnold Weinstein gave readings of their work and then,

> hard upon that event, the students in the Intermediate Creative Writing Seminar (goaded by the imminent departure for Hollins Abroad of LEE SMITH) presented samples of *their* work, in poetry and in fiction. Introduced by RICHARD DILLARD, their mentor, the students who participated were: JO BERSON, of Nashville, Tenn.; ANNE BRADFORD, of Houston, Texas; CURTISY BRIGGS,

21. Kiely would, at that time, be meeting with the other class in Rubin's house; Richard Dillard, personal interview.

of Merion Station, Pa.; ANNIE DOAK, of Pittsburgh, Pa.; ELLEN GEARY, of Chester, Va.; PENNY GRILL, of Racine, Wisc., CINDY HARDWICK, of Milwaukee, Wisc., KAREN LONG, of New Vernon, N.J.; BONNIE MOON, of Charleston, S. C.; and LEE SMITH (aforementioned), of Grundy, Va., and Paris, France. According to MR. DILLARD, the performances were met "with a chorus of hurrahs and envious boos."

Though public readings have since become common practice in writing programs, it was the first time students had given one at Hollins, and the students met the occasion with "knees knocking furiously." The advanced writing seminar, now feeling the competition from the sophomores and not to be outdone by them, gave a public reading later in March. The Hollins Group had already begun establishing new ground rules that challenged the older standards.[22]

Sophomore year was marked by the increased interlacing of writing and activities among these women. One event of this sort, recorded by Hardwick and friend Jeannette Purrington, was an evening of conversation about William Blake's "The Mental Traveller" to inaugurate a semester-long series. The conception for the evening arose from a method employed by English professor John Allen whereby class was conducted every two weeks by a panel of five students who had become specialists on a particular poet through extensive research. Each student wrote a paper on the poet's work and gave an oral presentation to the seminar. On this occasion, Hollins Group women ran and reported the event. Hardwick and Purrington reported that sophomore Annie Doak was master of ceremonies at the event attended by Allen, Sawyer, Dillard, George Garrett, and twenty students.[23] Such activities encouraged the Tinker women not only to write for performance but to write about each other, effectively converting the authority of academic study into the authority of students.

Publication of creative writing by the Hollins Group expanded during sophomore year as well. Anne Bradford had three poems, "The Return," "Ihknaton's God," and "In Her Memory," accepted for publication in *Southern Poetry Review*. The all-male University of Virginia *Plume and Sword* staff accepted three poems from Annie Doak: "Weekend," "Euterpe on Cam-

22. "Reading," *Hollins Columns,* January 1965, p. 2; Richard Dillard, personal interview; *Calliope's Comments* (May 1, 1965): 3.

23. Cindy Hardwick and Jeannette Purrington, "Students Teach Poetry to Allen, Sawyer, Dillard," *Hollins Columns,* March 4, 1965, p. 3.

Anne Bowles Bradford

pus," and "Northern Quebec—August"; the *Transatlantic Review* accepted Doak's poem "Overlooking Glastonbury." Short stories accepted by the *Plume and Sword* included Lee Smith's "The Auction" and Karen Long's "The Flower." In an unusual move, the literary society Grapheon inducted a sophomore, Annie Doak, into its ranks in May. Most encouraging for everyone was the fact that Shannon Ravenel (Hollins '60), an editor for Houghton Mifflin, stopped at Hollins on a scouting trip for promising young writers.

Junior year found the Hollins Group women specializing in their studies and in their publication activities. George Garrett announced the forthcoming publication of *The Girl in the Black Raincoat*, a collection that would include a poem by Annie Doak Dillard and stories by Richard Dillard and Henry Taylor.[24] Jo Berson was one of four students working on an independent study, "The Detective Story as a Serious Art Form," with Richard Dillard. Anne Goodwyn Jones worked with Sawyer on "Studies in Eliot, Rilke, and Stevens." The new staff of *Cargoes* included as readers Anne Bradford, Cindy Hardwick, and Annie Dillard. Lucinda Hardwick now joined Anne Bradford as editorial assistant on the *Hollins Critic*. The relationships were

24. A new graduate student and future Pulitzer Prize winner, Henry S. Taylor, studied southern women novelists with Louis Rubin. Taylor became quite close to his fellow writers in the writing seminars as well.

close, congenial, and focused on advancing the literary preparation of the student. The campus community was so small that social and academic lines blurred in the respect that student class projects often seemed the center of their social interests as well. Accordingly, students often pursued their literary interests with a vigor that at other times might be divided with purely social pastimes.[25]

By junior year, fewer of the bonding experiences of the Hollins Group involved exclusion because the women had made themselves vital to the life of campus publications. More frequently now, they willingly joined each other in high-spirited literary adventures, and those adventures sometimes challenged traditional perceptions about the proper roles of women. The event that most dramatically exhibits this challenging, collaborative spirit occurred during the summer before senior year and is worth describing at length. While Cindy Hardwick spent the summer after junior year in England and Europe on an English-Speaking Union fellowship at the University of London, her classmates Anne Goodwyn Jones, Nancy Beckham, and Lee Smith joined thirteen other Hollins women in making an eleven-day raft trip—à la Huckleberry Finn—950 miles from Paducah, Kentucky, to New Orleans, Louisiana.[26] At first, parents and school officials attempted to persuade the girls not to make the trip because it was too unsafe and too difficult to execute. "The obvious improbability, almost impossibility of undergraduate girls making the trip a reality spurred us on," claimed student Anne Megaro.[27] Motivated by the adult opposition and determined to test their limitations, the students planned and worked even harder to succeed at their project.

Each girl, as a sign of commitment to the project, paid $125 to pay for construction of the raft and $25 for supplies and food. In early June, the girls flew

25. According to *Calliope's Comments* (December 1, 1965): 13, "The student Editorial assistants are responsible for preparing the checklist of books and the biography of the writer to whose work the review essay in each issue is devoted, and also for keeping the subscription records"; Jones, telephone interview.

26. The itinerary covered from June 9 to June 20 and included Cairo, Illinois; Carruthersville, Missouri; Memphis, Tennessee; Helena, Arkansas; Greenville, Vicksburg, and Natchez, Mississippi; Baton Rouge and New Orleans, Louisiana. The ensign was a sailfish with a purple fin—a "huckleberry fin"; the girls wore T-shirts with rosebuds painted on them. Annie Dillard had been scheduled to make the trip but did not.

27. Earl G. Gottschalk, Jr., "Huck Finn Revisited: Youthful Adventure on Old Man River," *National Observer,* September 25, 1967, p. 1.

to Louisville and from there went by two station wagons to Paducah, where they first saw their raft, christened the *Rosebud Hobson.* There they met Gordon W. Cooper, a seventy-year-old retired river pilot, and two young men who would help with the heavier tasks. Quickly the trip became a media event: local stations televised the life preserver drill in the country club pool; strangers gave them hams, dinners, beer, even Ku Klux Klan literature; the Evinrude corporation gave a cocktail party and lobster dinner as a promotion of the trip; the Louisville *Courier-Journal* devoted an issue of the Sunday magazine to the trip. One Paducah man "wanted to write a book about us . . . but by astute questions Lee Smith discovered that all the man has written to date is 16 pornographic novels!" Nancy Beckham wrote of how one photographer persisted "in his efforts to get several of us who were in our bathing suits (we had washed our hair in the river) to line up for a 'cheesecake' shot. His comeuppance came when he leaned too far out to get the picture and fell in the water. Not one of us moved to help him once we saw he could swim."[28]

The *Rosebud Hobson,* a craft approximately 40 feet long and 16 feet wide, was named for a 1907 Hollins student from Paducah. It floated on 52 oil drums, relied on two 40-horsepower outboard motors for power, had two sweep oars for emergencies, and cost approximately $1,800 to construct. The galley was stocked with, among other things, 48 cans of tuna fish and 13 dozen doughnuts; refrigeration was an old-fashioned ice box; the bathroom was made with plumbing from an old Pullman train. The day before their departure the group met Lillian Hobson, the sister of Rosebud (Hollins '08), for whom the raft had been named. Departure was delayed for two hours when the girls discovered they had forgotten fresh water, kerosene, and their bedding for the trip, army cots. They used a camp stove for cooking and a bucket with holes punched in it for showering.[29]

Accompanying them on the *Rosebud* was a huge amount of publicity, which the young women thoroughly enjoyed. In Greenville, Pulitzer Prize winner Hodding Carter, an uncle of one of the girls, gave them supper and entertained them; in Vicksburg, Mayor John Holland gave each girl a souvenir piece of ammunition from the local battlefields and a silver copy of the Civil War battleship *Cairo* and treated them to a catfish and hushpuppy dinner.

28. Nancy Beckham, letter to Mrs. Carter, June 1966, in Fishburn Archives, Hollins College; Beckham, "The Remarkable Voyage of the Rosebud Hobson," *Hollins College Bulletin* (November 1966): 42.
29. Gottschalk, "Huck Finn," 1.

They did, however, face some difficult challenges: they were often plagued by winds, choppy water, cold nights, and drenching rains. Mosquitoes proved a special trial: "one girl claimed a record of 36 bites below the knee on one leg only." Nancy Beckham's eyes were swollen shut with bites. They washed their hair with garden hoses. Their luck remained mixed until the end. As they neared Baton Rouge, "one of the girls' fathers had helicopters drop a dozen red roses, a dozen pink carnations, a dozen white carnations, and a dozen Hershey bars" to them. Before entering New Orleans they had to stop for repairs after a towboat tore off the rear of the raft. Finally, on Monday, June 20, they arrived in New Orleans to a dockside champagne reception from the mayor and the Preservation Hall Olympia Band. Afterward, the financial aspect of the enterprise completely deteriorated. The students had hoped to regain their investment by selling the raft, but it broke from its moorings and was so damaged that it was sold for one dollar to a salvage company. The two outboard motors, valued at $1,200 total, were stolen. As a final consolation, the girls thought the trip itself had literary promise: "Hopefully, the trip will be recorded for the girls by an aspiring writer, Lee Smith of Grundy, Va., on board. She plans to write a short book about it. She said the book will be 'sort of a factual, funny deal, you know?' "[30] The book has yet to be written.

Although the girls began the trip as something of a lark, they quickly found meanings in it that they had never anticipated. It became a challenge to prove that they could succeed at a project their parents and school officials considered impossible; it instructed them in connections with the past, with each other, and with literature. The trip was billed as "the Last of the Great Experiments in Communal Living," where vanity would be outlawed and grubbiness would reign.[31] The organizers promoted this as an opportunity

> to exploit every possible avenue of learning about the Mississippi, so that they may most effectively relive its history. Various members of the group are Researching different aspects of the trip which they will share with the others on the way down, as mental activity will be of the essence.
>
> The planned "lecture series" includes such topics as astronomy, river cur-

30. Mary Bland Armistead, "Privacy 'Up the Creek' on Girls' River Jaunt," *Roanoke World-News,* June 24, 1966, p. 10; Henry Hurt, "Hollins Girls on 'Rosebud' See Vicksburg, Resume Trip," *Roanoke World-News,* June 17, 1966.

31. Tricia Neild, "Huck Finns Plan 'Cruise,' " *Hollins Columns,* May 3, 1966, p. 3.

rents and cloud formations, historical sketches of the ports to be visited, "piloting, seamanship, and small boat handling," Mississippi folklore, ghost stories and, of course, daily readings of *Huckleberry Finn.*[32]

Each young woman took an area of study about which she would report as they traveled. These women were talented at combining lighthearted adventure with serious intellectual pursuit.

The students were impressed that, for the people of Paducah, this trip was no trivial matter: "They took us seriously." Nancy Beckham likened their adventures—and misadventures—to those of Huck Finn. Captain Cooper was unflinching, she wrote, "when we reported, 'Sir, we just lost our second anchor,' or, 'Captain, we seem to be out of gas.' The only thing that seemed to upset him was having corned beef sandwiches for three meals one day." Memorable to Beckham as well was "being read to sleep from *Life on the Mississippi* and feeling that you were part of it." Annie Dillard's former roommate, Anne Megaro, had similarly poignant observations about the adventure: "Before the trip we thought if 16 people find it hard to maintain smooth relations on a campus, what will it be like on the tight quarters of a raft on the river? We formed an entity, found perhaps by such respect for the raft, the very idea of it, and automatically, effortlessly, lived up to it. It evoked something in us which we weren't at all sure we possessed." Megaro's comment about the difficulty of maintaining "smooth relations on campus" confirms that life among women on a small campus was not so idyllic that they could automatically expect to succeed at a difficult enterprise far afield. However, her words also confirm a certain ability of these women to allow their enthusiasm for literature and achievement to overcome the competition they normally felt among themselves. Again they overcame resistance in order to pursue their vision of literary experience, their interpretation of Twain's *Life on the Mississippi;* again a significant factor was that a certain group of people took them seriously. Resistance coalesced their motivation but encouragement sustained it.[33]

The Mississippi raft trip propelled the Hollins Group into their senior year with a spirit of exhilaration. The standard models of the past three years continued to challenge these young women. Hollins M.A. Sylvia Wilkinson

32. Ibid.
33. Gottschalk, "Huck Finn," 1, 21; Beckham, "Remarkable Voyage," 41, 45.

read on campus in November. Richard Dillard, Julia Sawyer, and John Allen, among other English faculty members, gave readings of their writing—as did student writers. Visiting writers included Howard Nemerov, William Styron, John Barth, and James Dickey. In the spring, "joining Dickey in discussing student poetry in the afternoon session were HENRY TAYLOR, poet, Hollins M.A. (1966), presently on the Roanoke College faculty, and JAMES SEAY, of the V. M. I. faculty."[34] Eudora Welty returned to campus in the spring to receive the Hollins Medal. But what proved different was that this senior class included the largest number of English majors to date; and now, as natural leaders of the student community, the Hollins women dominated Hollins publications. Annie Doak Dillard and Cindy Hardwick edited *Cargoes;* Lee Smith and Jo Berson edited *Spinster;* Nancy Beckham was editor in chief of *Hollins Columns,* with Anne Bradford and Cindy Hardwick as her coexecutive editors. The writing and activities of the group were in abundant evidence throughout the year. One could select almost any random issue of the *Hollins Columns* and find multiple notices by or about these women. Cindy Hardwick, Lee Smith, Annie Dillard, and Anne Bradford worked together in their creative writing course. Hardwick and Dillard talked and argued with each other through an independent study course with the Reverend George Gordh on mysticism, a study that was later to be a significant influence on Dillard's *Pilgrim at Tinker Creek.* Anne Bradford, Cindy Hardwick, Annie Doak Dillard, and Anne Goodwyn Jones were elected to Phi Beta Kappa. In the terms of MacKethan's metaphor, the Hollins women were taking possession of their garden and designing it to fit their purposes: they were in charge of publications and prepared to be their own storytellers.

Nancy Beckham, Jo Berson, Cindy Hardwick, Annie Dillard, and Anne Goodwyn Jones were reunited in Louis Rubin's course, "Studies in the Modern Novel," in which they studied Louis Rubin's favorite literary interest, Marcel Proust. By having his students explore the "new techniques of characterization and chronological form," Rubin hoped that the student would "be substantially equipped to explore the rich territory of modern fiction on her own." In a sense, the members of the Hollins Group were already shaping the terrain of that fictional world. Cindy Hardwick trained the attention of the

34. *Calliope's Comments* (May 1967): 14. Mississippian Jim Seay was one of George Garrett's star pupils at the University of Virginia. Tall, thin, and handsome, Seay wore a rakish black eyepatch. Lee Smith and Seay met when he came to Hollins College for a reading and, after her graduation, married.

Nancy Head Beckham

campus on the war in Vietnam in a poem entitled, "My Brother Used to Play." The central image in the poem read: "The night before he went to war, / He took his marbles / Out into the yard, / And shot them at the stars; / And watched, as one by one / They fell like just so many / Silent bombs to pierce the night." The maturity and realism of this image contrast strongly with "Dragon Slayer," Hardwick's freshman poem in *Beanstalks* about knights in shining armor. Another area in which the Hollins women shaped their terrain was in the selection of essays for the *Hollins Symposium*. Anne Bradford was on the selection committee of which Anne Goodwyn Jones was cochair. Ten student essays were selected from among forty-three recommended for consideration by members of the Hollins faculty. Jo Berson's essay on Proust won, as did Annie Dillard's essay on Emily Dickinson.[35]

A final event of their undergraduate careers exhibits the continuing independent spirit of this group, that same wild passion for experiencing literature. It occurred in October when the college newspaper announced that "slickers of any size, shape, or description" would admit one to a "read-in" in honor of the publication of *The Girl in the Black Raincoat,* an anthology edited by George Garrett that included poetry by Annie Doak Dillard. Richard Dillard commented for the paper, "We hope the party will hover between a Happening and an Event." According to one record, Henry Taylor wrote the first raincoat story, "And Bid a Fond Farewell to Tennessee," which initiated the fad. The women's rock group on campus, the "Virginia Wolves," played, and according to the *Hollins Columns,* the evening launched "Mr. Dillard's career as a mod entrepreneur, if such things be; Jim Seay's career as a folk hero; the Virginia Wolves' career as a fire hazard; and the erstwhile go-go girls' careers as erstwhile go-go girls." Richard Dillard contributed a short story to the collection, and Annie Doak Dillard had a poem, "The Affluent Beatnik." Literary critic Leslie Fiedler, novelist Fred Chappell, and poets Carol Kizer and David Slavitt attended the event and soon witnessed the then-legendary high spirits of the literary community when Lee Smith, Annie Dillard, and others "dressed in miniskirts and white boots . . . climbed into high windows behind the poets and performed go-go routines to the rhythm of the recitations." The *Calliope* report of the event confirms much of the story:

> It was all very gay, it was all very merry in the Main Drawing Room the evening of Tuesday, October 22. The occasion was a "read-in" in honor of publication of *The Girl In The Black Raincoat,* by Duell, Sloan and Pearce ($5.95), being a compendium of prose and poetry by numerous hands, every item of which at one point or another alludes to a girl in a black raincoat. Hollins writers were prominent in the collection—assistant professor RICHARD H. W. DILLARD, undergraduate and faculty wife ANNIE DOAK DILLARD, 1965–66 graduate student HENRY TAYLOR, 1965–66 writer-in-residence WILLIAM JAY SMITH, and next year's writer-in-residence SHELBY FOOTE. The collection was edited by

35. *Calliope's Comments* (May 20, 1964): 6; Cindy Hardwick, "My Brother Used to Play," ibid. (November 1966): 12; Hardwick, "Dragon Slayer," in *Beanstalks,* ed. Berson et al., 6; *Calliope's Comments* (May 1967): 7.

GEORGE GARRETT, associate professor of English at the University of Virginia and a member of the editorial board of *The Hollins Critic*. The "read-in" was like nothing that ever transpired in the Main Drawing Room before—a rock-and-roll band, a set of Go-Go Girls (all of them senior English majors), and much reading and singing.

George Garrett asked the young women to do a repeat performance at the Prism coffeehouse in Charlottesville, where they were less appreciatively received by the predominantly male audience. Senior year was marked by such literary playfulness, in which we see the wild exuberance of these women who took their writing with such great seriousness and who took their living with equally strong humor. The Hollins Group fed each other in this creative engagement with the literature they studied and the writing they produced.[36]

Ironically, senior year ended for the Hollins Group with signs that the writing life might be a passing phase for some of the women. Annie Dillard had early traded her student status for that of faculty wife; Lee Smith married James Seay seven days after graduation; Jo Berson married a month later. Cindy Hardwick, in fact, reported that "as the diamond stockpile among the class of '67 grows at a rate too depressing to publish, unattached seniors are beginning to wonder if there isn't going to be a 'rock' shortage soon." Others, such as Anne Jones, were going to graduate school for reasons ranging from " 'I can't quit now; I'm just getting the hang of it' to 'It beats working.' " As for herself, Hardwick wrote, "Cindy Hardwick is being interviewed for a job as a governess in East Africa where she will at last have a practical use for her bongo drums."[37] Early marriage, however, scarcely deterred most of these women from writing and writing careers. Nancy Beckham went to work for the *Washington Star* and now publishes *Government Computer News.* Anne Bradford Warner returned to Hollins to earn a master's degree, obtained a Ph.D. in English from Emory University, and now teaches at Spelman College in Atlanta, where she devotes her scholarship to black women writers. Jo Berson wrote for a Franklin, Tennessee, newspaper for two years before joining her husband in running a real estate business. Lee Smith balanced teaching and home life with progressively ambitious short story and novel writing.

36. Tunstall Collins, " 'Raincoat' Party Will Honor Authors," *Hollins Columns,* October 18, 1966, p. 1; Lee Smith, "Hollins Four Go-Goes to Beatnik Folk Tune," ibid., October 25, 1966, p. 4; Epps, "Learning to Write Can Be Fun," 1; *Calliope's Comments* (November 1966): 8; MacKethan, telephone interview.

37. Hardwick, "June Grads Are Never Sad," *Hollins Columns,* May 2, 1967, pp. 5, 7.

Annie Doak Dillard stayed at Hollins and earned a master's degree; within a few more years she won the Pulitzer Prize for *Pilgrim at Tinker Creek*. The writing life had become strongly rooted at Hollins.

When one reflects upon these collegiate careers, it becomes clear that the activities of the Hollins Group demonstrate a synthesis of two patterns of community formation: competition and collaboration. In cases such as *Beanstalks,* the splitting of the sophomore class, and the Mississippi raft trip, the women joined together to prove that they were capable of succeeding when others believed that they could not. They believed in their own powers. Collaboration was not the only link among these young writers. Competition with each other proved to be a highly motivating force as well. Richard Dillard has observed that Annie Doak Dillard was fiercely competitive and especially alert to Lee Smith's success in writing. Annie Dillard herself explains the competition more positively, stating that the Hollins writing program was successful during these years because "our teachers were so good and such wonderful people that we wanted their approval (or, at least I did), and Lee Smith was so talented it was exciting to be in the same state with her." About Cindy Hardwick's work Annie Dillard writes, "I always stayed real close to the texts in my papers. Once I read a Cindy Hardwick paper and was amazed by its intellectual sweep. I didn't know it was possible to think so freely. It was brilliant."[38] This mutual appreciation occurs countless times throughout the course of their undergraduate careers. Anne Goodwyn Jones wrote feature columns in the newspaper about race relations and student issues, and other writers such as Cindy Hardwick and Nancy Beckham wrote subsequent extensions and explorations of those arguments. Annie Dillard presented her senior essay to the *Hollins Symposium,* and board members such as Anne Goodwyn Jones read and accepted it. A blending of competition and collaboration was crucial. The competitiveness spurred the women to perform well for their peers and enhanced the confidence they felt about themselves and their writing. The collaboration, however, established the ties of congeniality that evolved into the women's network of criticism and support that has persisted to the present day.

This blending of individual achievement and collaborative effort evolved in a process by which the Hollins Group changed from outsiders to insiders and gradually began to take over the campus publications. The collegiate

38. Annie Dillard, letter.

Lucinda Clay Hardwick MacKethan

newspaper careers of Cindy Hardwick and Anne Goodwyn Jones—women whose later scholarly work parallels each other's—illustrate two of the ways by which the women became insiders. When Hardwick felt her first deep bout of homesickness as a freshman, Louis Rubin consoled her and then promptly asked the editor of the school newspaper (for which he was the adviser) to solicit Hardwick to write an article. Never having worked with a newspaper before, Hardwick was surprised to discover that she took genuine pleasure in newspaper writing. She became a regular reporter and had to do the routine assignments such as writing about the conversion of a faculty house to a student dormitory, as well as the lead story announcing the arrival on campus of the new writer-in-residence, Irishman Benedict Kiely.

Often Hardwick's articles were humorous; some of them reflected the social constraints that still pressured the young women. In March of 1965, she wrote an article that represented her first in-print questioning of administrative policy. Apparently the student body was distraught that the May Cotillion had to be held on campus without liquor being served. Hardwick maintains a subtly humorous tone in her report, but an undercurrent of questioning marks the article as well. On another point, she made some rather wry observations about the artificiality of the social practice of college "mixers," which she compared to the game of Monopoly. Gradually, Hardwick had more leeway to pursue her own interests rather than an obligation to handle the routine reporting assignments, a change suggesting that she had made the transition from outsider to valued contributor in the publications at Hollins. Though the Hollins Group maintained their mild counterculture, this alteration from outsider to insider was a significant step in establishing themselves as leaders within the larger college community. This transition occurred for these women because they persistently threw themselves into the writing necessary to feeding these organizations: Hardwick had paid her dues by willingly taking on the routine, relatively unglamorous assignments such as covering the swim club activities. She and the other women succeeded because they put themselves in the service of these publications and thereby became essential to the running of them.[39]

The other writer whose newspaper writing became progressively more prominent at Hollins was Anne Goodwyn Jones. As was true with several other Hollins writers, her opening gambit with publication was collaborative. Early in her sophomore year, Jones and two other students signed a letter to the editors of the college paper complaining that "the *Hollins Columns* has failed in its obligation to educate students concerning issues in the presidential elections." The challenge brought a rather stinging reply from the editor: " 'The Hollins Columns' is not obliged to 'educate students concerning issues in the presidential elections' or on the 'philosophy of the future role of our country'; a college newspaper is not equipped to substitute for a metropolitan

---

39. Hardwick, "Students Voice Various Reactions to Possibilities of Future Dry Cotillions," *Hollins Columns*, March 25, 1965, p. 3; Hardwick, "Mixer Monopoly! A Game to Win," ibid., October 28, 1965, p. 4.

or national newspaper. Students are obliged to educate themselves and may do so by consulting regularly any of the newspapers or current periodicals available in the library."[40] Clearly not satisfied with the limitations implied by that response, Jones took on a more individual role for herself in responding later in the month, writing a lengthy article attacking Goldwater on his defense policy and supporting Johnson on civil rights and welfare issues. Her article included specific percentages of increased megatonnage of nuclear warheads; descriptions of how that megatonnage was distributed; an analysis of Goldwater's reasons for voting against the Civil Rights Act of 1964; and specific statistics on incomes and standards of living for poverty-level families. Jones's actions later influenced another member of the Hollins Group, Annie Dillard, to help register city voters for the Goldwater/Johnson election. Jones, who had been politically active even in high school, remained true to her interests as the one member of the Hollins Group who wrote consistently about current matters of social conscience.

In February of 1965, Jones returned to write in the "Open Forum Column" of the *Hollins Columns* concerning the dangers of student apathy. A flurry of writing from Hollins Group women soon followed Jones's article. Cindy Hardwick, Jeannette Purrington, and two other young women signed a letter to the editor voicing their concern and disappointment over student apathy. The theme that Jones had sounded clearly found resonance with Hardwick. Nancy Beckham felt moved as well; her article for the April 22, 1965, issue recorded that she and two other Hollins students had participated in the anti-war march on Washington, D.C. Beckham's record of the Washington protest and the repeated urgings of Hardwick and Jones constituted new voices of political conscience on campus. Jones would often return to this issue of student apathy: "It is not that we lack at Hollins the possibility for controversy, the potential for vital discussion, the other sides of the question. It is that we are unable or unwilling to ask with honesty the questions that are meaningful." It is far too easy to become caught up in unexamined lives. "Instead," she continued, "we live in our 800 individual worlds" and "silently fear there is nothing worth a damn." A frequent theme in Jones's writing was the failure of students to become involved in intellectual and political struggle. She chastised students who failed to avail themselves of lectures on conserva-

40. Anne Jones, Melissa Kinsey, and Sharon Whittle, "If Students Uneducated Our Fault?" ibid., October 8, 1964, p. 2.

tism and on the New Left. Lee Smith tells a perhaps apocryphal story that one day while women were sunbathing on the roof of a dormitory, they looked over into the courtyard to see Jones, along with a lone history professor, picketing in protest of the war in Vietnam.[41]

In February of 1966, Jones began writing a regular column entitled "Scriptiunculae," and for it she wrote articles ranging from a collection of haiku to the political implications of prejudice. The first issue she addressed was the question, "Are We Honor Bound?" and concerned a search following a recent honor code infraction in the Randolph dormitory:

> When I first heard about the Randolph fiasco, I fumed and raged and thought of WW II movies, Dragnet and several nightmares. And so, it seems, did many in Randolph. It is no wonder. Confinement to your room with little explanation during exams, dark rooms with people in them who shine lights on your hands, the planting of treated money with the hope that it will be stolen— these methods smack of something sinister. Guilty until proven innocent, maybe. Or, fight force with force, evil with evil, the act of stealing with the aura of suspicion, tension and mutual mistrust. The whole idea is repugnant; it was mishandled to boot; and nothing good came of it. Except that we know the thief is not a Randolph girl—and that, I thought, was our original assumption anyway, under the honor system.

It revealed the "failure of a system based on trust," she wrote.[42]

Jones seemed the writer most clearly aware that some conflict was healthy and natural. In March she boldly supported a recent resolution that urged the integration of Hollins. In April she again reflected upon the complacency of the student body and actively complained that even the modest number of student petitions had been "squelched" by President Logan. In her final column of the year, Jones examined the conflict over whether attendance should be required at chapel talks: "It is dishearteningly typical to see that students are more eager to complain about requirements than to exercise the freedom which they already have, which is the privilege of hearing and responding to

41. Anne Jones, "Open Forum," ibid., February 25, 1965, p. 3; Nancy Bryan, Ginny Byrne, Cindy Hardwick, and Jeannette Purrington, letter to the editor, ibid., March 25, 1965, p. 6; Anne Jones, "Problem of Apathy Is Perennial," ibid., February 22, 1966, p. 2; Lee Smith, personal interview, July 25–26, 1991.

42. Anne Jones, "Jones Gives Look at Japanese Haiku," *Hollins Columns*, May 10, 1966, p. 2; Jones, "Prejudice Is Political Danger," ibid., May 3, 1966, p. 2; Jones, "Are We Honor Bound?" ibid., February 15, 1966, p. 2.

Anne Goodwyn Jones

serious thought dealing with subjects highly relevant to the growth of the student and largely ignored in the daily grind. No wonder chapel is required. 'They' know we don't care enough to go of our own choice, to endure a little 'religion' or whatever you want to call it for the sake of something we consider to be worth our time." Jones herself found the talks to be educational opportunities that others were missing because they were so concerned with their supposed rights: "Anyone who doesn't care enough to go and see what's offered has no right to complain that her freedom has been limited. She's already forfeited it." Considering Jones's deep concern with human issues, it was no surprise to find her during senior year as cochair of the Religious Life Association, whose members did tutoring and other community work in impoverished sections of Roanoke.[43]

Interestingly—and as was true for many members of the Hollins Group—the longer Jones wrote for the *Hollins Columns,* the more frequently she wrote humorous articles as well. Humor and playfulness seemed to be signs that the women felt supported enough to risk being silly. In one column she advocated a Spring Tinker Day which would, she claimed, strike "at spring fever's roots: spring. And, once cured, we could work again. Our work would be in on time

43. Anne Jones, "Word Play," ibid., March 8, 1966, p. 5; Jones, "Legislation Was Squelched," ibid., April 12, 1966, p. 2; Jones, "Motivation Is Our Problem," ibid., May 17, 1966, p. 2.

again. Our souls and bodies would attend class *together* again." She even took herself humorously in assessing the value of the day: "Those who have latent activist tendencies could vent them all on this one massive Cause. And organized marches, complete with posters and pamphlets, could be arranged on Tinker Top. You could write your cause in big letters on the mountain and airplanes would see it."[44] However, the overwhelming majority of Jones's articles were the works of a woman who sought to remind a school of its social conscience: individualism operated in support of the community.

Implicit in any theory about women's communities is the question of whether the goals of such communities are qualitatively different from all-male or gender-mixed writing groups. The Hollins writing community proved that individual aspirations could be employed in support of peers. The Hollins Group women were seeking to find their voices in the face of a paternalistic social and literary tradition, and their peers were crucial sources of support. Again, Anne Goodwyn Jones and Lucinda Hardwick MacKethan are exemplars of this feminist impulse in the Hollins Group. Since graduation from Hollins, both women developed independent scholarly careers but have demonstrated a few marked similarities to each other. Both women did graduate study at the University of North Carolina at Chapel Hill at the same time. The Chapel Hill area has, in fact, become something of a gathering place for Hollins alumnae such as MacKethan, Smith, and Shannon Ravenel as well as being the location of Louis Rubin's Algonquin Press. Both women completed their doctorates with Rubin as director. MacKethan's dissertation became her first book, *The Dream of Arcady: Place and Time in Southern Literature*. Jones's dissertation also became her first book, *Tomorrow Is Another Day: The Woman Writer in the South, 1859–1936*. Rubin invited MacKethan and Jones to write essays for *The History of Southern Literature* (1985), which he edited. Both MacKethan and Jones have made southern writing—particularly southern women's writing—a central concern of their intellectual study: their first journal articles were about Lee Smith's writing; their most current books explore the relationship of southern women to the traditions of fiction and storytelling. A few examples from their scholarly work illustrate how the Hollins influence and connections persist.

Jones's book, *Tomorrow Is Another Day*, is a study of the literary manifestations of southern womanhood. Her introduction suggests that she has, as Ru-

44. Anne Jones, "Celebrate Spring on Tinker," ibid., March 22, 1966, p. 2.

bin advocated, written from her own experience: "Every book is shaped by its writer's experience and predilections; this one is no exception. I grew up in the South, and thus I have known firsthand both the appeal and the threat of becoming a southern lady. Like many southern white women of my generation, I felt the fissures of southern life as personal rifts, ultimately requiring personal choices. The image of the lady awed and angered me; I went to the cotillions and to the civil rights marches, enjoying the privileges of southern white womanhood while pursuing the contradictory dream of freedom and equality."[45] Jones has reclaimed in this book seven women writers whose works—with few exceptions—have scarcely been given serious scholarly treatment. Jones begins her analysis with a survey of the literature concerning the southern lady and then addresses various stereotypical aspects of the image—the perfect lady, the bad little girl, and others—as they appear in selected novels of these women writers. Because of the fine quality of her research and analysis, Jones's book has become one of the most frequently cited studies in feminist and new historicist criticism on southern women's writing. In a similar fashion, in 1983, Jones wrote an article that helped to establish the literary reputation of her classmate, Lee Smith. In "The World of Lee Smith," Jones gives a feminist reading of Smith's fascination with activities such as cake-baking, quilting, and hairstyling: "Often as not, the metaphor for art in her stories comes out of women's culture; not only does it shape life but it is useful as well, like cakes or quilts or hairstyles. Her tendency to prefer traditionally female immanent art to traditionally male transcendent art parallels her preference for the spoken to the written word." Jones observes that Smith's writing not only brings attention to women's culture and voice but also gives sharp observations about the particular constraints of southern life: "What she hears is the sometimes heroic, sometimes comic, sometimes sneaky and petty ways in which Southern women and men try to salvage a sense of self within a system that tries to define that self for them."[46] In Smith's writing and Jones's criticism, one sees not only a continuation of their collegiate writing about the heavy constraints that southern culture has placed on women but a continuation of the literary collaboration that marked their collegiate careers.

45. Jones, *Tomorrow Is Another Day*, xii.
46. Anne Goodwyn Jones, "The World of Lee Smith," in *Women Writers of the Contemporary South*, ed. Peggy Whitman Prenshaw (Jackson, Miss., 1984), 252, 271.

Lee Smith's writing has also been the subject of Lucinda Hardwick MacKethan's scholarship. In 1982 Rubin, as coeditor of the *Southern Literary Journal,* asked MacKethan to write an article that became "Artists and Beauticians: Balance in Lee Smith's Fiction." Briefly, MacKethan argues that Lee Smith's fiction is deeply feminist because it reveals that the ordinary, daily work of women is a special form of art. To analyze Smith's writing is, states MacKethan, an intriguing proposition, one in which she feels no privileged insight: "Lee as writer has always seemed very separate from Lee as friend. In my mind it was always easy to separate the writer from the person I had lunch with, and it has remained that way, so that when I talk about her work I don't feel like I'm talking about my friend's work. I'm talking about a writer named Lee Smith who I don't feel like I really know at all. So separating the two has always been very easy." Still, even the thematic concerns of these two women seem similar. In both *Oral History* and *Fair and Tender Ladies,* Smith has explored the significance of storytelling and the epistolary mode for southern women seeking to discover their own lives and voices. MacKethan describes similar interests in *Daughters of Time:* "My idea for this book came about through voices, the voices of southern women storytellers who, in my personal experience as well as in many of my favorite books, have helped me to discover who I am. I still hear my grandmother's Kentucky voice; as we sat on her front porch in the summer, glasses of iced lemonade in hand, she would explain to her exiled granddaughter who belonged to what family. . . . I have tried to keep my mother's voice; her letters to me, beginning the year that I left home to go eight hundred miles away to college." As is true with Jones and Smith, MacKethan's interest and insights into Smith's work continue to reflect a concern with the confining roles imposed upon southern women and an interest in the writing that such women have been able to accomplish.[47]

The Hollins writing community was, then, a balance between individual literary aspiration and collaborative feminist spirit. In print and in action, the Hollins Group challenged the constraints put on them by the traditional cultural definitions of women. Though individualistic, even competitive with each other about their writing, they were so committed to understanding and improving the status of women at Hollins that supportive feminism became a pattern in their later work. If aftermath provides any sort of substantial proof of community, then the subsequent network of influence main-

47. MacKethan, telephone interview; MacKethan, *Daughters of Time,* 1.

tained by the women of the Hollins Group stands as powerful evidence of such a community. In fact, the Tinker diaspora is an impressive story of women continuing to collaborate with each other after leaving the hotbed of creative activity. For MacKethan, her friends/critics were crucial: "Somehow when I left that community of readers, I didn't keep writing [poetry]. I was, I think, writing for them. . . . And when they weren't there anymore to read it in that context, I just didn't have the energy to do it." Over time, however, the Hollins Group women have reestablished their relationships as supportive and critical readers for each other. Initially, Rubin created postgraduate opportunities for these women to stay in touch with each other and to analyze each other's writings; now the women themselves naturally and readily maintain those connections. MacKethan studies Lee Smith's creative writing and cites Anne Goodwyn Jones's scholarly writing in *Daughters of Time*. In *Tomorrow Is Another Day*, Jones thanks Lee Smith for reading several draft versions of the book. In 1992, both Annie Dillard and Lee Smith published new novels, and each has noted that the other made some contribution to the novel. Smith acknowledged Dillard's contribution of a song title, "Two Lefts Don't Make a Right," to *The Devil's Dream*. Dillard credits Lee Smith with advice that helped her to write her first novel, the newly published *The Living:* "She told me 6 or 7 years ago that she wrote from very long (40- or 50-page) outlines; she planned novels in great detail before she began writing sentences. I used this same method on my first novel, *The Living,* and would have been lost without it. She 'de-spookified' the process." In 1967, Louis Rubin observed that graduation seemed to place a seal upon the ties of Hollins women: "The graduating classes cleave together unto death; they are indissoluble. I recall one husband of a recent Hollins graduate saying plaintively to me . . . : 'I knew I was marrying a Hollins girl, but I didn't realize I was marrying an entire class!'" Hollins women are, concluded the young man, "'awe-inspiring . . . bright-eyed Minervae.'" The ties of affection and aspiration hold together a network of individual women working together toward similar goals.[48]

That the Hollins Group attended a private southern women's college certainly confirms Fox-Genovese's classist charge about women's communities; and yet, despite her objections, it is relevant to consider what it means for any

48. MacKethan, telephone interview; Jones, *Tomorrow Is Another Day,* xvi; Annie Dillard, letter; Rubin, "Hollins College," 10, 12.

Louis D. Rubin, Jr., also made the 1967 *Spinster.*

core group of women to contribute to the lives and writing of each other. Here was a community of white women who shared the benefits of education made possible by a middle- or upper-class economic status. They chose to attend a southern women's college because it represented personal values and professional goals that each had already claimed for herself—in this regard Fox-Genovese is accurate in describing such choices as motivated by class and individualist goals. Her comments are also accurate that a community such as the Hollins Group gathered because of individual decisions about academic and professional choices: MacKethan confirms that "we were not in any way a follow-the-leader type group. We were all very individualistic."[49] However, the sisterly atmosphere at Hollins tempered that competitive spirit until it shared a fruitful tension with collaboration. As a result, these women became campus leaders, confident writers, and supportive colleagues. Hollins did not produce the talent but created conditions most favorable to the growth of the

49. MacKethan, telephone interview.

talent: courses and publications provided public spaces in which women could explore and voice their thoughts; mentors and peers offered them criticism and support.

Finally, by ignoring the temporal dimension of a community, Fox-Genovese's argument misses a significant cohesive element. The claims of the Hollins community have gained more emotional and real strength with passing years precisely because the women have come to value the sense of community more than their individual importance within that community. Competition is subsumed within support. Annie Dillard makes a thoughtful observation about their strong continuing network of support: "Of course I write blurbs for their books and talk them up. I talk to a lot of people, and can try to steer invitations and offers to friends. 'Network of support' sounds like a trendy term to describe the ordinary kindnesses of friendship which include men as well as women."[50] Since the 1960s, these women have been shaping a complex, continually changing community based in part on sentiment but also on a genuine respect and appreciation for the writing craft. For writers such as Smith, Jones, and MacKethan, the cultural positioning of southern women has increasingly become a stronger, shared theme of their professional writing.

What was the nature of the writing community at Hollins from 1963 to 1967? Clearly, these were not the women whom William Golding described as "obsessive note-takers" hoping to "avoid the sheer agony of having to think for themselves."[51] Yet living on the cusp of an age combined for these women a unique power with a taunting sense of limitation. As Lucinda MacKethan's evocative image suggests, the women of the Hollins Group were young women moving beyond the role of daughter and into the role of storytellers and scholars. They had the potential to be their own blend of upstarts and women of taste yet still faced real institutionalized limitations upon their actions. Inspired and challenged by other Hollins writers, they undertook to listen to their own voices. The telling measure of the Hollins community is evident in their continued support of each other. They were, indeed, women who took possession of their own gardens, imagining and designing much of their education at Hollins and, in later years, drawing on that experience and that comradeship to write about women's issues. Their competition, of itself,

---

50. Annie Dillard, letter.
51. Golding, "The Glass Door," 142.

did not undercut the importance of their community; it was merely one of the ways they defined themselves in relation to others. Far from being consumed by the flame of creative intensity, these women discovered themselves warmed by it throughout their writing careers. Their community did not exist simply at one campus at one particular point in time but has spread across the country and across time, all held together by a concept they still perceive as *Hollins.*

4

ANNIE DILLARD
The Pilgrim at Tinker Creek

One night, however, back in Pittsburgh, I had a dream about Hollins. The dream was about the beauty of the little creek that ran behind the old snack bar and out behind the library. The dream was so haunting I changed my mind . . . and applied [to attend Hollins]. . . . It was a miracle I got in.

—Annie Dillard, letter

This Tinker Creek! . . . These are the waters of beauty and mystery, issuing from a gap in the granite world; they fill the lodes in my cells with a light like petaled water.

—*Pilgrim at Tinker Creek*

*W*hen *Pilgrim at Tinker Creek* won the Pulitzer Prize for general nonfiction in 1975, Annie Doak Dillard was not yet thirty years old. This exceptional achievement quickly established an international reputation for Dillard that the other members of the Hollins Group have yet to rival. Contemporary reviews of her writing ranged from suggestions that her natural peers were William Blake and Albert Einstein to the recurring, re-

Annie Dillard at the time of the publication of *Pilgrim at Tinker Creek* in early 1974.

markably unliterary observation that Dillard was "extremely good-looking." Dillard's fame and fortunes rose at a meteoric rate: 37,000 copies of *Pilgrim* were sold within two months of first publication; the book went through eight printings in the first two years; paperback rights and Book-of-the-Month Club selection brought her $250,000 within three months. Fans of the book treated her as a guru or "female Castaneda" and began besieging her with mail and speaking requests. For her part, Dillard was nonplussed that this book that had taken her eight months to write had entirely eclipsed *Tickets for a Prayer Wheel,* the book of poetry that had been published the month prior to *Pilgrim* and had taken her five years to write. The attention proved almost unnerving: "I'm starting to have dreams about Tinker Creek," Dillard commented soon after the book's publication. "Lying face down in it, all muddy and dried up and I'm drowning in it. Ever since I made a symbol of it." She had, she thought, "shot my lifetime wad. *Pilgrim* is not only the wisdom of my 28 years but I think it's the wisdom of my whole life."[1]

Pilgrim at Tinker Creek did indeed reflect the wisdom of Dillard's twenty-eight years as daughter, wife, woman, student, and writer. Though her performance of these roles may have often been conventional, Dillard nearly always regarded herself as living at the margins of convention. Along with her Hollins Group peers, Dillard had felt at home at Hollins where they were "betwixt and between" the social roles assigned to women.[2] There she could create her own definition of herself with little interference. A rebellious debutante, a student who married her professor, a faculty wife who wanted to legitimate her writing ability with the college faculty, Dillard found herself attracted to, and modeling herself after, writers who dealt with liminal experiences. *Pilgrim at Tinker Creek* eventually became a troubling vision for Dillard, in part because interpreters of the book attempted to settle its meaning—and her own as its author. Tinker Creek had so completely "filled the cells" of the writer that book, voice, and writer seemed to share the same meaning; and the critical efforts to secure specific meanings for them worked against the ambiguous marginality that was central to Dillard's personal worldview.

Although Dillard has described herself as a writer in the New Critical tradition, two of the central literary features in *Pilgrim*—her persona and the idea of circumference—are liminal features more evocative of a destabilized literary tradition. "The essence of liminality," argues Victor Turner, "is to be found in its release from normal constraints, making possible the deconstruc-

1. Annie Dillard, *Pilgrim at Tinker Creek* (New York, 1974), 274; *Book-of-the-Month Club News*, April 1974, p. 2; John F. Baker, "Story Behind the Book: 'Pilgrim at Tinker Creek,'" *Publisher's Weekly*, March 18, 1974, p. 28; Jeannette Smyth, "Annie Dillard: Southern Sibyl," *Washington Post*, May 19, 1974, sec. G, p. 1. In sheer quantitative terms, *Pilgrim* has ensured that Dillard has not been out of print since it was first published. By 1987 it had sold more than 655,000 copies and had been reprinted in five countries. See Linda L. Smith, *Annie Dillard* (New York, 1991), 1; Smyth, "Southern Sibyl," G4; Anna Logan Lawson, "Thinker, Poet, Pilgrim," *Hollins* (May 1974): 12; William McPherson, "A Conversation with Annie Dillard," *Book-of-the-Month Club News*, April 1974, p. 25.

2. Turner, *Ritual Process*, 95.

tion of the 'uninteresting' constructions . . . [into units,] which may then be reconstructed in novel ways." Perhaps, given her self-image, it was natural for Dillard to write in a literary form that obscured the traditional distinctions between fiction and autobiography, between the temporal and the eternal. Her poetry, her memoir, and above all, her essays, subvert the characteristic differences between writer and persona; all flirt with the notion that the "I" of this piece is certainly just a persona but is also strikingly like Annie Dillard in her habits and beliefs. Or as one of Dillard's models, Emily Dickinson, cleverly disclaimed in a letter to Thomas Wentworth Higginson barely a century earlier, "When I state myself, as the Representative of the Verse—it does not mean—me—but a supposed person." Arguably, all of Dillard's life and writing have been part of a rebellion, and the costs have often been exacted in personal and spiritual uncertainty that is reflected through careful self-representation in her writing. But beyond autobiographical interest, the liminality in her fiction serves to demonstrate yet another literary strategy by which women have explored possible literary and cultural alternatives to their life experiences. The persona "Annie Dillard" experiences and describes thoughts and events that the real Annie Dillard had only heard about or studied or imagined: the persona gave her thoughts and actions fuller room to range than she found in her daily life. The personal and literary progress of this pilgrim at Tinker Creek provides us with evidence of how Dillard's apprentice work was a necessary preparation for her greater professional achievements such as *Pilgrim at Tinker Creek*.[3]

Dillard almost taunts the reader to distinguish between autobiography and fiction in her writing. *An American Childhood* is, ostensibly, an autobiographical work; yet it is also an artfully crafted retroactive anticipation of a constructed "Annie Dillard" who appeared over a decade earlier in *Pilgrim at Tinker Creek*. She observes, near the beginning of *An American Childhood*, that on April 30, 1945, Hitler died and Meta Ann Doak was born in Pittsburgh, Pennsylvania. This remark about a coincidence of chronology pri-

3. Victor W. Turner, *On the Edge of the Bush: Anthropology as Experience*, ed. Edith L. B. Turner (Tucson, 1985), 159–60; Emily Dickinson, *The Letters of Emily Dickinson*, ed. Thomas H. Johnson and Theodora Ward, 2 vols. (Cambridge, Mass., 1958), 2:410. See Daly, "Liminality and Fiction," 83. Richard Dillard, personal interview, notes that *Pilgrim at Tinker Creek* was especially a product of reading about nature. In *The Writing Life* (New York, 1989), 34, Annie Dillard observes that writing the book in a library carrel at night affected the nature of the book.

marily indicated Dillard's war-baby status; but her thoughtful selection of a single detail also creates an extravagant metaphor for a woman at the threshold of her life. This remark about her embarkation upon life at the death of a dictator seems to foreshadow a fictional character as much as it represents a statement of autobiographical fact. Her family portrait in *An American Childhood* reveals a restless, adventurous family. Her grandparents had been part of that nineteenth-century migration from Europe that had settled so many Germans in the Ohio Valley. Theodore Ahrens, great-great-grandfather of Dillard, had founded American Standard Corporation in 1848; and as a consequence, Annie and her two younger sisters could expect to have a life of considerable financial comfort. Their father, Frank Doak, Jr., an only child, apparently relied on that security, because in 1955 he quit his job with the family corporation and sold his holdings to take his 24-foot cabin cruiser down the Mississippi. A fan of jazz and of Jack Kerouac's *On the Road,* Doak hoped "to relive Mark Twain's *Life on the Mississippi,* his favorite book, and to visit New Orleans, the birthplace of Dixieland jazz. After six weeks he got lonely, sold the boat, and flew home, having traveled no farther than Louisville, Kentucky. When he returned to Pittsburgh, he became business manager of a recording studio." His idealism and intellectual iconoclasm had made a practical concession to the constraints of a conventional way of life.[4]

In a similar way, Dillard's mother, Pam Lambert Doak, combined social convention with intellectual ambition. Pam Doak pursued the more traditional role of the homemaker, but her personal tastes and behavior were eclectic and intellectually charged. She decorated the house with taste that reflected the influence of Calder, Gauguin, and African artists; she, like her husband, was a passionate reader; like him, she had elevated joke telling to an art form. Pam Doak also had a strong liberal social conscience: she once disciplined Annie severely for repeating to their maid a racist phrase learned from a neighborhood boy. Perhaps her most significant literary legacy to her daughter was her fascination with the sounds and phrasings of language. Dillard wrote that her mother "picked up every sort of quaint expression" from mountain phrases to "Scotticisms"; for seven or eight years she improvised

---

4. Annie Dillard, *An American Childhood* (New York, 1987; reprint, 1988), 16; Linda L. Smith, *Annie Dillard,* 4.

gags with the phrase "Terwilliger bunts one"; "the drama of the words 'Tami-ami Trail' stirred her."[5] The intellectual playfulness and nonconformity of such parents seemed to encourage Annie's capacity for experimenting and for questioning the world which she inhabited.

This questioning stance toward the world informed many of Annie Doak's youthful pursuits: from a very young age she made herself an observer of the world around her. Fascinated by the studies possible with her micro-scope, she collected boxes of rocks, insects, and other natural phenomena. She spent hours making mental grids of the town and constantly locating *herself* on those maps. And she developed the habit of wide and voracious reading to shape her record keeping: her secondary school reading ranged from public health and epidemiology to Emerson's idea of the Over-Soul, and Christian pacifism. The book that proved most suggestive for her later nature writing was *The Field Book of Ponds and Streams*, "a small, blue-bound book," wrote Dillard, "printed in fine type on thin paper, like *The Book of Common Prayer.*" The comparison was fitting: nature and mysticism would become inextricably intertwined in her first essays. *Pilgrim at Tinker Creek* would begin with seemingly innocent observations of natural phenomena, but each observation would quickly become the point of departure for dis-quisitions on scientific facts and meditations on the spiritual and mystical be-liefs of great philosophers and Christian theologians. One striking result of *An American Childhood* was that it ensured that the reader would see a partic-ular foreground to Dillard's writing about nature and religious belief.[6]

Childhood, as Dillard portrayed it, was not only a process of coming to consciousness about nature and ideas but a time for learning about society as well. Like her future classmate Lee Smith, Doak attended the Presbyterian church, went to church camps, and generally followed the social patterns of her class. The Pittsburgh society in which the Doaks moved, however, seemed like a social dictatorship for young Annie. "The country-club pool," Dillard wrote, "drew a society as complex and constraining, if not so enter-taining as any European capital's drawing room did. You forgot an old woman's name at some peril to your entire family." The social life of the girls centered upon neat points such as learning how to wear and hold white gloves. We girls "were all on some [social] list . . . for life," wrote Dillard,

5. Annie Dillard, *American Childhood*, 36, 111.
6. Annie Dillard, letter; Annie Dillard, *American Childhood*, 81.

"unless we left."[7] Even within this rigid social structure, certain events seemed oddly juxtaposed, creating a divided nature in Doak. For example, in the year she turned ten, her father was making his very nonconformist move of leaving his job to float down the Ohio and Mississippi Rivers; at the opposite end of the spectrum, she was enrolling in the prestigious Ellis School for girls. Doak would hear her teachers—many of whom were recent émigrés from war-torn Europe—describe the horrors of war and the potential apocalypse of nuclear war, and then she would go to dancing lessons. Her education and rearing did not seem to connect the issues of gender, power, or politics in any comprehensive way.

Like many youthful rebels in the early 1960s, Annie seemed to identify with her parents' idealism and intellectual iconoclasm and to rebel against their failure to act out those beliefs in a thoroughgoing way. Increasingly she chafed at the traditional social roles assigned to women and, at age sixteen, discovered that she was a very angry adolescent: "I was getting angry, as if pushed. I morally disapproved most things in North America, and blamed my innocent parents for them. . . . When I was angry, I felt myself coiled and longing to kill someone or bomb something big. Trying to appease myself, during one winter I whipped my bed every afternoon with my uniform belt . . . as a desperate discipline, trying to rid myself and the innocent world of my wildness." She began to openly resist the expectations of what a "good" young woman should do. She fell in love with "oddball" boys, began smoking, got into a drag-racing accident, and to her parents' consternation, quit the church. She began thinking about the fact that "we students outnumbered our teachers. Must we then huddle here like sheep?"; she gained the reputation of being a student who "'works only on what interests her.'" In her reading, her tastes turned to Rimbaud and, like him, she decided she was a damned romantic. When she was suspended from school for smoking, her parents finally expressed absolute bewilderment about what to do with her. They wanted her "to go south [to college]—'to smooth off my rough edges,' they said. The phrase gave me the creeps." Her minister was able to "lure [her] back [to the church by loaning her] the writings of C. S. Lewis," and she remained tractable enough to yield to her parents' desire that she attend a southern women's college.[8]

---

7. Annie Dillard, *American Childhood*, 67, 89.

8. Ibid., 222–23, 231, 232; Annie Dillard, letter; Linda L. Smith, *Annie Dillard*, 6.

Doak chose to visit Randolph-Macon Women's College, Sweet Briar, and Hollins. Hollins had initially captured Doak's interest because a Hollins alumna, Marion Hamilton, was headmistress of the Ellis School and was a brilliant woman after whom Doak aspired to model herself. Hamilton urged Doak to consider the school; later she also told Dillard that she "sent all her problem children" to Hollins. Doak was also impressed by the fact that in 1962, William Golding was Hollins' writer-in-residence. The college was clearly a writing center, and Doak intended to be a writer. A third factor attracting Doak was not nearly so ambitious a reason: like her future classmates Lee Smith and Cindy Hardwick, Doak was delighted to learn that Hollins did not have a math requirement. Overall, her parents were assured that Hollins not only appealed to their daughter but reflected their own values, combining intellectual independence with social convention. Nevertheless, after touring Hollins, Doak decided to attend Randolph-Macon, primarily because she thought she could not handle the work load at Hollins: "It seemed more serious academically than the other schools I visited—terrifyingly so." What changed her mind, she later wrote, was the dream, quoted at the chapter beginning, that proved so haunting that it compelled her to reverse her early decision. Still, a fear stayed with her about this southern women's college. She did not want to have her rough edges smoothed: "I had hopes for my rough edges. I wanted to use them as a can opener, to cut myself a hole in the world's surface, and exit through it. Would I be ground, instead, to a nub? Would they send me home, an ornament to my breed, in a jewelry bag?" The social ambience of the school seemed equally as formidable in its way as the intellectual challenge of a college with a nationally renowned writing program.[9]

By many accounts—even her own—at this stage in her life the angry, passionate young Annie Doak was undirected. It was "college, and theology in particular [that] channeled [her energies]," observes critic Mary Cantwell.[10] Studying nature with an intent, unwavering gaze had become a well-established habit for Doak, but the sophisticated reflections about theology, the capacious Thoreauvian metaphor of Tinker Creek, and the persona were discoveries made at Hollins. In fact, the literary achievement of *Pilgrim at*

9. Annie Dillard, letter; Annie Dillard, *American Childhood*, 243.
10. Mary Cantwell, "A Pilgrim's Progress," *New York Times Magazine*, April 26, 1992, sec. 6, p. 36.

Tinker Creek is in no small measure a gauge of the coherence in her own life that Dillard had discovered at Hollins. In her friends, she had found support for her writing aspirations, competition to hone her writing skills, and peers who shared her questioning stance toward conventional social standards and authority. With her professors, she discovered models of the writing life, guides to literary experimentations, and supports who helped her understand her identity as an observer of the world around her and as a writer. But ultimately, the act of writing is a solitary activity, and part of the experience of each of the women of the Hollins Group consisted in making her own personal progress in this endeavor.

At Hollins, Doak changed from being an angry daughter into a sister who competed with and supported her peers. Without recapitulating the description of her interactions with the women of the Hollins Group, I find it still pertinent to observe that her undergraduate career exhibited that competitive/collaborative spirit characteristic of the women in the writing program. She admired Lee Smith's stories, "which she seemed to produce by magic," and that admiration was tinged with envy as well. Enterprises such as the Black Raincoat Party allowed high spirits to overcome the edginess created by competition. Like her peers in the Hollins Group, Doak began writing letters to the *Hollins Columns* during freshman year, though she never wrote for the newspaper with the regularity of her classmates. For the most part, her contributions were serious. She coauthored a letter in support of a trimester system as a way of relieving the pressure of multiple required courses during freshman year,[11] and cosigned another letter protesting the move to abolish the point system for disciplinary action. By senior year, she alternated with Lee Smith in writing a regular column entitled "Out of My Mind": her columns regularly attacked President Logan for vetoing student-passed legislation and complained about what she described as silly restrictions

---

11. Annie Doak and Dibba McConnell, letter to editor, *Hollins Columns*, February 13, 1964, p. 2. Doak and McConnell wrote, in part:

As freshmen we now find ourselves confronted with a mass of superficial data on five mostly unrelated (and often required) courses. We have to "stuff" our schedules with courses in which we have little interest in a frantic attempt to leave our upperclassmen years comparatively free for concentration in our major fields.

In reference to a trimester system for Hollins we heartily echo your words: "Such a change can not be so overwhelming and monumental a task, provided the college is willing to accept the responsibility of making significant decisions."

placed on women's behavior at the college.[12] As was true with the other women of the Hollins Group, she took advantage of the school newspaper as a forum for criticizing the administrative policies that she found dictatorial to women.[13]

Doak's social interaction with the women of the Hollins Group eased the anger and helped her relax and enjoy the life of the college. However, her college life differed markedly from the lives of her classmates when she married one of her professors during the summer following her sophomore year. Certainly the most personal of literary influences on Annie Dillard was Richard H. W. Dillard, the professor she married on June 5, 1965. The only written records of the marriage, the poems in Richard Dillard's *News of the Nile,* describe some of the personal life of the young couple and create the impression of a marriage both highly intense and intellectual.[14] Doak's marriage represented both a rebellion against and a capitulation to the conventional social expectations that Hollins held out for its women. At that time an early marriage to a professor was certainly a rebellious act and must have caused some consternation within the faculty, if not within the Doak family. John Allen, acting chair of the English department, considered it important to state the department's sentiments about the event: "To the latter announcement [about the wedding], I may add that Miss DOAK is also an excellent student and English major. The English Department regards the match as a very sound one, as it will keep MR. DILLARD at Hollins at least until Annie's graduation (in 1967), and thereafter will hopefully keep Annie on as a faculty wife. Never have we congratulated any couple more sincerely than RICHARD H. W. DILLARD/META ANNE DOAK!" The marriage had a calming effect on Doak: Lucinda Hardwick MacKethan observes that it seemed to settle her, ease her agitated spirit, and deepen the quality of her poetry. At any rate, after

12. Annie Dillard, "'Education Be D——d!'" *Hollins Columns,* October 11, 1966, p. 2.

13. Annie Dillard, letter; Richard Dillard, personal interview; Doak et al., letter to the editor, *Hollins Columns,* April 29, 1965, p. 2; Annie Dillard, "SGA Lacks Real Powers," ibid., September 29, 1966, p. 2; "Dillard Advocates End to Mockery," ibid., October 4, 1966, p. 2ff.

14. See Richard H. W. Dillard, *News of the Nile* (Chapel Hill, 1971). The one experience of their marriage that Annie Dillard has especially remarked upon was that Richard introduced her to the scholars William R. and Mina Robinson. After rearing her children, Mina Robinson pursued a career as a molecular biologist; and William's admiration for Emerson led Annie Dillard to revalue Emerson. The Robinsons impressed the new wife because in them she observed contemporaries who had successfully combined "the notion that one could be a serious thinker and have a lively crowd of kids" (Annie Dillard, letter).

the question of marriage seemed solved, Annie showed greater concentration on the writing about nature, religion, and literature that mattered so intensely to her eventual career.[15]

Despite her reluctance to discuss their personal lives together, Annie Dillard remains generous in crediting Richard Dillard with helping her understand many of the intricacies of writing and literature. She writes: "The influence of Richard H. W. Dillard? I was married to him for 10 years; he was my education. I don't remember life before Richard. Like Louis Rubin and George Gordh, he was so kind and good and innocent that I never wanted to be anything else. (I couldn't have withstood the pressure of early 'success' without such examples.) Richard liked a kind of intellectually sophisticated literature, an ironic, self-referential, playful literature that I soaked myself in perfectly happily. (Later I began to realize that while I liked it, I didn't like it best. In fact, I was hopelessly sincere.)" Although she sometimes attempted to assimilate Richard Dillard's literary tastes, Annie Dillard conceded that one of the traits that made Richard her "best critic" was that with *Pilgrim* he did not attempt to change her ways of writing to conform to his own ideas. Perhaps one of the most useful pieces of advice that Richard Dillard had given her, Dillard concluded, was the admonition to "'Keep 'em guessing!'" Interestingly, although Annie Dillard called her husband her "best critic," he did not have a significant influence on *Pilgrim at Tinker Creek.* His literary agent handled the *Pilgrim* manuscript, but Annie Dillard noted at the time that he "makes no decisions for me and only gives 'leave it in or take it out' advice when pressed.'" The marriage itself did not really survive the winning of the Pulitzer Prize. Perhaps the relatively small measure of Richard Dillard's direct influence on the *Pilgrim* manuscript was an indication of the degree to which the marriage was already strained. Annie Dillard's writing had always shown more attentiveness to nature than her husband's writing had; in the latter years of the marriage, her work reflected an increasing concern with religious mysticism that her husband's writing did not even consider. The divergence in interests between husband and wife was yet more evidence of Annie Dillard's resistance to traditional social roles for women.[16]

Dillard's marriage altered some aspects of her life, but her friendships with her classmates were remarkably unchanged. About these she wrote:

15. *Calliope's Comments* (May 1965): 9; MacKethan, telephone interview.
16. Annie Dillard, letter; Lawson, "Thinker, Poet, Pilgrim," 12.

After I was married, it used to be a great treat for me to hang around the dorms. Nancy [Beckham] and I kept very late hours; I remember roaming the halls of Tinker dorm at three or four in the morning & wondering how people could stand to sleep & miss so much fun. We used to play scrabble in French—she had a French scrabble set. If you drew a "W," you were in trouble. Apart from "wagon-lit," which was improbable, about the only thing you could do with it was the *tour de force* "WAQF," which we found in Larousse. It means "Turkish blue-collar worker." [I] pined for the long nights in the dorms and in the snack bar. But Richard was as fine a friend as one could wish, and I was to spend many years of long nights in the snack bar with graduate students, telling jokes and singing.[17]

As a student, she became increasingly more focused on her studies. She became a reader for the literary magazine *Cargoes* and, by senior year, was one of the editors; she was selected for *Who's Who Among Students in American Universities and Colleges* and earned admission to Phi Beta Kappa. In sum, Dillard's marriage did not dissolve the bonds of friendship and competition that she had already established, and it was that intense involvement in the publications and activities of the writing community that continued to hone her writing skills.

The literary orientation of the Hollins writing program had a complex role in contributing to the development of Hollins Group writers such as Dillard. The New Critical theory that dominated the larger scholarly world was taught at Hollins as a theory that emphasized literary technique, the way a poem or novel worked its effects, and the training of this literary theory effectively produced at Hollins a new generation of talented and independent southern women who wrote about their own life experiences. It is unclear whether Dillard fully appreciated the underlying theory of literature on which New Criticism depended, but she clearly learned a great deal from it about writing as a craft. New Criticism reflected for young Dillard the attentiveness to language that she had already learned from her mother. It also seemed especially suited to what Dillard perceived as her intellectual needs and temperament at the time. She felt intellectually challenged and inspired by a method of reading that enforced such a rigorous attention to the literary text:

New critic[i]sm was good for writers. It implied that the writer's job was to produce coherent texts. It prized concision. It ignored politics, gender, class. It im-

17. Annie Dillard, letter.

plied that someone would read the text and discover its structure and internal relationships. It prized "the artist"—"the poet"—rather too highly, I thought, setting him up in the place of a priest who transmitted society's highest values, etc, which snobbery appalled me, so that after 4 years I stopped writing and didn't take creative writing at all my M.A. year. (I think. At any rate I didn't write a creative thesis.) . . .

We never read texts because they were written by women or by men; we read them for their intrinsic interest. New criticism, which was the school we were taught, eschews political or any extra-textual readings of texts. As such, it was the best possible critical training for writers.[18]

Few undergraduate programs at the time taught anything different. The discipline required by close study of language and internal relationships in a piece of literature appealed to Dillard's personal need for focus and direction in her intellectual growth; she accepted the New Critical opinion that good writing was based on absolute literary standards and that the literary standards of the day were gender neutral. The writing techniques of the New Critical school were instructive and empowering for Dillard, training her to write the highly structured, coherent texts that would become her hallmark. As we shall see, her essays on Dickinson and Thoreau are models of the New Critical approach, focusing on imagery, philosophical concerns, and the overall strategy of an author.

Naturally, Dillard's initial contacts with the Hollins writing program included faculty members in the English department. Like the other members of the Hollins Group, Dillard also developed personal and professional relationships with professors, relationships that seemed to make significant contributions to her writing as it developed during those collegiate years. She has observed that "it isn't the teaching of teachers, I think, so much as their example, that strikes students." Several professors in particular seemed important to young Doak as adult models of the intellectual life that was possible for her. When Louis D. Rubin, Jr., first met Dillard, he found her to be a "very sophisticated young lady" and a "helluva good student." He also found her to be very intense. It was no mere excuse Dillard offered Rubin in saying that she couldn't talk about *Catcher in the Rye* in class because it was "too personal" a book. It was very close to her own personal experience.[19]

18. Ibid.

19. Ibid.; Rubin, personal interview. Rubin opens his article "Thomas Wolfe: Homage Renewed," *Sewanee Review* 97 (1989): 261, with a retelling of this anecdote about Dillard, though he named her only in the personal interview with the author.

For her part, Dillard looked to Rubin as an example of how teachers should treat students: "I was no great personal favorite of his as Lee and Cindy clearly were. (I was a smart-ass.) I took half his American lit and his modern novel; he ran the creative writing seminars in his basement Wednesday nights, and showed us the hospitality I try to pass on to my students. He had the view that your students were your students *for life*. You helped them get into graduate school, get jobs, get published, get sane—whatever they needed, forever. This insight has been crucial to my own teaching." Louis and Eva Rubin were faculty members who early befriended Richard and Annie Dillard when they were first married. For Dillard, however, Rubin was primarily—and importantly—an adviser to her. She cites one occasion on which she found Rubin's advice about her writing career to be more perceptive than that of her parents: "My parents knew that I was going to Hollins to major in English & write poetry. They hoped I would go on Hollins Abroad [study abroad program], too. Louis Rubin advised against it, if I was serious about the English major; he said I'd lose the thread of my thinking and fail to learn the field in depth. He was right. It was good advice." She also admired his enthusiasm about literature. He was, she wrote, "inspirational, especially on Proust. He said once that by the time we were *five* years old, we had all the experience necessary to write the greatest literature. The writer doesn't need more experience—the writer needs to know what to do with it. Louis Rubin, and George Garrett, and Richard H. W. Dillard stressed to us that living writers were still producing 'American literature.' Literature wasn't over." Rubin's perspective encouraged Dillard to think of herself as one of those writers who was producing American literature.[20]

Some professors provided Doak with the critical discipline she was seeking. John (Lex) Allen was another professor who saw the troubled intensity in freshman Doak, and he helped direct her to find an outlet through poetry. "Lex Allen taught a completely extraordinary freshman creative writing course that changed my life," Dillard wrote. "I think it was the analysis of the poem 'Maiden with Orb and Planets' (Nemerov) that lifted off the top of my skull—look what humans can do! I was eighteen. How grand it would be to write complex, powerful poetry. How witty Lex Allen was, how familiar with all of it!" Allen's introduction to technique was a crucial starting point, be-

20. Annie Dillard, letter. Dillard writes that "George Garrett asked for a poem of mine when I was a sophomore, and then another soon after, and *published* them. It was a shock. His idea was not to throw raw undergraduates to the lions, but to ease them over the terrors of publication! He edited *The Girl in the Black Raincoat* anthology."

cause what ultimately proved most helpful to Dillard was the rigorous discipline required by the quality and quantity of reading and writing assignments she had at Hollins. There she developed the habit of taking notes on her reading, a habit she has continued to the present day. She has also observed: "We got in the habit of reading literature. We got in the habit of thinking about what we read. We wrote carefully. John Moore marked every typo; it gave me the impression that my little undergraduate papers were to be taken seriously. . . . We had lots of papers. I always wrote over 100 pages of papers every semester for my junior, senior, and master's years. By the time I got out of Hollins, all I could *do* was write papers. I thought of *Pilgrim at Tinker Creek* as a series of 20-page papers." Of the notable papers, she remembers ones on Donne's "Anniversaries," E. T. A. Hoffman, Tillich's idea of prayer, St. Teresa of Avila, Ibsen, and World War I poets.[21]

Julia Randall Sawyer was an important model for the women of the Hollins Group and for Annie Doak Dillard in particular because she was a "woman who has committed her life to her art." When Sawyer's book of poetry *The Puritan Carpenter* was published, Annie Doak Dillard considered that she had found a style of poetry from which she could truly learn: "Julie's slant rhymes, her carefully stressed lines, her voice alternately hectoring and lyrical—these things influenced me." By all accounts, Sawyer cut a dramatic figure as a woman entirely devoted to writing and literature. For her, to be a writer meant to be cursed with the greatest of burdens and the highest of vocations. As Sawyer expressed it in the poem "A Curious Fire," though "all fires are lit by five / Fingers that hold the match of time / To flesh and bone, and all fires burn," the inspired life is "a curious fire [that sings] in my bones." This real passion about writing also sustained an intense interest in the work of her students. Even after Dillard graduated from Hollins, Sawyer read, marked, and commented on her poetry. She was, wrote Dillard, a model of "extraordinary generosity." Sawyer's example of passion combined with discipline appealed to Dillard as a way of life for herself. From a passionate, directionless young woman, she was turning into an intense, disciplined writer. About Randall she wrote, "She loved poetry; she believed in and led the dedicated life." These words became true for Dillard herself as well.[22]

The professor who became Dillard's primary reader for *Pilgrim at Tinker*

---

21. Ibid.

22. Richard Dillard, personal interview; Annie Dillard, letter; Julia Randall Sawyer, *The Puritan Carpenter* (Chapel Hill, 1965), 51; Annie Dillard, letter.

Creek was John Rees Moore, another faculty member who had come to Hollins during John Everett's aggressive restructuring of the college in the 1950s. Dillard found his approach to literature to be highly intelligent and congenial, and so she took his literature courses, undertook independent study with him during three different semesters, and wrote her master's thesis with him. Moore, for his part, was supportive of Dillard's work. He encouraged her to publish her senior essay on Emily Dickinson, and the mere suggestion from him "heartened" her about her future as a writer. He and his wife took a personal interest in Dillard as well; and she saw them, again, as models: "generous, wide-spirited, well-traveled people who lived—as so many people at Hollins did—outside the clamor of popular culture." What impressed her most about this professor, however, was his courteousness to students and his attentiveness to their writing: "John had the most stunning way of treating us as colleagues. It is this more than anything that will stick with me: the amazing respect with which he treated student opinion, and the extreme, if time-consuming, courtesy with which he so gently brought a wrong-headed student around in class. Sometimes I'd wake up in the middle of the night with the abrupt realization that some gentle, winsome speech John Moore had made me that morning had essentially been saying I was wrong, dead wrong, and wrong again." Moore was Dillard's "formal literature teacher. It was to him I turned for my master's thesis, even though I wasn't writing in his field. . . . He is . . . one of those few readers on Earth you can trust." When she finished a chapter of *Pilgrim at Tinker Creek,* she brought it to him for his careful reading and thoughtful advice. One specific piece of advice that Moore offered about the manuscript was that Dillard should be direct with her intentions. Dillard had always considered, as New Criticism seemed to argue, that strong writing had meanings that were well hidden, "like Easter eggs." Moore "suggested I enlarge the first chapter of 'Pilgrim at Tinker Creek' to make clear, and to state boldly, what it was I was up to. I disagreed, but I did it anyway. It was good advice." If *Pilgrim at Tinker Creek* may be said to have had one primary reader, that reader was clearly John Rees Moore.[23]

The individual who had the most influence on the substantive ideas of *Pilgrim at Tinker Creek* was Annie Dillard's mentor in religious studies. George Gordh, Methodist minister and professor of religion, had come to Hollins in

23. Annie Dillard, letter; Annie Dillard, "John Moore: A Sense of Proportion, a Gracious Heart," *Hollins* 36:1 (October 1985): 9; Annie Dillard, letter; Annie Dillard, "John Moore," 9.

1951 in the first wave of hiring done by President Everett. His graduate degrees were taken at the University of Minnesota, the Southern Baptist Theological Seminary, and the University of Chicago. To the students, Gordh's mind seemed to encompass all of civilized thought, "from Plato to Popeye," wrote Dillard.[24] Doak took his survey history of Christian thought during sophomore year and subsequently tried to take every course with him that she could. Often his courses had no required reading: Gordh dictated detailed outlines to students of the subjects of his lectures.

The number of similarities between George Gordh and Dillard reflect the kinship of their spirits, her conscious imitation of practices and philosophies she admired in Gordh, and some instructive insights into her own ideas and writing. In matters of personal style, teacher and student shared a marked tendency to eschew affectation and subordinate personal importance to what each regarded as the more important issue, the ideas at hand. Dillard wrote that Gordh was an unpretentious man, preferring not to be called "Dr." but "Mr." Another modest expression that captured Dillard's fancy was Gordh's use of the word *folks:* " 'Tillich,' he would say, 'has the notion that folks, because of this finitude, are living inauthentically.' Down this would go into the notebooks, right in the middle of the Latin and Greek." Dillard, when faced with the acclaim occasioned by winning the Pulitzer Prize, struck a similar stance: " 'I'm not eager to talk about myself, I'm eager to talk about the book. This book is wonderful and I'm just me. Emerson had this notion of the transparent eyeball, and that's what I am in the book—a tinted window to look through.'" This disclaimer about the importance of the writer reveals Dillard as a far more settled writer than the "damned romantic" of her high school years. It also reveals her as a New Critic attempting to discount the autobiographical influence in the book by arguing that the text existed independently of context.[25]

Beyond matters of personal style, however, Dillard was fascinated by "the clarity of [Gordh's] mind, and the great, stunning sense he made of a welter of materials," that is, theology. He "required us to *know the material* upside-down and sideways: Compare the Christology of Augustine and Niebuhr. Trace the idea of God as Being."[26] Each year Gordh taught a humanities

24. Annie Dillard, "On George Gordh's Retirement: An Unsolicited Testimonial," *Hollins* 27:6 (1977): 14.

25. Ibid.; McPherson, "Conversation with Annie Dillard," 4.

26. Annie Dillard, letter.

course, and each year he set himself a personal goal of learning all that he could about one staggeringly broad topic such as the history and ideas of government as developed in western civilization. In preparing for writing *Pilgrim*, Dillard set a similar goal for herself of doing extensive research, eventually amassing over a thousand note cards on all of the natural phenomena she would later describe in her book.

Beyond Gordh's extraordinary capacity to master a body of knowledge, Dillard seemed taken by his *way* of thinking about ideas. As she described it, he had a "mind so supple that it could become the mind of each thinker in turn." For many people, such a judgment would have the air of cliché about it; but to Dillard, assembling her personal philosophy about the intense relations between seeing and understanding, Gordh's capacity to inhabit the mind of another thinker was a revelation. In "Sojourner," an article that appeared in the *Living Wilderness* in 1974, Dillard describes this capacity with wondering admiration when relating her one experience of entering the mind of a weasel:

> Our look was as if two lovers, or deadly enemies, met unexpectedly. . . . It emptied our lungs. It felled the forest, moved the fields, and drained the pond; the world dismantled and tumbled into that black hole of eyes. . . . He disappeared. . . . I don't remember what shattered the enchantment. I think I blinked, I think I retrieved my brain from the weasel's brain, and tried to memorize what I was seeing, and the weasel felt the yank of separation, the careening splashdown into real life and the urgent current of instinct. He vanished under the wild rose.

Her disengagement with the weasel's mind echoed a fear she had when studying Gordh: "His answers were perfect . . . , his engagement with other minds complete; but I always was in dread that, right before our very eyes, he would strip all his gears." Dillard seemed attracted to the idea of being fused to a great power—by intellect to Gordh or by spirit to the weasel—and equally horrified at the danger of losing her self-contained individuality through such metaphysical unions with the Other. The subject matter of that powerful attraction/fear played out in *Pilgrim* through the admiration and horror the persona feels at seeing God's power expressed in nature.[27]

27. Annie Dillard, "George Gordh," 14; Annie Dillard, "Sojourner," *Living Wilderness* (summer 1974): 3—this article also appeared as "Living Like Weasels" in *Teaching a Stone to Talk* (New York, 1982); Annie Dillard, "George Gordh," 14.

The effect on Dillard of teachers and friends from the Hollins community was both substantial and long-lived. She had come to Hollins with a great deal of talent, intelligence, and confusion. Sawyer taught her the value of words well chosen; Moore taught her the discipline of clarity and organization; and Gordh taught her the importance of broad and detailed knowledge. These professors took a personal interest in her work that extended beyond the requirements of their job. Through her studies she developed habits of reading and writing that were congenial to her serious temperament and that channeled her intelligence. The rigorous standards established by her mentors were reinforced by the competition she felt with peers such as Cindy Hardwick, whose writing seemed to her to be finer than her own. The kindred thoughts and writing of Anne Goodwyn Jones in the *Hollins Columns* confirmed Dillard's sense that women should not passively accept unfair social constraints. Contrary to Turner's view of liminal entities as "passive or humble," these women regularly confronted authorities and established a sisterly community in the interstices of the existing social structure.[28] Above all, these women maintained friendly ties that led them to develop a pattern of collaborative support that would last a lifetime. Neither exclusively individualistic nor cooperative, the Hollins community nurtured its students to find their own definitions of their lives and their writing. Given this habit of self-definition, it is scarcely remarkable that Annie Doak Dillard created and tested personae in her writing at Hollins.

It is intriguing to consider that the woman who would gain her fame as a prose writer worked so diligently and prepared herself so expressly to follow the model of Julia Randall Sawyer and become a poet. She was genuinely appalled that her book of poetry was forgotten when *Pilgrim at Tinker Creek* was published. Writing poetry honed Dillard's writing skills, allowing her to examine her ideas early in a compressed form. Certain poems show Dillard consciously working with personae that seem strikingly close to autobiographical in tone or subject matter. Two such poems, appearing in *Beanstalks* during her freshman year, reveal a young woman testing the role of the artist. "Weekend," which Doak wrote under the humorous nom de plume Norma Dee Plum, is a brief poem, fifteen lines in length. In it, a female narrator describes, in slice-of-life form, a couple's weekend spent in Washington, D.C. Initially, the narrator luxuriates in the splendid isolation the two of them feel

28. Turner, *Ritual Process*, 95.

as they tour the city: "At the National Gallery we alone understood art." But the idyllic weekend is "no longer smooth" after her friend tells her "How frightening were his dreams and [after] I remembered / My own life." This persona feels avant-garde and superior to the ordinary people around her. The poem concludes with the woman returning home alone by bus and virtually dismissing the significance of the weekend: "On the way back my bus had a flat in Lynchburg; / I was two hours late, sticky and cold, but someone / Covered me as I slept with a brown overcoat— / Or I might have minded the trip."[29] Again, the studied ennui of the persona reflects a character who sees nonchalance as the mark of the romantic figure. Doak's method in the poem is interesting to examine in that it shows the apprentice writer working to create a voice that the reader can see through: here, the Holden Caulfield figure tries to express deep emotion with a studied nonchalance. The young college sophomore was pleased to have the poem accepted for publication in *Plume and Sword,* a national literary magazine published in Charlottesville, Virginia.

The second *Beanstalks* poem, the twenty-four-line "Euterpe on Campus," is another instance in which Doak tentatively works with a persona who blends autobiographical elements with fictional ones. Again, the poem portrays a persona whose conception of herself as a poet is so self-conscious that it verges on the melodramatic. In this poem, however, Doak treats the persona with more ironic distance than she does the persona in "Weekend." Conceiving of herself as inspired—hence the allusion to Euterpe, Greek muse of tragedy—the narrator walks to the duck pond on campus, finds a "proper tree" underneath which she sits "where she could be seen from the road," arranges her skirt and hair, and then turns her attention to her subject matter, the ducks. She seems to find a theme when all the ducks turn and peck a small black duckling; but suddenly the ducks turn on her and chase her away. Back in her dormitory room while drinking a Coke, she reflects that "not even the ducks understand me."[30] The narrator's ironic treatment of the persona creates sufficient distance for the reader to see the poem as gently mocking self-conscious artists.

At the same time Doak wrote this ironic view of the self-conscious artist, her poetry was beginning to reflect some significant changes in her views of

29. Annie Doak, "Weekend," in *Beanstalks,* ed. Berson et al., 14.
30. Annie Doak, "Euterpe on Campus," ibid., 9.

writing and of writers. In the spring 1964 *Cargoes,* Doak continued her exploration of the role of the writer through a fictional interrogation of Rimbaud, the compellingly dark and deeply romantic poet Doak had discovered during her early reading. The narrator in the poem "Rimbaud" asks the poet whether his mystical vision of colors and the "fever dreams learned in the night's horror" were worth the sacrifices of his life. Rimbaud's visions, Doak writes, were "harmonies [transcribed in the] brine" of tears, purchased by "eat[ing] your life and suck[ing] its poisoned essence."[31] This poem reflects Dillard's life-long interest in the role of the seer. Rimbaud provides her with one model of a *voyant* who penetrates the mysteries of infinity and thereby becomes the voice of the eternal. Later in her undergraduate career, her study of Emily Dickinson would alter this notion of the seer and her relation to the infinite. But at this point in her thinking, Doak was fascinated by the romantic figure who purchased vision at the cost of everything else in his life. The poem shows her artistic vision consciously turning inward, searching to discover whether the path of enlightenment followed by the artist-as-mystic can offer meaningful insights to a community of readers that extends beyond herself.

The first poems printed at Hollins under the name Annie Dillard—"Baltimore Oriole" and "Song for Myself"—reveal Dillard attempting to combine her interest in nature with the emotional power she has discovered in love and art. Rimbaud's continued influence on Dillard is reflected in the first poem, which begins with an epigraph from Rimbaud—"Au bois il y a un oiseau, / Son chant vous arrête et / Vous fait rougir" (In the woods is a bird / whose song stops you and / makes you blush)—and then describes the black and orange Baltimore oriole as a bird "wild as fire light" whose song threads its way through many significant memories of the persona's life. The narrator of the poem recalls the unusual instances in which she has heard the song of the Baltimore oriole and wonders if her daughter will hear this bird and be enchanted with its song. She then traces several encounters with the bird and records the persona's increasing knowledge of nests, mating, and migration. Dillard then concludes the poem by combining a rather sentimental love scene with a Rimbaudesque description of the beauty of the bird's song: "He [her lover] pressed my hand, and again today / It was a green morning, an orange and black morning, / a blue and purple, red and yellow morning." The second poem, "Song for Myself," alludes to Whitman's "Song of Myself" and

---

31. Annie Doak, "Rimbaud," *Cargoes* 51:2 (1964): 13.

is a short, rather whimsical poem on the need of the persona to live in nature. That need is so great, she writes, "If I can't live in the wild, wild world / Then the world will come to me." The poem becomes a Whitmanesque catalog of the various ways she will bring nature into her house. She proposes to incorporate the world within her house by "flood[ing] the whitewashed cellar / Until it's a raging sea," by "paint[ing] stars on the ceiling," and installing moles and birds and bears in the halls and on the mantles. These two poems show Dillard writing about nature with a Rimbaudesque passion, but they also show a young writer at work struggling to strengthen theme and to develop control of her work.[32]

With the winter 1963 issue of the college literary magazine *Cargoes*, Doak also began publishing poems that described liminal or threshold experiences in which the narrator inhabits a world that seems outside of the usual structures and constraints of reality. In these poems, the imagination is a borderline realm where conventional rules of understanding don't apply. "Alice" is a whimsical twelve-line question-and-answer poem about Alice of Wonderland attempting to recall the confusing experiences she had beyond the looking glass. The second poem, "Northern Quebec—August" is a fourteen-line dream sequence in which the narrator guides the reader to a mountain lake in the north woods where, from a boat in the center of the lake, one can watch— or imagine—naked Indian boys moving silently among the trees on the shore. Although these two poems are not complicated, they are striking because they reveal Doak beginning to write about an imaginative edge to life, in which reality blends with fantasy or the present disappears to reveal the ghosts of a past existence. The poems lack the mystical underpinnings that will become central features in *Pilgrim at Tinker Creek*, but they do show Doak beginning to experiment in her writing with her personal interest in flouting conventional understanding.[33]

Dillard did not publish poetry in this vein again until nearly two years later, in two poems that are among the few published during her college years that reflect upon marginalizing experiences expressly related to women. "Monica at the Window" is essentially a portrayal of the family life of a young woman who is sensitive and artistic. The only discordant image in the

32. Annie Dillard, "Baltimore Oriole" and "Song for Myself," ibid. 53:1 (1965): 15–17.
33. Annie Doak, "Alice" and "Northern Quebec—August," ibid. 51:1 (1963): 12.

poem occurs in the final lines when Monica stands at the window sketching a faceless nude woman upon the steamy panes of glass. In contrast with the rest of the poem, in which Monica appears successful and well integrated into her family life, this ending suggests that she is a young woman who is somehow separate, restricted: ". . . her moving / Reflection glows pale in the steam, the glass / Reflects dim, then clear, in the lines of the woman, / A curved broken image of Monica drawing." The second poem, "for PLD" (her mother, Pam Lambert Doak), seems to be a straightforwardly autobiographical poem about a transitional point in her own life: the preparation for her marriage to Richard Dillard. The poem is a reflection upon the wedding veil that has been passed from generation to generation in her family: "I never expected this, / To be suddenly cast with all the maidens / Of time, to sound again the singing / Of the first marriage feast." Though the persona initially wants to resist the pattern—to "refuse to bear children" and thereby refuse to pass on the veil and dress—she decides that she will "accept the old wine, / Gladly. I cannot deny all my countless mothers." As in many of her works, this poem is noteworthy for again reflecting a persona in a fleeting pivotal moment. If only for an instant, she considers resisting the traditional expectation dictated by social convention and ritual. Interestingly, the persona frames this yielding to conventional expectations about marriage as a refusal to deny "my countless mothers" who have enacted the ritual for generations past. Ironically, the honoring of a matrilineal heritage is an implicit yielding to a tradition shaped by paternalism. If read as autobiography, the poem reveals a rebellious spirit muted by convention.[34]

One of the final published poems of Dillard's senior year combined her experiments in liminality with the personal subject matter that had inspired so much anger and protest in her own life. Included in George Garrett's collection *The Girl in the Black Raincoat* was Dillard's poem "The Affluent Beatnik." Here again, the poem has a tantalizingly autobiographical flavor or self-consciousness to it in the description of the persona. Like her idealistic parents, Annie Dillard seems to portray her persona, perhaps herself: "The affluent beatnik, bred to pour tea, / Shuns her pearls for beads of dried almonds / And, unladylike, straddles the footstool, / Sipping liqueur in her blue jeans." This young woman "Look[s] out past the stables to the millions /

34. Annie Doak, "Monica at the Window" and "For PLD," ibid., 52:2 (1965): 21–22, 24.

In the city, and mourn[s] their lives loud / From the carpeted room." The poem is a critical representation of a rebellious woman for whom protest is a fashion statement more than a commitment to action.[35]

Given Dillard's success as a prose writer, what is the significance of this undergraduate poetry? First, Dillard's experience of apprenticing in one genre and succeeding professionally in another was not an atypical pattern among the writers of the Hollins Group. Lucinda Hardwick MacKethan apprenticed in poetry and journalism and became a literary scholar. Lee Smith apprenticed in newspaper feature writing and short stories and yet has become most noted for her novels. One genre seemed to cut across the grain of the second and produce a more complicated vision by combining their insights. In Dillard's case, poetry seemed especially suited to channeling the power of her intense temperament, imposing a discipline upon her to order and compress her language. One of the recurring tributes to Dillard's prose in *Pilgrim at Tinker Creek* has indeed been that it approximates poetry. Dillard's undergraduate poetry allowed her to work out in a compressed format many of the issues that concerned her: questions about self-consciousness and the role of the artist; moral concerns about the obligations of the socially privileged; issues of how to understand nature and our relationship to it. Certainly Dillard could and did write about these issues in her undergraduate essays. Poetry, however, gave her discipline, concision, and the habit of working from metaphor. Nothing seems clearer in *Pilgrim at Tinker Creek* than the pattern of describing natural phenomena in exacting detail and then treating those phenomena as metaphors embodying mystical truths. Dillard's undergraduate poetry trained her in a disciplined way of seeing that eventually proved versatile enough to accommodate her self-consciousness as an artist and her visions of nature, science, and mystical religion.

In particular, these undergraduate poems also show Dillard's struggle to gain technical control of voice in her writing. In these poems, often the voice of the narrator is so strong that it overpowers the other elements. Alternately rebellious, cynical, self-deprecating, or passionate in tone, the speaker is always an observer of the world around her. She consistently keeps a distance so that she can study life without being drawn into it in some uncontrolled way. She even maintains a distance from any people or creatures who enter her

---

35. Annie Dillard, "The Affluent Beatnik," in *The Girl in the Black Raincoat*, ed. George Garrett (New York, 1966), 340.

poems: she watches Monica at the window, studies the affluent beatnik who mourns for the poor, records the habits of orioles. In *Pilgrim at Tinker Creek,* the persona will still have a strong voice and still be an observer, but Dillard creates a more sympathetic voice and balances that voice more carefully against the subjects being observed. The persona in *Pilgrim* will identify with her subjects more than distance herself from them. These early poems do not show that control and empathy, but they do show Dillard gaining clarity in articulating the issues that concerned her.

It was not until she wrote her senior and master's theses that Dillard discovered the two organizing principles that would structure *Pilgrim at Tinker Creek.* Remarkably, of the hundreds of pages of criticism written on *Pilgrim,* only the Twayne study of Dillard contains even a single sentence about her master's thesis on *Walden* that was her early exploration of a structure for *Pilgrim;* no criticism mentions her equally formative study of Emily Dickinson. These two apprentice works show Dillard discovering the techniques that organized her professional work: Thoreau's use of Walden Pond as a literary vehicle for his metaphysical writings and Dickinson's notions of circumference and of persona. From them she learned how to conflate the genres of autobiography, novel, scientific treatise, and religious meditation; she saw in the example of Tinker Creek a metaphysical entity existing at the edge of infinity; and she studied a disciplined narrative voice that was part persona, part author. A writer who lived her life at the edge of conventional expectations discovered in these works the ideas and forms that would allow her to blur successfully the boundaries of her writing.

The first of these formative works was Dillard's senior thesis on Emily Dickinson, a product of an independent study project with John Rees Moore. Entitled "The Merchant of the Picturesque," the essay was selected for inclusion in the *Hollins Symposium,* a student scholarly journal published by Hollins and edited during Dillard's senior year by, among others, Anne Bradford and Anne Goodwyn Jones. In brief, Dillard traces in Emily Dickinson's poetry a pattern "of description and disappearance. The poet describes something—usually something good or beautiful—then 'kills it off' in a variety of ways. It dies, or, more frequently, it is translated into a vague 'beyond,' a beyond that holds both death and all the unattainable secrets of life." The first half of the essay examines specific examples of this pattern of description and disappearance in Dickinson's poetry. The pattern may take the form of death: Mother Nature is portrayed as a housewife arranging the world into order with her broom of death; a flower is "'canceled by the Frost.'" In other instances, things just "go away": Elijah rides away "'Upon a Wheel of Cloud'"; butterflies "'stepped straight through the Firmament.'" In Dickinson's scheme, writes Dillard, the "beyond" to which subjects such as flowers and butterflies disappear is coded as the word *circumference*, "the edge of infinity which surrounds the world of time and touches it at its farthest limits":

> Symbolically, the sea and the sky are almost interchangeable, although the sea tends to represent the more frightening, overwhelming aspects of infinity—the death that is its prerequisite—and the sky tends to represent the more mysterious and beautiful aspects of infinity—death's release into freedom, into heaven and knowledge of the sacred mysteries. The word "circumference" comes to stand for both the sea and the sky, the boundary of time and eternity. An example taken from a situation that recurs in the poems illustrates the paradox embodied in the word: a ring of mountains opens onto either an infinite stretch of sky above or sea below. The mountains are a kind of enclosing, inhibiting "circumference," and the infinite stretches of sea or sky beyond are also "circumference."

In this scheme, any liminal experience—faraway places, sunset, the sea, the sky—is a threshold touching on the eternal. As such, the liminal experience, argues Dillard, occurs on the periphery of cosmic meaning and subverts the usual ways of knowing about God. And once this transgressive moment occurs, the liminal is no longer at the margins but becomes part of the center of meaning: once we see beneath the disguise of nature, we discover ourselves facing a divine revelation.[36]

The second part of the essay turns to what Dillard sees as the expansive movement of nature. Interestingly, although the focus is on nature, the role of the observer is equally significant: "Things move away from the poet's range of vision and out towards infinity, the circumference of the natural world. Nature moves towards death; landscapes open out on more distant landscapes. . . . The poet gets left behind, feeling that her humanity is her severest limitation." The poet, then, is painfully separate from nature because she is self-conscious and nature is unconscious. She is caught between ways of understanding, losing insight at the very instant she feels on the verge of gaining

---

36. Annie Dillard, "The Merchant of the Picturesque: One Pattern in Emily Dickinson's Poetry," *Hollins Symposium* 3:1 (1967): 33–42.

it. In an explanation evocative of her own remarkable moment of communion with the weasel, Dillard writes that "Dickinson cannot help but feel that if this separation were somehow bridged, if some level of communication could be established if only for an instant, then she too could feel a part of her own world." As the poems stand, however, the poet can only be tantalized by the glimpses of infinity that she sees in nature.[37]

Dickinson had no "single, all-embracing system" in her poems, observes Dillard. In fact, she writes, "Dickinson is not given to great systems of logical thought" but rather operates by mood or whim. The pattern in Dickinson's writing is that "the natural world moves away from the poet only in unconscious obedience to the laws of time—of motion—so that as it fades away it seems to be rejoining an infinity that consists less of 'nothin[g]ness' than of the infinite motion of the things of time." It is that "seeming" quality that proves crucial to Dickinson's scheme, judges Dillard: unconscious nature *seems* to be a part of infinity. Eternity is a "trickster," writes Dillard, "revealing only enough of himself to make his audience aware of how much more he is concealing." She concludes, "The natural world is a beautiful and cruel peep-show, a burlesque directed by a half-malicious God who turns out the lights just as the fans are about to part."[38] This image of the cruel peep show is one that Dillard later employs for her purposes in *Pilgrim*.

The second extant essay remaining from Dillard's prose writing at Hollins is her master's thesis, completed under the supervision of John Rees Moore for her degree requirements in May 1968. The thesis, "Walden Pond and Thoreau," was a study of Walden Pond as a structuring device for Thoreau's *Walden*.[39] The epigraph, "a blue sky can reflect in a lake," was taken from Gertrude Stein's *How to Write*, and as Dillard develops it in the essay, the epigraph seems to aptly link Dillard's reading of Thoreau and of Dickinson. In this study, however, Dillard is already forming her own ideas of how circumference—or infinity—may *seem* to be reflected in a natural phenomenon such as a pond or a creek.

In a tough New Critical reading of Thoreau, Dillard critiques the writer—as she did Dickinson—for lack of rigor in forming a logical system.

37. Ibid., 37, 38.
38. Ibid., 9, 40–42.
39. Annie Dillard, "Walden Pond and Thoreau" (M. A. thesis, Hollins College, 1968).

She argues that he scarcely notices the wildlife, only noting creatures in "glimpses"; his social satire is "scattered in bits and pieces, never sustained or directed"; his is "not a commitment to a way of life but an extended vacation."[40] What she does find intriguing and worthwhile about *Walden*, however, is how the pond, as "focal point, the beginning and end of all excursions, contributes cumulatively to the architectural construct of the pond as mythic image." The pond is an extremely versatile vehicle for thought because it is the locus of a threshold whose meaning is uncertain. And in conflating her ideas about Dickinson with those about Thoreau, Dillard seems to anticipate her own treatment of Tinker Creek. She describes the pond as a liminal place of ambiguous meaning: "It is the source and the milieu of all life, necessary to the survival of the flesh and of the harvest; it is cleansing, refreshing, and sacramental. But water kills in surfeit; the deluge and the flood traditionally mean a more complete devastation of human life than a conflagration, earthquake, or hurricane. Great bodies of water suggest a vastness that mirrors a still eternity beyond time or that terrifies by its desolation."[41] In places such as Walden Pond and Tinker Creek, the infinite power in the universe reveals both its felicity and its terror, the dark threat that complements any benevolent vision of God.

The characteristics of this body of water are central to its meaning as well. The purity of the water connotes holiness, Dillard argues, and certainly Walden Pond is Edenic. Its purity links it to "an eternal sphere quite apart from the flawed history of human endeavor."; it is "a pearl of great price, the kingdom of spiritual reward on earth." Pure water, she observes, "cannot foster secrecy" and so encourages forthright observation and admiration. A second trait of the pond is that it is a microcosm of life. Again seeming to anticipate *Pilgrim at Tinker Creek*, Dillard observes that "the pond is a miniature of all

40. Dillard similarly criticized the devotees of Thoreau who, out of some "sheer loyalty to *Walden*," go on "writing articles about it, joining Thoreau societies, visiting Walden Pond, or, lobbying for the Thoreau postage stamp, reading mediocre poetry and dull travelogues"; ibid., 2. In 1987 she wrote the archivist at Hollins to affirm that any scholar had permission to read her thesis except the Thoreau scholar Robert Richardson: "If by any chance a scholar named Robert Richardson, from Colorado, asks to see my master's thesis, DON'T give it to him! Don't let him see a copy! . . . This guy's Thoreau biography, *Henry Thoreau: A Life of the Mind*, is the best biography I've every read. . . . I sure as heck don't want him reading my dumb stuff"; Annie Dillard to Tony Thompson, Fishburn Library Archivist, July 17, 1987. Ironically, Dillard later married Richardson.
41. Annie Dillard, "Walden Pond," 4, 6.

nature and of *Walden* itself, structured on the cycle of one year." The pond seems to suggest constancy because of its continuity in time; but though Walden Pond is a constant feature in Thoreau's life, it is actually quite changeable and sensitive, as is life itself. This sensitivity touches on the eternal, argues Dillard: "[the pond] moves, guided by its own secret impulses, and is moved, a vast Aeolean harp on which the winds of heaven play." This *seeming* paradox of constancy and transience evokes the paradoxical nature of time itself: "The pond absorbs the notions of time, subsumes them, and even redeems them in its fulness." This last feature of the pond—being time-bound yet timeless—is essentially a moral one, Dillard suggests. Ultimately, humankind is called to be attentive to the pond and to treat it with respect because it is "the eye of heaven watching the deeds of men." The pond is a measure of earthly human activity that is linked to eternal spiritual activity, "two kinds of thing[s] at once. It is of earth and it is of heaven." As the edge of infinity, the site where God may be known, the pond represents, in Dickinson's terms, circumference.[42]

Although Dillard studied Thoreau's treatment of Walden Pond with keen interest, she did find limitations in his discussion. Some complaints are minor. At one point she expresses some impatience with Thoreau's notion that ice-cutters and others who use the pond somehow profane it if they do not approach Walden with the appropriately reverent attitude. In reacting to Thoreau's horror that the village people used the water of Walden to wash their dishes, she writes that "when the water of Sandy Pond was piped into the village instead of Walden water, Thoreau voiced no objection; Walden water is sacred, apparently, because of Thoreau's personal associations with it and its setting. (And what did Thoreau wash *his* dishes with?)" A more significant flaw Dillard finds in Thoreau's analogic treatment of the pond was an issue raised in her essay on Dickinson's work. "There is," Dillard writes, "a feeling in *Walden* that the depth of a man's character corresponds to his apprehension of eternity," that one can somehow connect with eternity by apprehending it in natural phenomena such as the pond. This apparent connection is illusory, she suggests, although in this essay she is not explicit about the nature of the illusion. Rather, clinging to the pond metaphor, she simply explains that sometimes "clouds, mist, or night obscure the face of the sun, and man's soul seems hidden, its purpose obscure. At such times the pond's depth seems a

42. Ibid., 15–20, 33, 37.

menace, concealing perhaps unknown terrors, the sea-monsters of human nature." Certainly the "sea-monsters of human nature" are an obstacle to a connection with eternity. But Dillard will not identify in this thesis what she considers to be the greatest obstacle to knowledge. Only later in *Pilgrim* will she discover that she has appropriated part of Dickinson's view that the "natural world is a beautiful and cruel peep-show, a burlesque directed by a half-malicious God." [43]

Despite the limitations she sees in Thoreau's conception of Walden, Dillard does draw some conclusions that she will use in *Pilgrim*. "Walden Pond," she writes, "has its meaning for Thoreau not only from his personal association with events concerning the pond, but from the physical fact of the pond itself. The pond is a 'fact' of nature, and facts are beautiful as well as true." Dillard's analysis of Thoreau's description of the intersecting measurements of the pond really anticipates her own conception that in a study of nature "the instruments of the scientist merge and fuse with the prophet's holy pen" in finding divine revelation through discovery of natural law. It is Thoreau's inability to preserve distinctions between facts and poetry that she finds especially compelling and true: "Poetry, for Thoreau, is moral philosophy," and the meaning that Walden derives is "from its physical, factual attributes." Hence, in the final pages of her thesis, Dillard qualifies her initial critique of Thoreau: "Thoreau's going to Walden to live was not so much a retreat from a way of life he disliked as a positive pilgrimage to a way of life he liked. It was a 'tune in,' not a 'drop out.'" It represented his spiritual quest to eschew the uncertain wisdom upon which civilization was constructed and to "[build] on piles of his own driving, on solid ground." And finally, for Dillard, it represented the type of liminal metaphor she was seeking in order to structure a complex first-person narrative that articulated her ideas of the blurred, artificial distinctions among nature, science, and mystical religion. [44]

Working with these same ideas from her undergraduate studies, Dillard immediately began work on a book of poetry, *Tickets for a Prayer Wheel*, which actually constituted the final experimentation with the themes she would explore in *Pilgrim at Tinker Creek*. Five of the twenty-four poems were from her undergraduate days, and Dillard organized them all into sections that created the effect of a religious triptych. Not surprisingly, the themes that critics

---

43. Annie Dillard, "Merchant of the Picturesque," 34, 31, 32.
44. Ibid., 9, 35–37.

identified in these poems were ones drawn from her college essays: "the intricacy and detail of nature, the changing lights of consciousness, the mystery of time's relation to eternity, the futility of asking questions about God, and ultimately, through all the poems, the poet's urgent longing for a God who is hidden." In *Tickets*, however, Dillard did begin establishing certain new patterns that were repeated in *Pilgrim*. One pattern consisted of the persona noticing the presence of a natural phenomenon such as a wood duck and then developing her thoughts into a meditation on a religious theme such as a feast day. The poems, like the college essays, are texts heavily weighted with literary and philosophical allusions ranging from the Bible to Borges to Muir. And of course, the poetry was consistently written from a first-person point of view. Among the dominant themes of this volume was, again, the central concern that Dillard discussed in her writings on Dickinson and Thoreau: what is the relation of nature to the infinite? In both *Tickets* and *Pilgrim*, Dillard uses the image of a burning tree to show how the speaker, like Moses and the burning bush, discovers some evidence of God: "The presence of God: / he picked me up / and swung me like a bell. / I saw the trees / on fire, I rang / a hundred prayers of praise. I no longer believe / in divine playfulness." This God is, like Dickinson's, infinite, hidden, half terrifying, and—above all— *seemingly* knowable through natural phenomena.[45]

These patterns of writing and the subjects of her earlier essays come together in *Pilgrim at Tinker Creek*. She had taken from Thoreau the central organizing principle—the pond/creek—that allowed her to merge her life experiences with her epiphanies about nature and her meditations on mystical theology. Critics such as Marc Chenetier rightly draw many points of comparison with *Walden:*

> the activity of the narrators, who both inhabit spartan lodgings; whose isolation ranges from the relative (Dillard) to the symbolic (Thoreau); whose existence explores a common sort of social and natural "in-betweenness" . . . ; [whose studies are] mediated by a fair amount of bookish knowledge. Further, both claim the autonomous nature of their quest . . . ; their narratives are given in the first-person to promote such an independent stand; and they make wide use of the available range of rhetorical moves (I, you, we, me . . .) to promote

45. Lynn Martenstein, "Author Localizes Book Setting, Recalls Undergraduate Years," *Quadrangle* (March 7, 1974): 5; Nancy Lucas, "Annie Dillard," *Dictionary of Literary Biography: 1980*, ed. Karen L. Rood, Jean W. Ross, and Richard Ziegfeld (Detroit, 1981), 184; Annie Dillard, *Tickets for a Prayer Wheel* (New York, 1974), 123–25.

didactic purposes (from Thoreau's "preachifying," as Hayden Carruth has put it, to Dillard's "the-point-I-want-to-makes"). Both start from a desire to question reality radically: Thoreau, "determined not to live by faith if we can avoid it" (W 113), answers across the years a woman who knows that we "live by fiction." Both seem to adhere to the idea that "no way of thinking or doing, however ancient, can be trusted without proof" (W 111) . . . ; both, therefore, veer away from sentimentality as much as possible and stand convinced that "the poem of creation is uninterrupted." (W 168)

Each of these points reflects an elaboration upon points Dillard had already considered in her writing. Dillard's view startled reviewers, though, because it reversed the archetype of the machine in the garden: in *Pilgrim* Dillard presented "the unexpected onslaught of the natural world into the civilized one." This disruptive quality of nature produces surprise in the observer and confounds all conventional expectations of what nature should do and mean. To substitute the word *woman* for *nature* in the last statement would reveal that Dillard's attitude about nature is consistent with her resistance to the conventional definition of women.[46]

Although *Pilgrim* echoes some of the structure of *Walden,* the Dickinson influence is so pervasive in Dillard's book that, ironically, the more striking view of nature draws upon Dickinson's Christian mysticism—even upon the tradition of Christian mysticism—more than it does upon Thoreau's thought. Nature is, she writes, "very much a now-you-see-it, now-you-don't affair" that has God in it everywhere. Critic Linda L. Smith describes Dillard's perspective as a way of seeing God, first through the via positiva and then through the via negativa. The first view searches to experience God by contemplating God's nature; the second view maintains that God is inscrutable and that one can only "experience God by completely emptying the mind and the soul." This argument reconciles the seemingly conflicting notions that God can create both beauty and horror in nature. Critic William J. Scheick describes Dillard's book as exploring the "liminal edge as a *hemline* between eternity (spirit) and time (matter) in nature." Terror and beauty intersect in this space or circumference that Dillard creates "between verbalizing the seen (revealed surfaces) and seeing beyond what can be verbalized (concealed depths)." But as Dillard's Hollins writings show, circumference is

46. Marc Chenetier, "Tinkering, Extravagance: Thoreau, Melville, and Annie Dillard," *Critique* 31 (1990): 162; Gary McIlroy, "Pilgrim at Tinker Creek and the Burden of Science," *American Literature* 59 (1987): 71.

always out of the poet's range of vision: unconscious nature is God teasing the self-conscious observer. "Our whole life is a stroll—or a forced march—through a gallery hung in trompes-l'esprit," she writes. The creek is the via positiva in its physical richness and its metaphorical capaciousness; it is the via negativa in its inability to reveal through fact the eternal toward which it gestures.[47]

In studying nature, the persona "Annie Dillard" discovers not only evidence of God but a vision of her own place at the edge of mortality and the infinite: "I look at the water: minnows and shiners. If I'm thinking minnows, a carp will fill my brain till I scream. I look at the water's surface: skaters, bubbles, and leaves sliding down. Suddenly, my own face, reflected, startles me witless. Those snails have been tracking my face! Finally, with a shuddering wrench of the will, I see clouds, cirrus clouds. I'm dizzy, I fall in. This looking business is risky." In studying the water of Tinker Creek, she is a mystic who sees her own face as part of the vision of death (the tracking snails) and the infinite (the sky). This discovery of her place in this liminal experience moves the persona away from Dickinson's image of God as mere trickster to a sense of awe at divine revelation: "Divinity is not playful. The universe was not made in jest but in solemn incomprehensible earnest. By a power that is unfathomably secret, and holy, and fleet."[48] Once a woman receives her own revelation of herself as part of the infinite, she can no longer allow her vision to be bound by the limitations of the culture that had once defined her.

One of the cultural limitations that Dillard resists in *Pilgrim*, argues critic Suzanne Clark, concerns gender. The relationship between *Walden* and *Pilgrim* is more accurately a case in which the woman author "cit[es] the male subject to provide the facts of expertise and the context of culture . . . and then works [the elements of this male culture] at a bias, calling up and undoing their cumulative hold." Or, as Frederick G. Waage observes, "a woman, cursed by ignorance and exclusion," can see incongruities of which the male observer is unaware. Her marginal position in life allows the woman to see the water—life—differently, and Dillard's construction of her persona is the technical expression of a writer subverting male culture by cutting it at a bias. In creating a sustained, partly autobiographical persona in works such as *Pil-*

47. Linda L. Smith, *Annie Dillard*, 17; Annie Dillard, *Pilgrim*, 17, 84, 279; William J. Scheick, "Annie Dillard: Narrative Fringe," in *Contemporary American Women Writers*, ed. Catherine Rainwater and William J. Scheick (Lexington, Ky., 1985), 52–53.

48. Annie Dillard, *Pilgrim*, 24–25, 278.

grim at Tinker Creek, Dillard's almost invariable use of first-person narration and autobiography represents a resistance to being defined by others.[49]

As Shari Benstock and others have observed, women have exploited the authority of the genre of autobiographical writing "as a means by which to create images of 'self' through the writing act, a way by which to find a 'voice'—whether private or public—through which to express that which cannot be expressed in other forms." Male autobiographies have traditionally enjoyed a relative clarity because the subject readily occupied the center of the text; the prevailing culture validated the voice. However, Benstock argues, "the self that would reside at the center of the text is decentered—and often is absent altogether—in women's autobiographical texts" because women have not had the luxury of an individual identity. That is, as Susan Friedman explains, "Women develop a dual consciousness—the self as culturally defined and the self as different from cultural prescription." The dual consciousness of women, then, argues for a form that confounds the traditional conception of autobiography. Dillard's narrative strategy draws on a poststructuralist notion of representation. Her persona, a partly autobiographical figure, is a collection point for personal memories or stories told to her; it is her own voice speaking against the conventional wisdom of a culture that attempts to enforce constraints upon women, upon writing, even upon understanding itself.[50]

A partly fictional figure, the persona in *Pilgrim* seems Dillard's calculated self-representation. Through this literary subversion in her first-person narrative and her blurring of the lines between author and persona, essentially, Dillard becomes reinvented as the character "Annie Dillard." Hers was the voice of a woman who found much of her life to fall between those traditional positions assigned by social convention and literary expectation. Though reared in sophisticated circles, Dillard felt outside of those interests; though she aspired to a professional writing career, she yielded to social convention and married before graduating from college; though trained as a poet, she es-

49. Suzanne Clark, "Annie Dillard: The Woman in Nature and the Subject of Nonfiction," *Literary Nonfiction: Theory, Criticism, Pedagogy,* ed. Chris Anderson (Carbondale, Ill., 1989), 115; Frederick G. Waage, "Alther and Dillard: The Appalachian Universe," *Appalachia/America: Proceedings of the 1980 Appalachian Studies Conference* (Johnson City, Tenn., 1981), 204.

50. Shari Benstock, ed., *The Private Self: Theory and Practice of Women's Autobiographical Writings* (Chapel Hill, 1988), 5–6, 20; Susan Stanford Friedman, "Women's Autobiographical Selves: Theory and Practice," ibid., 39.

tablished her reputation in prose. Dillard has never made such dichotomies of these conditions. Indeed, they represent the permanent condition of liminality that has characterized her life as a writer and as a woman. In this respect, *Pilgrim* is the quintessential instance of Dillard's obscuring the traditional line between writer and first-person narrator. In blurring these distinctions, Dillard disorients her readers, forcing them to confront the subjective nature of all self-representation, whether it be a narrative voice created by the author or a divine revelation offered in nature by God. Arranged in essaylike chapters, the book made little pretense to appearing as fiction; however, as a restructuring of actual experiences and philosophical concerns of Dillard, it also denied being fact. Rather, it was a personal and spiritual journey whose paths extended outside of the confines of the endpapers. A behemoth that has both fostered and haunted Dillard's entire writing career and professional success, it is a book closely tied to Dillard's personal experience. The work began and ended as Dillard's personal struggle to establish her identity as a writer.

Dillard's identity and self-representation were an issue at every stage of *Pilgrim at Tinker Creek*. At the time of the publication of *Pilgrim*, Dillard was blissful, happily crediting the supportive community in which she worked: "'Hollins is wonderful; everybody's writing. It makes you feel like writing is a natural thing to do. It also kind of puts a pressure on you to come into the snack bar and talk about your novel.'" But her compliments also included an edge of anxiety, a concern with competing well: "'I was married when I was 20—unformed—and I guess he [Richard] licked me into shape.' But [added the interviewer] an exemplary husband can make his wife self-conscious about her own work in the same field. Annie Dillard couldn't join the snack bar conversations about novels in progress. 'I didn't have the right,' she says. 'I wasn't a professional. I was just a housewife.'" At heart, despite her disclaimer that she believed good writing would be considered for its merit and not because of gender, Dillard did believe that the publishing world was difficult for a woman writer. She considered hiding her female identity by submitting the manuscript as "A. Dillard" because she didn't think that a book of theology written by a woman would be accepted: "'It's a book of theology, and I can't think of a single book of theology written by any woman except Simone Weil.'" Richard H. W. Dillard, who had already published three books of poetry, had his agent, Blanche Gregory, look at the early chapters, and Gregory encouraged Dillard to submit the manuscript under her full name. Louis

Lapham, then editor at *Harper's* magazine, immediately bought the chapter on praying mantises.[51]

But as soon as the book was published, Dillard had to resist other cultural stereotypes. The subject matter of the book encouraged some reviewers to leap to traditional assumptions that a southern writer was somehow untutored about modern life. Because she lived in southwestern Virginia, interviewers asked her if she "rode a mule to the post office or if her father was a coal miner." One executive explained to her that a drink "on the rocks" meant a drink with ice. Local journalist Jeannette Smyth heard Dillard's assessment of her reception: "[Dillard] told the hometown papers that New Yorkers 'assume I'm a chipmunk who does automatic writing and doesn't know what I wrote. I've got it all against me. I'm a woman and I'm from the South.'" Eudora Welty openly wondered in the *New York Times* what Dillard was about: "I honestly do not know what she is talking about at such times. The only thing I could swear to is that the writing here leaves something to be desired." Other reviewers chose to portray Dillard as an environmentalist or a counterculture figure of the 1960s: the well-known photographer Jill Krementz took publicity photographs of Dillard in Bob Dylan's apartment; book reviews compared her work to Rachel Carson's. At this latter comparison Dillard finally attempted to assert her own view of herself: "Rachel Carson had a Ph.D. and was a scientist, and I am not. She . . . was disseminating information and I am disseminating a vision, and it's completely different." *Pilgrim* seemed to have created multiple authorial representations, all of which at various times were forced upon Dillard by a public determined to see a certain type of writer behind the voice they heard.[52]

Part of Dillard's reaction to these definitions applied to her by the larger culture seem an attempt to control the meaning of the book. She established its sources: the Bible, she stated, was the greatest single influence on it. She described it as "'a meteorological journal of the mind'—Thoreau's phrase. It's a book of the spirit.'" She also attempted to explain the way it should be read: "'*Pilgrim* works artistically or not at all, really. It works as a novel or as a poem

51. Smyth, "Southern Sibyl," G4; Annie Dillard, notes to author, September 3, 1996.

52. Katherine Weber, "PW Interviews Annie Dillard," *Publishers Weekly*, September 1, 1989, p. 68; Smyth, "Southern Sibyl," G4; Eudora Welty, "Meditation on Seeing," *New York Times Book Review*, March 24, 1974, p. 5; McPherson, "Conversation with Annie Dillard," 4.

works—you know, with imagery carried through the whole thing. The images gather meaning.'" And if anyone had missed the point, she stated specifically, "'I'm interested in the poetry of the fact.'" Because the book was so closely linked to her as a person, by defining the terms upon which the book operated, she could hope to control the definition of herself.[53]

A second action Dillard took was to provide elaborate self-representations of her life as a woman writer. In *The Writing Life,* she describes the process of writing *Pilgrim at Tinker Creek* during the Watergate summer: "I had a room—a study carrel—in the Hollins College library, on the second floor. It was this room that overlooked a tar-and-gravel roof. A plate-glass window, beside me on the left, gave out onto the roof, a parking lot, a distant portion of Carvin Creek, some complicated Virginia sky, and a far hilltop where six cows grazed around a ruined foundation under red cedars" This account instructs us on several points. Unlike her classmate Lee Smith, who by this time was wedging in her writing around schedules of husband and children, Dillard was fortunate to have, in Virginia Woolf's phrase, some money and a room of her own. The virtues of time and financial support at least seem to have made some difference in allowing Dillard to succeed at her work early in her career. Second, much of Dillard's research and writing for this project were accomplished behind the plate-glass windows and walls of Fishburn Library. This point does not undermine Dillard's accomplishments as a naturalist, but it does qualify the label to show that her work is a carefully researched and measured type of writing, a product of hardworking intelligence, not of mystical inspiration alone. The young naturalist did not disdain her view of the parking lot: "From my desk I kept an eye out," for "intriguing people, people I knew" were coming and going and capturing her speculations. To a woman who was a part of this community, even the view of the parking lot held its own possibilities.[54]

In her self-representation and despite her anxiety about being "merely" a faculty wife, she still credits the small community at Hollins College with supporting her as a writer. She had a key to the library so she could come and go whenever she wanted; she had conversations with former professors and

53. Lawson, "Thinker, Poet, Pilgrim," 12; McPherson, "Conversation with Annie Dillard," 4.

54. Annie Dillard, *Writing Life,* 27–28.

got their comments on her work—all cheerfully offered gratis to a former student. Still, in the end, the wrestling with the angel remained a formidable, solitary pursuit. This image of herself as a writer is worth quoting at length:

> When I flicked on my carrel light, there it all was: the bare room with yellow cinder-block walls; the big, flattened venetian blind and my drawing taped to it; two or three quotations taped up on index cards; and on a far table some ever-changing books, the fielder's mitt, and a yellow bag of chocolate-covered peanuts. There was the long, blond desk and its chair, and on the desk a dozen different-colored pens, some big index cards in careful, splayed piles, and my messy yellow legal pads. As soon as I saw that desktop, I remembered the task: the chapter, its problems, its phrases, its points. This night I was concentrating on the chapter. The horizon of my consciousness was the contracted circle of yellow light inside my study—the lone lamp in the enormous, dark library. I leaned over the desk. I worked by hand. I doodled deliriously in the legal-pad margins. I fiddled with the index cards. I reread a sentence maybe a hundred times, and if I kept it I changed it seven or eight times, often substantially. . . . I opened the blinds a crack like eyelids, and it all came exploding in on me at once—oh yes, the world. . . . My working the graveyard shift in Virginia affected the book. It was a nature book full of sunsets; it wholly lacked dawns, and even mornings.

She was correct that her working habits were reflected in the book. The prose style reflected her delight in exploring the comparatively loose genre of prose: "When I switched from poetry to prose, it was like switching from a single reed instrument to a full orchestra. I thought: 'My god, you can do everything with this stuff. You can do everything you do with poetry, and more besides.'" This record also reveals that the "Annie Dillard" of *Pilgrim* who seemed to spend her days in nature was not entirely the same Annie Dillard who was often closeted for long hours working in Fishburn Library.[55]

In sum, Dillard's conception of the first-person narrator throughout the corpus of her writing is strikingly parallel to the hide-and-seek show of God's in nature. The essential feature of nature—according to Dickinson and Dillard—is that God is a trickster, on one hand offering a personal revelation and, on the other, withdrawing that offer. In *Pilgrim at Tinker Creek* and her other works, Dillard alternately poses as narrator and as autobiographer. This changeable persona creates an experience that leaves her readers in the uncer-

55. Ibid., 30–31, 34; Cantwell, "A Pilgrim's Progress," 36.

Annie Dillard, date unknown

tain, sometimes uncomfortable position of not knowing what exactly to believe about the story. These efforts to control her self-representation, however, are a logical literary expression reflecting the life of a woman who has continually resisted being defined by others. The fact that she obscures the line between persona and writer draws more upon her belief in circumference than in traditional modes of autobiography. The individual is, like Tinker Creek, the site where the divine and the finite meet. If readers cannot cleanly make a distinction, then Dillard has succeeded in recreating the experience of a woman discovering an inscrutable God at Tinker Creek. However, if readers can accept the uncertainty of the liminal persona, then they have gained a deep insight into the unsettled and unsettling lives of women writers.

The record of Dillard's life after Hollins is evidence that *Pilgrim at Tinker Creek* did change in her life. Other contracts soon followed; part of the manuscript was even published in *Sports Illustrated.* The book was published on March 13, 1974, and by June she had a commission from *Harper's* to retrace Darwin's voyage to the Galapagos Islands, an offer to review Evan Connell's theological poetry, and as many magazine and television interviews as she cared to accept. She had dedicated *Pilgrim* to her husband Richard, but the ten-year marriage ended in 1975, the year she won the Pulitzer Prize. She then moved to Western Washington University in Bellingham to be writer-in-residence, and her life on the nearby islands provided her material for the book she likes best, *Holy the Firm*. Her research about the Bellingham area also lead to a long piece of fiction entitled "The Living" that appeared in *Harper's* in 1978. That fiction piece was expanded in 1992 into her first novel, *The Living*, in which she hoped to "create a coherent work of art, a Thomas Hardy novel." While she was at Western Washington University, she met and married Gary Clevidence, an anthropology professor at Fairhaven College. With him she had her only child, Cody Rose. In 1979 she moved to Wesleyan University in Connecticut, where she has remained as a distinguished visiting professor. Dillard notes that she met "'her third husband, Robert D. Richardson, Jr., after she'd written him a fan letter about his book *Henry Thoreau: A Life of the Mind.'*" They had "'two lunches and three handshakes' and then married" in 1988. Richardson and Dillard both taught at Wesleyan University until Richardson's retirement in 1994. Dillard has, in recent years, become writer-in-residence at the university. She still sometimes plays second base on the Wesleyan faculty softball team, the Hamstrings, a name echoing the faculty band, the Hambones, at Hollins College. She has won, among other awards, the Washington State Governor's Award for Literature, a nomination for the National Book Critics Circle Award for *An American Childhood*, the Connecticut Governor's Award for Literature, the Milton Prize for literature, and the Campion Award, an international award for literature.[56]

Annie Dillard has remained an articulate poet and essayist who has indeed led the dedicated life. Her passion for disciplined meditation and her belief in mysticism eventually led her to convert to Roman Catholicism when she was in her forties. She has enjoyed wide success as a writer, and her essays have been quoted and anthologized as frequently as those of any living writer. Yet even now, at least two Annie Dillards still exist. A contemporary interviewer describes the writer in this way: "What she is, despite some readers' fond fuzzy dreams to the contrary, is an extremely well-read intellectual who

56. Annie Dillard, "Footfalls in a Blue Ridge Winter," *Sports Illustrated*, February 4, 1974, pp. 73–80; Annie Dillard, "The Living," *Harper's*, November 1978, pp. 45–64; Bob Sipchen, "Down-to-Earth Writer Inspires Awestruck Devotion," *Richmond Times-Dispatch*, July 3, 1992, sec. D, p. 7; Cantwell, "A Pilgrim's Progress," 40, 42.

grew up in an elegant Pittsburgh household; her ancestors founded American Standard. She chews her fingernails and tries not to smoke, she adores jokes, even dumb ones, likes to dance, cares about her friends, prizing kindness above many other traits, and she comes across as both knowing and deliberately un-chic. She is a self-described 'old-timey liberal Democrat' who sometimes works the polls on election day. She is really not an environmentalist first and foremost, she defends hunting, and she is far more concerned about affordable housing than acid rain." The literary figure "Annie Dillard," however, began in the first-person narratives she created for herself in her Hollins writing: rebel, artist, naturalist, mystic. The internationally recognizable Annie Dillard is the woman who, on the day she won the Pulitzer Prize, was "walking along Tinker Creek looking for a cynthia moth, showing some kids what poison ivy is, helping the same kids across the bridge and cutting her finger carving an avocado." One image continues in flux; the other is constant. Captured in an ambiguous first-person narrative form, the literary "Annie Dillard" has become as much a metaphor as the creek she once portrayed.[57]

57. Weber, "PW Interviews," 68; Ben Beagle, "Pulitzer Author Prizes Privacy," *Roanoke Times,* May 6, 1975, p. 1.

5

LEE SMITH
Fair and Tender Lady

*T*he frame to Lee Smith's 1992 novel, *The Devil's Dream*, describes the reunion of a family of country singers in Nashville, arranged by a granddaughter, singer Katie Cocker. The novel itself is structured as an "album" of "songs" that tells the history of this family from Grassy Branch, Virginia; but before these song-stories begin, Katie gives an observation that seems descriptive of Smith herself:

> When Katie Cocker answers a question she leans forward on her stool and speaks right to the one who asked it. She looks you dead in the eye. "That's a pretty complicated question for me to answer," she says now, slowly, to the woman from the BBC. "I have to admit, there was a time when all I wanted to do was get out of that valley. I was just dying to get away from home. What I didn't understand, all those years when I was waiting for my life to start, was that it had already started. I was already living it! Those were the most important years, and I didn't even know it. But I was real young then, and foolish, like we all are. I wanted to be somebody different, I wanted to be me, and I thought that the way to do this was to put as much distance as possible between me and Grassy Branch. So I did that. And I took some chances, and I got knocked down flat a couple of times—I guess I'm Phi Beta Kappa at the School of Hard Knocks!—but I'd get right back up, and keep on going. I made a lot of mistakes.

Lee Marshall Smith in the 1967 *Spinster*

I thought I had to do it all by myself, see. It took me a long time to understand that not a one of us lives alone, outside of our family or our time, and that who we are depends on who we were, and who our people were. There's a lot of folks in this business that don't believe that, of course. They think you can just make yourself up as you go along. The trick is to keep on moving. But I can't do this. I come from a singing family, we go way back. I know where we're from. I know who we are. The hard part has been figuring out who *I* am, because I'm not like any of them, and yet they are bone of my bone."[1]

1. Lee Smith, *The Devil's Dream* (New York, 1992), 14.

Like Katie Cocker, Smith had to travel a chronological and physical distance from Appalachia before she could—in her phrase—"get a purchase on it." As a teenager, Smith simply wanted to escape from the circumscribed life of Appalachia. By the time she was an adult, she had virtually reversed that position and, as the author of books such as *Oral History, Fair and Tender Ladies,* and *The Devil's Dream,* has made Appalachia both substance and metaphor for her explorations of self and of other in American society.

The "others" who have become the central subjects in Smith's fiction are most frequently women. One constant feature in the development of Smith's writing has been her increasingly open consideration of the victimization of women in American society and the way women have learned to overcome that condition. One can almost draw a direct line tracing the evolution in her thought from her earliest published short story, "Wading House," to her most recent novel, *The Devil's Dream.* Her early stories describe girls and young women who have been literally or figuratively silenced, limited, or raped. Her later novels reveal women who have resisted cultural restraints, found their own voices, and succeeded at unique life goals that oppose conventional expectations. Her motivation for treating this subject comes from her personal experience of resisting the culturally imposed image of the southern lady. At Hollins she met peers who confirmed her ideas that women should resist the constraints put on them by convention, friends who supportively criticized her writing, and professors who encouraged her to write about what she knew. There she did "take some chances" and get "knocked down flat a couple of times," but the writing community's encouragement to persist in writing about her own worldview helped her to build her personal critique of the treatment of women.

The beginnings of Smith's exploration of self and other seem rooted in her family upbringing in the remote western Virginia village of Grundy, and they involved the tension between the middle-class standards of education and gentility the Smiths sought to maintain there. Lee Marshall Smith was born November 1, 1944, to a thirty-seven-year-old home economics teacher, Virginia Marshall Smith, and her thirty-six-year-old husband, Ernest Lee Smith, a small business owner. Her mother "was what they refer to in Grundy as a 'foreigner,'" one from outside this mountain area.[2] Virginia Marshall had left Chincoteague Island to become a schoolteacher, fell in love with Ernest

2. Ken Ringle, "A Southern Voice, in Her Own Write," *Raleigh News and Observer,* December 9, 1988, sec. D. p. 1.

Smith, and like Ivy Rowe's parents in *Fair and Tender Ladies,* eloped with him. In a sense, the woman from Chincoteague genuinely was—and remained—a foreigner in the Appalachian town of Grundy, and perhaps to herself as well. The culture of Grundy was so radically different from that of eastern Virginia that if the historical mountaineer-flatlander antagonism could have a true embodiment in an individual woman, it would have been Virginia Marshall Smith.

Virginia Smith aspired to be a lady, and as Anne Firor Scott and others have demonstrated, the southern lady was one of the holiest relics of antebellum southern life to which an aristocracy in distress clung. In Lee Smith's mind, her mother was a woman very much a product—and a victim—of this cultural standard: " 'I grew up to some degree feeling that if you didn't fit right in, if you didn't conform, you would go crazy. My mother, see, came from eastern Virginia and she was always trying to be a lady, and there was this notion that if you fit right in, if you were a lady and went to a nice school and married a doctor and so on, that that was somehow comforting and would somehow keep you from going crazy. But the idea of being artistic was being outside of norms in a certain way, and it was sort of dangerous.' " Even after Virginia Smith moved to the western part of Virginia, she remained bound to aristocratic conventions and expectations, though she was physically cut off by distance and the Appalachian Mountains from the eastern Virginia society she admired. Mountain life presented her with its own real restrictions and constraints. Lee Smith has commented that her mother "always felt oppressed by the mountains, closed in; she often complained that the sun never hit our yard until about eleven, because of the steepness and closeness of the mountains. Not only were we surrounded by the mountains, but also by my relatives—my aunt and uncle Dennis in the house to our left, my Belcher cousins on our immediate right, my Venable cousins and more Dennises across the road, and still more Smiths up and down the river." People knew if their neighbors went to the drugstore even before they returned home from the errand. Smith uses the image of the mountains as a metaphor for the cultural entrapment of women that is reflected in her fiction. In contrast to Annie Dillard's writing, in which nature leads one out into infinity, many of Smith's novels present the image of a woman closed in by mountains.[3]

From her father's side of the family, Smith acquired certain tools for her

---

3. Virginia Smith, "Conversation with Lee Smith," 791; Lee Smith, Appalachian State University commencement address, Boone, N.C., May 19, 1991.

literary work: an Appalachian heritage, a storytelling tradition, and a pro-
clivity for following one's own mind. Ernest Smith was always, notes Lee
Smith, "kind of a maverick. He had gone away to the College of William and
Mary to play football one season and acquired some notions" of what he
wanted from life,[4] one of which was the eastern notion of what it meant for
his daughter to be a proper southern lady. He had her attend Episcopal or
Methodist churches, rather than what he considered the indecorous Southern Baptists or Pentecostals. He sent her away from home to live at a private
girls' school in Richmond rather than have her stay in a school and an area
that might allow her to be content with standards regarded as lower by the
social elite that Richmond represented. He also held some personal, fanci-
ful notions including marrying a "foreigner" and, like the character Grant
Spangler in *Black Mountain Breakdown,* reading poetry to his daughter.[5]
Smith "grew up hearing lively, long-winded discussions about politics and
community affairs on the front porch of her home" as her father, uncle, and
grandfather sat and drank iced tea. Bits of these stories appear in Smith's later
fiction in incidents such as the murder of Babe Rowe in *Fair and Tender Ladies.* She has also used in her fiction details of Ernest Smith's Ben Franklin
store and gossip of the county that gained an airing in their house during her
grandfather's forty-year tenure as county treasurer. From them, too, Smith
began innocently collecting the story elements that would appear in later
writing: she noted that "people were always getting killed. There were people
whose fathers would be killed or their brothers shot. . . . I have a real high tol-
erance for violence in a funny kind of way because of that." She remembered
"showing these coal mine kids how a flush toilet worked"; she discovered that
her best friend was pregnant in ninth grade. Despite this family history and
cultural heritage, Lee Smith did not remain a docile listener to tales but often
rebelled, resisting cultural standards and working to become a teller of her
own stories in her fiction.[6]

If the essence of southern gentility was the ability to subordinate unruly

---

4. Ringle, "Southern Voice," sec. D, p. 1.

5. Not only did the poetry prove memorable to Lee Smith, but other reading and conversation did as well. Virginia Marshall Smith read to her daughter from the *National Enquirer,*
sparking what would become a long-term interest in sensational events and in the creation of
personae. Lee Smith, personal interview.

6. Ibid.; Michelle Lodge, "Lee Smith" *Publishers Weekly,* September 20, 1985, pp. 110–11;
Dorothy Combs Hill, *Lee Smith* (New York, 1992), 5; Ringle, "Southern Voice," sec. D, p. 1.

passions to the demands of etiquette and convention, then the Smiths had difficulty sustaining the illusion. The Smith family strained with the effort to maintain gentility in a small Appalachian town. Frequent emotional breakdowns scarred Smith's childhood. As it has for many women, writing came to have therapeutic value for Smith. In reflecting on this point, she recalls to critic Virginia Smith that there had been " 'a lot of mental illness in my family. Once when I was a girl, both my mother and my father were in separate psychiatric hospitals at the same time. My father was overworked and had a nervous breakdown; my mother was always anxious and had colitis and every now and then would get into a "state." I was fourteen; I was staying with my aunt when my mother was in Charlottesville in the hospital.' [Lee] Smith feared that she, too might go crazy until a doctor assured her that she wouldn't. 'Probably for me, writing has been totally therapeutic, because anything that I am really worried about I just write about. So I never have to act it out in my life.' " The southern code of gentility would have urged reticence in discussing such emotional breakdowns, and writing was a way to break out of the silence and isolation. Lee Smith realized only in retrospect that *Black Mountain Breakdown* was really about the breakup of her first marriage. Similarly, she has observed that she wrote *Fair and Tender Ladies* to create a role model for herself when she was facing difficulties with her teenage sons and the impending death of her mother.[7]

Ironically, for all the silences she had perceived in her upbringing, Smith appreciated the rich oral heritage of storytelling in the South. Writing was an early vocation for her: "I was always sure that I would write. It's all I ever wanted to do," she has observed. She wrote her first "novel" at age eight on her mother's personalized blue stationery. The story, *Jane Russell and Adlai Stevenson Go West in a Covered Wagon,* was constructed around the two celebrities she admired most at that time. She had seen Jane Russell movies in the local theater owned by her uncle Curt, and the actress seemed a natural female counterpart to the politician. According to Smith, "The plot was that they went West together in a covered wagon, and once there, they became— inexplicably—Mormons" and married. Though her parents were supportive of her writing, as she became a young woman they were concerned over whether this choice of vocation would somehow undermine her financial se-

7. Virginia Smith, "Conversation with Lee Smith," 791; Lee Smith, "In Her Own Write," lecture at Virginia Museum, Richmond, March 7, 1990.

curity; they frankly hoped she would marry a banker. Still, they were aware that she had some exceptional ability and worried that Grundy High School would not provide the intellectual challenge that she needed.[8]

Grundy was—and is—a small town of fewer than two thousand people, and Lee Smith grew up surrounded by her relatives, the Dennises, Belchers, and Venables. Though she was a town girl, all county children went to the same school, and from them Smith began acquiring a sense of the poverty and deprivation that poor mountain folk suffered. By high school, Smith showed all signs of becoming a willing participant in the culture. She won "a beauty contest at Grundy High, . . . frosted her hair and went to revivals and funerals as her characters do." She has observed, "My father was afraid I would marry my high school boyfriend. Which I probably would have," had her parents not decided to sent her to a private girls' school in Richmond. Interestingly, when Smith finally left Grundy, she had come to regard the Appalachian town as provincial, a place far too narrow for a young woman of high energy and independent thought. Like her character Katie Crocker, only later when she had achieved some detachment did Smith discover that she had already begun her writing life and that this provincial town was central to it.[9]

Smith's personal experience of "otherness" occurred when, in an ironic reversal of her mother's experience of "foreignness," Smith boarded in her junior and senior years at the prestigious St. Catherine's Girls School in Richmond, Virginia. Though she had "felt hemmed in by those mountains and my 42 immediate relatives" in Grundy, at St. Catherine's she experienced "culture shock in . . . encountering the genteel arrogance of wealth." She was from a substantial middle-class family, but she found boarding school and its behavioral expectations for young women unsettling. Many of her classmates were evidently rich and socially assured beyond her imagining. She had not been clearly aware of a class system in Grundy, since the rich owners of the mines lived elsewhere, "so at St. Catherine's I encountered this whole world I didn't even know existed."[10] In this setting, Smith had good reason to identify herself with her less privileged Grundy neighbors: measured by the stan-

8. Mark W. Scandling, "Profiles of Three North Carolina Writers" (M. A. thesis, University of North Carolina at Chapel Hill, 1979), 16; Lee Smith, Appalachian State address; Scandling, "Profiles," 16.

9. Laura Alderson, "You Can Go Home Again," *Hollins* (April 1981): 23; Ringle, "Southern Voice," sec D. p. 1.

10. Ringle, "Southern Voice," sec. D, p. 2.

dards of upper-class Richmond, they all looked alike. Later this adolescent culture shock would translate directly into the story of Brooke Kincaid in *Something in the Wind* and indirectly into the character of Richard Burlage in *Fair and Tender Ladies*. But in the two years Smith attended St. Catherine's, none of these observations found its way into print. In fact, Smith never published any creative writing in the school literary magazine.

As a high school senior, Smith was accepted by early decision at Bryn Mawr, but her mother didn't want her to go north. "I went to Hollins," she concludes, "because of its writing program, and because it was close to home, too."[11] This remark reveals a good deal about Smith at the time of her matriculation at Hollins. First, in yielding to parental desires to stay in the South and "close to home," she—as would be good breeding and good sense for a young southern woman—deferred to the wishes of her parents. That two of her choices were Bryn Mawr and Hollins indicates that the family had financial resources and particular interest in the advantages of attending women's colleges respected for intellectual challenge and social prestige. And finally, Smith's decision indicated that she knew she wanted to pursue her interest in writing.

Smith chose Hollins, but felt ambivalent about it, as did many young women in the mid-1960s. It had a nationally recognized writing program that would be a significant support for her. But it was even more socially difficult than St. Catherine's had been. Smith was constantly getting into scrapes that, by today's college standards, would scarcely hint at disciplinary action. In this respect, paternalism still persisted in shaping social behavior at the school, binding women students in a way male students never had to consider. The fact that Smith was continually getting into minor trouble— sneaking in after curfew, visiting the local truckers' hangout—suggests the extent to which Smith chafed at the constraints. Though a semester expulsion for missing a curfew while in Paris chastened Smith, she was still her own woman: two weeks before graduation she was "campused"—confined to campus—for coming in late after a party. Despite these social constraints, the women's college offered Smith freedom from the inequitable competition that still characterized coeducational institutions and from the daily coed life that might excessively distract her attention from writing. Smith herself judges that if she had not attended a women's college, "if I had gone somewhere like East Tennessee State, I might have gone after cheerleading and

11. Edwin T. Arnold, "An Interview with Lee Smith" *Appalachian Journal* 11 (1984): 240.

never written a word." Or, as Richard H. W. Dillard more dramatically puts it, Hollins held Smith "back from being a wild thing, a wild creature of the night." At a women's college, Smith could stay focused on her writing and on publication strategies. And at Hollins she discovered a sisterly community that encouraged her to break free from the social constraints upon her to be a good southern daughter and lady. She came to Hollins to write, and the Hollins community quickly recognized, encouraged, and shaped that potential.[12]

It is a tribute to her own talent and to the educational force of Hollins' writing program that Smith could ultimately tap into her background and find a vehicle for her thoughts. The creative writing courses at Hollins propelled Smith toward a more formal perception of what her literary voice in fiction might be. Smith initially resisted the advice to write about the life she knew because she couldn't write about her life experiences in Appalachia with any depth. Not uncommonly, freshmen writers seek exotic plot lines for their stories. Glad to be away from home, they eschew as boring the subject matter with which they are most familiar. Smith has described her own initial apprentice work as romanticized:

> The problem was that I thought I had to think up something exciting, something glamorous, to write about. One of my early main characters, I remember, was a stewardess in Hawaii named Cecile. Or occasionally I came up with a story strong in theme—which, in my case, meant sappy and melodramatic. I am reminded of my story about the whole family that died in a fire on Christmas Eve and when the rescue squad arrived, the only thing left intact was a little music box among the ashes playing "Silent Night." C– for that one. My teachers kept telling me, "Write what you know," but I didn't know, for a long time, what that was.

Smith later translated that freshman writing experience into her 1991 story "The Bubba Stories." Her protagonist, would-be writer Charlene Christian, can find nothing of interest in her own life to serve as subject for her writing: "I used to climb up on the tin roof of our house and turn slowly all around, scanning the horizon, looking for . . . what? I found nothing of any interest, just flat brown peanut fields that stretched out in every direction as far as I could see, with a farmhouse here and there. I knew who lived in every house. I knew everything about them and about their families, what kind of car they

---

12. Ringle, "Southern Voice," sec. D, p. 1; Rubin, personal interview; Lee Smith, personal interview; Richard Dillard, personal interview.

drove and where they went to church, and they knew everything about us." The fictional Charlene Christian, who entered college in 1963 (as did Smith herself), creates a fictional older brother, John Leland Christian III— Bubba—about whom she tells numerous wild and outrageous stories in order to impress her girlfriends "at a small women's college in Virginia." But her writing teacher, Mr. Lefcowicz, "kept giving me B's and C's and telling me, 'Write what you know.' I didn't want to write what I knew, of course. I had wanted to write in order to *get away from* my own life." The lessons of the freshman had, years later, become the material for humorous irony in the mature writer's short story.[13]

The central problems for Smith were to find the subject, language, and voice through which to describe the life she had observed. It was due in part to the interests of the Hollins' writing program, which—drawing upon the technical interests of New Criticism—gave such attention to language and theme that Smith felt liberated. She observes, "[Louis] Rubin's great strength is that he cares passionately about theme; he won't stand for work that's not about something. It can be technically very good, but if there's no heart there, he'll tell you right off." Here Smith developed the habit of beginning her writing with her characters: "I feel like I have to know all the people before I can possibly know what will happen."[14] This attentiveness to character development has become a hallmark of Smith's later writing in that she draws marginalized individuals—beauticians, housewives, mountain folk, and others—toward the attention of a popular audience and into the focus of literary critics.

The intellectual experience that finally persuaded the freshman Smith that Grundy could provide "the stuff of fiction" was reading southern writers like Welty, O'Connor, and Faulkner. These writers used the material that was available to them, and it was material that Smith could recognize in her own experience.[15] Smith later wrote:

13. Lee Smith, "The Voice Behind the Story," in *Voicelust*, ed. Allen Wier and Don Hendrie, Jr. (Lincoln, Nebr., 1985), 93; Lee Smith, "The Bubba Stories," *Southern Review* 27 (1991): 115–35.

14. "Lee Smith," *Contemporary Authors* 119 (1987): 345, 346.

15. In October of Smith's freshman year, Flannery O'Connor visited the campus and told the young writers that "what your work is comes about because of what you are, and what you believe . . . The author works through the concrete; he affects the senses, then the emotions, and finally the intellect." Jill Abbott, "Flannery O'Connor Discusses Writing." *Hollins Columns*, October 24, 1963, p. 3.

I came upon the stories of Eudora Welty and Flannery O'Connor. It was as though a literal light bulb snapped on in my head . . . because I realized that these writers hadn't been anywhere I hadn't been, and didn't know anybody I didn't know. Now that was arrogant, but when you're eighteen years old you are arrogant, and anyway it didn't matter. For the first time I began to have a sense of what I knew, of what my subject might be. I remembered a man in Grundy, up in the mountains where I'm from, telling me how, if you buy a woman a set of new teeth, she'll leave you every time. I remembered ladies sitting on the front porch engaged in endless discussion about whether somebody did or did not have colitis. I began to think I might have something to say. Something about families, and about daily life, and small towns, and kids, and about expectations and reality and that point where they collide, because that's the point—I realized this much later—where the story happens. . . .

[After reading Welty] Suddenly I sat down and wrote a story about some women sitting on a porch all afternoon drinking iced tea and talking endlessly about whether one of them did or did not have colitis.

And guess what? The teacher liked it. My class liked it. And best of all, I felt good when I wrote it. For I knew, in my deepest heart of hearts, that it was somehow *true*.

Smith's mature writing clearly shows the impact of Welty. As Virginia Smith suggests, "Her fiction, like that of Eudora Welty, springs from the minutia of existence and the comic and poetic rhythms of speech." Lee Smith's 1985 review of Welty's *One Writer's Beginnings* could apply to her own writing as well: that it "embrace[s] the gross world in all its lovely and awful specific detail." Welty is, in fact, something of a litmus test for Dillard and Smith: all three writers certainly do "embrace the gross world in all its lovely and awful specific detail"; but in contrast to Dillard's work, the writing of Welty and Smith turns outward to society, stories, and multiple narrative perspectives. In her mature fiction, Smith, like Welty, has come to create artistic themes from the domestic and social ritual of women's lives. Eudora Welty visited Hollins and gave a reading during December of Smith's freshman year, and Welty's unpretentious manner left a lasting impression upon young Smith that writers didn't have to be affected in their writing or in their living. It was a manner that Smith adopted in her later career.[16]

16. Lee Smith, "Voice Behind the Story," 93–94; Lee Smith, Appalachian State address; Virginia Smith, "Conversation with Lee Smith," 229; Lee Smith, "Eudora Welty's Beginnings," *Southern Literary Journal* 17:2 (1985): 120.

Unquestionably, then, in Smith's mind the example of writers such as Welty and O'Connor proved to her that extraordinary drama exists in the lives of ordinary people—and that professional writers do successfully write about such dramas. The technical advice and personal encouragement to write, however, came from her Hollins professors. Smith herself links the discovery of her voice to the instruction and support of Louis Rubin and Richard Dillard, and mementoes of affection extended well into her professional career in the form of book dedications and acknowledgments. Rubin claims no credit for Smith's improvement and success: "She may have learned some technique and craft, but she already had the talent. I couldn't do much more than encourage her, and that's half the job." Smith disagrees: "I would say he has been the major influence on whether or not I kept on writing. It was all up to him. He was constantly encouraging me, even when I would write terrible stuff." Rubin also clearly influenced the direction of Smith's literary interests by exposing her to Welty, O'Connor, and Faulkner. It is Richard H. W. Dillard, however, who thinks he may have provided some technical advice to Smith: he found her to be a gifted writer but one who worked so quickly that she skipped the details. That observation about attention to detail, Dillard suggests, was his primary contribution to Smith's craft. The writing environment to which these teachers contributed seemed far more important to Smith because it was an atmosphere particularly suited to her: "In so much of academic life . . . people become terribly impressed with themselves. But at Hollins there was this great spirit of play. Which, of course, is what creativity is really all about. They made you feel like you could do anything." This "open space" at Hollins was what she had seldom felt in Grundy or in Richmond.[17]

Part of that open space to experiment with her life and her literary voice was made possible by the women of the Hollins Group. The audience of women was important to Smith partly because they recognized, enjoyed, and often shared her irreverence for social convention. In a sense, the students in the writing program constituted a modest counterculture on campus, often rebelling against the circumscribed setting of Hollins that appealed so much to their parents. They were significant critical readers for her as well. About the members of the Hollins Group she has commented, "'That was really

17. Scandling, "Profiles," 18; Richard Dillard, personal interview; Ringle, "Southern Voice," sec. D, p. 1.

nice, because when you're starting to write you really do need to have readers. You can't sit off in the closet and do it, unless you're Emily Dickinson. You have to have somebody reading and responding.'" The writing students were taught by a method that provided a model that Smith now follows in her own creative writing courses. She observes, "You can't really teach writing. What you do is provide a forum." The Hollins Group has continued as a support and a forum for Smith. Her later writing gained a deservedly broader critical following, in part, because of the illuminating essays written for important southern journals or collections by critics Lucinda Hardwick MacKethan and Anne Goodwyn Jones. Annie Dillard, with the force of her considerable reputation, has publicly described Smith as "the best of the younger generation of Southern writers." Jones and MacKethan in particular have produced strong critical analyses of Smith's writing, criticism that moves beyond personal interest to sincerely held and incisively given assessment. Such criticism is an extension of that intelligent and supportive women's writing community at Hollins.[18]

Smith first captured her critical audience at Hollins because of her humorous writing. Already apparent was her keen eye for tangible detail and mimicry, her gentle-hearted presentation, and her irreverence for paternal and pseudoreligious authority. The collegiate newspaper career of Lee Smith at Hollins does not tell us about her later competence to work for the *Richmond News Leader* or the *Tuscaloosa News* so much as it provides a fascinating view of her early experiments with humor that offers not only entertainment value but social critique. Humor has always been a genre with an inherent capability of suggesting criticism while deflecting serious retort. Because southern ladies have historically been restricted from making direct criticism of the cultural standards that defined them, humor seemed a natural outlet for Smith. Critic Nancy Walker argues that "women's humor is an index to women's roles and values, and particularly to their relationship with American cultural realities." She continues, "For women to adopt this role means that they must break out of the passive, subordinate position mandated for them by centuries of patriarchal tradition and take on the power accruing to those who reveal the shams, hypocrisies, incongruities of the dominant culture. To be a woman and a humorist is to confront and subvert the very power

18. Scandling, "Profiles," 17, 26; Annie Dillard quoted in brochure for 13th Annual Literary Festival, Old Dominion University, Norfolk, Va., 1990.

that keeps women powerless, and at the same time to risk alienating those upon whom women are dependent for economic survival."[19] In a sense, the woman humorist works within the same social tensions as does the southern lady: she may have an opinion at variance with the dominant culture, but she must express it with tact or great wit in order to maintain the polite social surface. Similar to Annie Dillard's use of a persona, Smith's use of humor allowed her criticism to range more freely than it could in her daily life. Smith's newspaper writing at Hollins reveals her often using humor not only to entertain but to be irreverent about religion, to mock the administration, and to rouse the student body to take their education seriously.

The newspaper articles of Smith's freshman year range from pure entertainment to light satire, but in each case she experimented with taking widely accepted cultural codes and restructuring them to express a more personal or irreverent purpose. A light parody of the Twenty-third Psalm concerns sunbathing practices on the campus. Another satire attacks the excessive strictness of the point system of rules on campus, which she sees as unfairly restricting the women.

During sophomore year Smith collaborated with her friend Karen Long on a series of articles. One article, "The Night That Goodheart Passed: A Parable of Social Pressure; or, On Selfseeking," reflected the class consciousness that stung Smith in Richmond and would be a continuing concern in such novels as *Oral History*. It may also represent critical self-appraisal, for during that academic year Smith's parents presented her with the gift of a Porsche and sent her to study in the Hollins Abroad program. In this program, students spent the first academic semester studying at the Sorbonne in Paris and then traveled as a study group throughout Europe. Smith elected to join the program and, in a manner reminiscent of *Our Hearts Were Young and Gay*, became the foreign correspondent for the *Hollins Columns*. Smith feigned continual culture shock about her travels. For example, the cafes, she noted, were not simply places for eating but stages upon which to enact personal dramas, particularly the drama of the romantic artist: "You get used to knocking over the tables because they are so petites and you are becoming so fat. Here are some things to do in a cafe: (1) practice looking very bored; (2) practice looking very sad; (3) scribble violently in a little mauve notebook and

19. Nancy A. Walker, *A Very Serious Thing: Women's Humor and American Culture* (Minneapolis, 1988), 7, 9.

eat passionately so that everyone will think you're a pauvre young writer, un-honored and unsung upon this foreign strand. When you smoke in a cafe you have to blow the smoke at the ceiling and stare at it reflectively for a while and have a vision, and then sigh." But even the traveler's culture shock has an edge of restlessness about the restrictions upon the young women: "But quelle hor-reur! We had to start classes immediately, please, and they are all in French. So we have to etudier beaucoup and we are desolees because the only time we can see Paris is at night and then it is dark. We hear it's a nice looking town, though." The high-spiritedness, however, brought both foreign correspon-dence reports and Hollins Abroad to an abrupt end for Smith. For acting out her rebellion against the social discipline—staying out all night in a cafe talking to a young man—Smith was sent home from Paris before the Hollins group left France to travel across Europe.[20]

The distraught young woman even had to wait a semester to reapply for admission to Hollins. Louis Rubin—who often protected students in the writing program from excessive administrative punishment—comforted Smith, assured her that she would be readmitted, and to help her use the time profitably, secured a job for her with his friend James J. Kilpatrick, the editor in chief at the *Richmond News-Leader.* This journalistic internship later served Smith well, helping her secure work at the *Tuscaloosa News*, but at the time, she was trying to recover from her shock at being expelled. Because she was lively, a friend of Rubin's, and living on her own in a boarding house, the Kilpatricks welcomed Smith into their home and family gatherings. Al-though she did not share the conservatism of the segregationist and already famous author of the column "A Conservative View," Smith was impressed by the modern, feminist marriage of the Kilpatricks.[21] Here was the first in-stance in which she had observed an equal division of household responsibili-ties between husband and wife, and the experience made a lasting impression on her. Kilpatrick and his wife, Marie Louise Pietri, treated the wife's art—sculpting—with the same importance that they treated Kilpatrick's journal-

20. Lee Smith and Karen Long, "The Night That Goodheart Passed: A Parable of Social Pressure; or, On Selfseeking," *Hollins Columns*, November 12, 1964, p. 2ff.; Lee Smith, "H. A. Learns Art of Gorging in France and How to Be French Tom Joneses," ibid., March 18, 1965, p. 3; Lee Smith, "H. A. Finds Paris Is 'Tres Formidable!'" ibid., February 25, 1965, p. 3; Rubin, per-sonal interview.

21. Lee Smith, personal interview.

ism. This family provided a model for Smith, encouraging her to see that a woman could be a wife and mother and artist as well.

During junior year, Smith was readmitted to Hollins and returned to writing for the *Hollins Columns,* but her first article, "What, Me Worry?" was markedly more serious than her previous ones—perhaps reflecting the recent experience of working on a newspaper or the testing of a new critical strategy by a recently punished student. Smith, Anne Goodwyn Jones, and the other women of the Hollins Group now seemed to represent a minority voice on campus aware of the developing student movement elsewhere. Smith openly wondered whether Hollins students were aware of the perilous condition of academic freedom:

> Evidently a nationwide student movement is taking place. But we never ignite ourselves before meetings of the Curriculum Committee; we never go limp in the lunch line; we never even try to stamp out the common cold in Salem. . . . We are a paragon of modern student life. And we treasure our fetishes, as on Tinker Day when we worship our geographical barriers. . . .
> Why did all those people at Berkeley carry on as they did?
> Why is that cute Straughton [*sic*] Lynd socially unacceptable to UNC?
> What is academic freedom?
> Does the Curriculum Committee really eat its young?
> Are Hollins students LIVING A LIE?

Later in the month, Smith would again chastise her peers, for poor attendance at a lecture by Howard Nemerov. The humor still flickers in these articles, but the social challenges implicit in her earlier writing were no longer submerged by a gentle wit. By March of junior year, however, Smith had fully regained her in-print humor, ending the year with a parody of Julia Randall Sawyer's dramatic romanticism and James Joyce's style entitled "Rejoyce." Here Hollins (Holland) is playfully romanticized and pointedly criticized for being a womb. This "placenta for girls" proves to be most difficult in the spring when the girls have to study (stutter) for exams and to diet away the winter weight gain. Their impulse is to sit in their rooms (wombs) and gaze with a sense of fatality (fetality) on the world (whirled). The humor had returned with this piece, but the usual disruptiveness and underlying challenge to authority marking the earlier newspaper features were conspicuously absent, as though the punishment for the Paris incident lingered as a reminder that flouting social conventions was not always funny. At any rate, during her junior year the demarcation of Smith's newspaper writing was clear: she discussed serious social issues in straightforward prose and confined humor more closely to the area of pure entertainment.[22]

Senior year would be the test of whether that schism continued in her newspaper writing. During the summer, Smith had gone on the Mississippi raft trip. The year itself began with great promise, with Smith and former roommate Jo Berson as coeditors of the college's yearbook, the *Spinster.* The yearbook proved to be an upstart edition in which senior women posed in garb ranging from raincoats to fur coats and in settings ranging from rooftops to Jeeps. Smith's newspaper writing, however, still retained the caution that developed during junior year. Throughout the year Smith wrote a fairly regular feature column entitled "Out of My Mind" and followed much along the serious lines of the column written by Anne Goodwyn Jones during the previous year. Subjects ranged from Vietnam to a worried consideration of why young women wanted to identify with models such as Twiggy and Jean Shrimpton. The October 4, 1966, column was an entirely sober essay questioning the new dean's warning that "We must see that [students] don't learn about moral or ethical freedom the hard way." Smith responds with serious anger:

> Several things are wrong with this statement.
> In the first place, morality is not the most important thing at Hollins. The Chapel is not the Hollins Navel. . . . Ideally speaking, the center of Hollins should be the classrooms, and for many of us it is.
> In the second place, moral conformity already exists at Hollins. Our attitudes and our actions are, as a rule, uniform. We brush our teeth, study and eat leafy green vegetables. We don't ask for unreasonable things like psychedelic chapel services, but we reserve the right to determine our own private and individual moral codes.
> We do not intend to be Very Bad. We do not intend to be Bad at all, in fact. We are so conditioned that, by this time, most of our decisions will be boringly correct anyway. But as long as our own personal moral codes are not harmful to the community as a whole, and as long as we break none of the stated rules, we cannot be forced to synchronize our private morals. . . .
> This column is not intended as a criticism of Dean Jackson. It is intended as

22. Lee Smith, "What, Me Worry?" *Hollins Columns,* February 15, 1966, p. 3; Lee Smith, "Rejoyce," ibid., May 3, 1966, p. 2.

a criticism of the whole concept of moral conformity. . . . We would rather have a chance to mess up, or clean up, our own lives.

This is a Solemn Warning. We had better watch out, and draw all of our wagons into a circle before we get morally conformed. Or else one morning we may wake up to find that moral conformity has been splashed all over Hollins like a big can of grey Sherwin-Williams paint.[23]

Smith's social criticism is direct and distinctly unamused. Here she challenges the authority of a paternal administration to determine the social nature of the college community. Rather, she argues, the weight of responsibility should be shifted to the women themselves who should have the right to make their own moral judgments—"to mess up, or clean up, our own lives."

Though Smith had come to identify more precisely the restrictions upon women like herself, at this point she still felt uncertain as to the necessary extent of resistance. Women needed to act on their intellectual beliefs, she argued in another article: students at Hollins "over-intellectualize everything. . . . In this state we can't enjoy anything without simultaneously analyzing our enjoyment. We have to develop some sort of synthesis mechanism so that we can handle what we learn. If we are unable to do this, we might as well become beauticians."[24] In another article she also stated that "for the first time, women can do (and are doing) whatever they damn well please." But then she revises that thought and concludes that "it is just possible, you know, that the world's happiest women live in Scarsdale."[25] The final sentence of this commentary suggests the ambivalence Smith herself still felt about a contemporary culture that still seemed to reward women who chose either to have careers or to be mothers.

Smith's senior-year column also foreshadowed one other feminist vein in her professional writing. In *Lee Smith,* the first book-length study of Smith and her writing, Dorothy Combs Hill argues that Smith writes with an unconsciously intuitive bent toward mythology. In fact, Hill finds myth to be central to what she conceives of as Smith's agenda of recovering the feminine

23. Lee Smith, "Moral Conformity: Poor Conception," ibid., October 4, 1966, p. 2.

24. Lee Smith, "Lex and the College Girl," ibid., October 18, 1966, p. 2. Ironically, Smith in her later writing would come to admire the creative comfort that beauticians can provide as modern-day equivalents of Clarissa Dalloway. Smith worked as a beautician's assistant for three weeks to gain insights for her novel *Family Linen.*

25. Lee Smith, "Thought Might Negate Life," *Hollins Columns,* November 8, 1966, p. 2.

deity. A November column written by Smith would seem to give some credence to Hill's argument. Smith began the article with an evocative description of her sophomore writer-in-residence, Irishman Benedict Kiely. He was, she wrote, "the first to point out that the climbing of Tinker Mountain each October harks back to ancient times. It is a pilgrimage of sorts. It is above all a Dionysian ritual of nature worship, in which the Tinker Hats relate to the old Greek masks. But mountains are phallic symbols in anybody's book; and Hollins is a girls' school. Therefore, we must assume that the climbing of Tinker is related to the female's eternal quest to conquer the male and is, in fact, a memorial to this lofty ambition."[26] Looking about her, Smith then cited other rituals such Founder's Day, which she saw as a renewal of the Egyptian practice of worshipping the dead; Hundred Night, a celebration of the id; May Day, a fertility rite; graduation, an initiation rite of the questing hero. In this article she also described the primitive custom of decapitating young men to learn if they are wise, a practice about which Smith joked, "Perhaps this would make for a more interesting ceremony than the one [graduation] which we observe at present." She would later employ this exact image as part of the funeral scene in her novel *Something in the Wind*.

It could easily be argued that Smith never made a strong distinction between her journalistic experiences and her creative writing. Her contributions to the *Hollins Columns* were feature articles rather than hard reporting; later in life she quickly converted her reporting at the *Tuscaloosa News* into the novel *Fancy Strut*. In fact, while working on the *Tuscaloosa News* Smith developed the habit of writing her fiction in longhand to make a distinction for herself between creative writing and journalism.[27] The nature of her newspaper writing at Hollins probably contributed to the blurring of that distinction, and yet the significance of that writing experience should not be discounted. Regular publication validated her perception of herself as a writer. It provided her with multiple opportunities to test personae, perspectives, and literary techniques, and all with an immediate and responsive reading audience. Ultimately this newspaper writing allowed Smith to test the capabilities inherent in humor and to develop a gentle, perceptive, irreverent view of society that has become a hallmark of her mature writing. This youthful journalism indicated that she was a close observer of social details, that she disliked the demands of convention, and that she was eager to go beyond intellectualizing and throw herself into experience.

Smith aspired to be a novelist, though, and so even though it was gratifying to be published in the school newspaper, it was even more crucial to her to have her short stories accepted. *Beanstalks* was important for providing an early validation of that talent; *Cargoes,* the college's literary magazine, carried Smith's successive efforts. *Beanstalks* included the three-page story "The Wading House" (1963), a young woman's description of her loss of innocence occurring at the end of one summer when she was a small girl. The story appeared during sophomore year in *Cargoes* as "Little Arthur" (1964); finally, in her senior year, she expanded the story into novel length for her senior creative writing project, *The Last Day the Dogbushes Bloomed* (1967). In a similar pattern, "The Red Parts" (1966), a short story published in *Cargoes* during the fall of her senior year, was the precursor to her second novel, *Something in the Wind* (1971). Other early stories such as "Fatback Season" (1964) are important for showing Smith's technical experimentation with multiple narrators. "Miss Hawthorne and the Beautiful Song" (1965) not only shows O'Connor's influence but reveals Smith finally drawing upon her Appalachian heritage to create atmosphere and setting. Narrative elements of "White Parts; or, The Last Moments of Eula LeBel" (1967) appeared nearly twenty years later in her novel *Family Linen.* The common thematic thread that runs through all of these stories is victimization of women. Abandoning much of the humor that characterized her newspaper writing, Smith gives serious treatment in these stories to the various methods of abuse, confinement, and restriction faced by women.

Although Hollins had restricted some of Smith's activities, it had also provided her with the space, encouragement, and literary techniques to portray the deadliness of the cultural confinements upon women. The winter 1964 *Cargoes*—for which she, Annie Doak, and Cindy Hardwick were now readers—published "Fatback Season." In this short story, Smith—in contrast to Dillard, who worked with a single, ambiguous first-person narrator—began to depart from narrative conventions about linear narrative and monologic voice. The story has little action; instead, it records the thoughts and differing narrative voices of several individuals who are drawn by various circumstances to the vicinity of the same restaurant. The first narrator, John, sits with his wife, Beulah, in a small restaurant on the Eastern Shore of Virginia. Stopping at the bayside restaurant reminds John of the three years he was stationed at the naval base on Wallops Island, and suddenly he remembers the dream he and a friend shared of going to Florida: "But we never got around to it. Something came up." As he muses on his lost dream, Beulah notices the lights of the boats fishing for fatback fish in the dark. For his part, John watches the "kids sitting by the door . . . cutting up and acting the fool like kids will, barking at each other, and for a minute I wished I was a kid. If I had it all to do over again I bet I'd make it to Florida."[28] When he drives away, John views the lights of the boats in his rearview mirror and metaphorically looks back to his past as well. This connection of nostalgia to the fishing boats suggests that by giving up the dreams of his youth, John has led a life as uncertain in its direction as fishing boats searching for fish in the dark. John's reaction is echoed in the brief narration of a schoolteacher driving up the coast to Baltimore, who passes the restaurant, inadvertently slows down, and, in thinking of her class of third-graders who will face her the next day, grows nostalgic, also wishing that she could be a child again.

When these two adult narratives are complete, the narration then switches to that of a seventeen-year-old girl named Lisa, who, bundled up in a black raincoat, has taken her sister Amanda to the restaurant to get ice cream. During the course of this action the reader is privy to Lisa's constant flow of thought, which, she asserts, she can compartmentalize whenever she feels trapped by thoughts about her boyfriend Kirk: "My mind has a little zipper bag in it and if I know something will upset me I zip it up in the little bag before I have time to think about it." Like Scarlett O'Hara and other southern ladies who defer self-recognition until "tomorrow," Lisa has already learned to repress her feelings of confinement. At the restaurant, she chooses to sit in a booth so Amanda will not talk to the cheap-looking waitress. Then, to Lisa's surprise, a young man—Cedric O'Brien—sits down at their table. She feels "something somewhere in me [fall]. I heard the sound of the fall and I could feel the empty place where it had been." Later, Cedric's narrative will clarify the meaning of this incident: meeting him forces Lisa to feel the deadening force of conventionality that has already shaped her life. This realization creates a despair with which she is unprepared to cope. At that moment of realization, Amanda notices the lights on the fishing boats. "It's for catching fatbacks," claims Cedric. "They're these dumb fish and they jump right in

28. Lee Smith, "Fatback Season," *Cargoes* 52:1 (1964): 41, 42.

the boat when they see the lights. . . . They have to."[29] Immediately Lisa zips up "all the little rowboats up tight in my zipper bag" mind, an action whose metaphorical significance is that, like the fish who cannot resist the lights of the boats, Lisa will be unable to resist her obsession with doing what is socially proper. A final brief narrative by an adult—a truck driver—serves to complete the frame of the internal action occurring among Amanda, Cedric, and Lisa, and the story concludes with the sense that all of the characters feel an unhappy recognition of self in the plight of those dumb fish trapped in the deadly patterns of their lives.

"Fatback Season" shows Smith attempting to employ multiple narrators in her story, a technique that will mark later novels such as *Oral History, Fancy Strut,* and *The Devil's Dream.* In this narrative construction, Smith experiments with the oral idiom of rural speakers and with interlocking first-person narratives. The unifying element of the story is a restaurant, and the action revolves around this locus much the same way as action in *Mrs. Dalloway* revolves about the tolling of Big Ben in London. The individuals pass through or near the restaurant, and through those consciousnesses the entire experience is collected. In a sense, the restaurant is like the center of a spider web: the various narrators encounter the restaurant, and from that touch point spin out the thread of their thoughts, sometimes connecting at a shared moment with other narrators. All take notice of the unusual lighted fishing boats that dot the night in the channel just beyond the restaurant, and this dilation upon the fishing boats and fishing creates a resonance that echoes the larger structuring device of the story. Fishing becomes a metaphor for storytelling itself: the multiple narratives surround the restaurant like a fishing net, and only when they are all tied up or completed is the experience of the restaurant "caught" and hauled onto the deck of the reader's mind.

In "Fatback Season," a young woman is only one of several individuals to realize that she has been trapped by conventional expectations. With her first published work in an Appalachian setting, "Miss Hawthorne and the Beautiful Song," Smith begins to explore specifically the plight of entrapped women.[30] The story is set in Grundy, West Virginia, and concerns an old pi-

29. Ibid., 43, 45, 46.

30. Lee Smith, "Miss Hawthorne and the Beautiful Song," *Cargoes* 52:2 (1965): 37–47. Miss Hawthorne later appears, in name at least, in the novel *The Last Day the Dogbushes Bloomed,* although she will not appear as a fully developed character there. The occasional overlapping use

ano teacher, Mabel Hawthorne, a woman who fancies herself to be of tragic and romantic temperament. In the process of propelling her cat out of the house one rainy day, Miss Hawthorne's makeup gets wet and she reacts by remarking, "The rain touches my face with tiny fingers." Impressed by her lyric talent, she reenters the house and puts the words to music. "It was positively the most exciting afternoon she had spent," she decided, "since that time the mailman killed the snake in her front yard."[31] Then, in a scene reminiscent of Flannery O'Connor, Miss Hawthorne attends the Missionary Society meeting and stares distractedly at "the little pink baby Jesus on the wall of the Missionary Society Room." Suddenly gripped by poetic inspiration, she leaves her shocked friends with the announcement, "I have to go home . . . because the sap of life is IN MY VEINS!" and rushes home to add that new line to her song. The secret pleasure she derives from her song generates a certain wildness in her: "One night she bought a package of Chicken Chop Suey for two and ate it all by herself, blushing." The wildness finally encourages her to invite widower Horn for dinner, and she is inspired to add to her song yet again. Eventually Miss Hawthorne finds the courage to send her song to Diamond Discs of Nashville. Nearly wild with excitement, she boldly announces to the Missionary Society that she has written a song that Frank Sinatra will record. Suddenly her piano lesson business increases as does her exhilaration, and she becomes a town celebrity. Unfortunately, as events unfold, Miss Hawthorne's song is performed not by Frank Sinatra but by Hawkshaw Hawkins and the Foggy Mountain Boys. It becomes the "Country and Western Pick Hit of the Week"; but to Miss Hawthorne it is a horrific rendering of her romantic piece, and she is haunted by its sound everywhere she goes. She breaks off her friendship with widower Horn, stops teaching, buys eleven turkey TV dinners, and rations food to her cat and herself until she finally starves to death. In a very Smithian ending, the cat soon meets her demise under the wheels of the local Welcome Wagon.

The plot development of the story clearly reveals Miss Hawthorne as a woman whose life is constricted severely by small-town ways. Bolstered by her enchantment with a whimsical tune, she draws the courage to invite a

---

of names in Smith's fiction hints tantalizingly at a more complete fictional world along the lines of Faulkner's Yoknapatawpha County, but the pattern of her writing to date has remained closer to the method of this story: an attempt to capture accurately one well-defined event and place in Appalachian experience.

31. Lee Smith, "Miss Hawthorne," 37.

man to dinner and to confide to her women's club—the town gossips—that she is a songwriter. Her song has a liveliness and sensuality that is absent in her life until she creates a romantic illusion more palpable than her earlier imaginings: the unfounded assertion that Frank Sinatra will record her song. Like a Blanche DuBois, she crumbles when that illusion is shattered. Technically, Smith reinforces this theme by juxtaposing the hopeful lyrics of Miss Hawthorne against the prosaic grounding of small-town life in such cultural phenomena as the Piggly Wiggly market and country music; against these realities, Miss Hawthorne's romanticism seems ludicrous. Ironically, these physical realities seem trite when set against the real tragedy of Miss Hawthorne's aborted life.

The influence of O'Connor becomes even more pronounced in a story that is centered on a character who is clearly an early version of the raped, mentally retarded Fay of Smith's *Family Linen* (1985). Smith's "White Parts; or, The Last Moments of Eula LeBel" is the story of a woman who literally eats herself to death as a response to forced incest.[32] The story opens with a description of Eula LeBel resting near death in an old home that is now physically surrounded by a horseshoe-shaped Piggly Wiggly; in fact, the back door from her house opens directly into the canned foods and dairy sections of the store. Eula LeBel, a silent, mentally retarded, 342-pound woman, simply watches television and eats. Her sister Stella, viewing it as her "Christian duty," tends Eula, reads the Bible to her, and keeps feeding her at a constant rate. Their brother Bennett comes to visit, but his primary response to Eula is irritation that she has not gone ahead and died so he can bulldoze the house and expand the Piggly Wiggly parking lot.

Eula is oblivious to Stella and Bennett, but the soap opera she watches on television periodically touches her eccentric thought processes. First, it prompts her to recall how her brother Bennett would steal her after-school treat when she was a small girl, much as he is now trying to take her house. She is sent into a spasm of small fits by scenes on the television of a man and a woman kissing and of another man driving off in a car. Stella responds—as she does whenever Eula has a fit—by giving her more to eat. Yet in these fits Eula has flashbacks to earlier events in her life: how she was not allowed to attend school after eighth grade and how her brother Bennett took

32. Lee Smith, "White Parts; or, The Last Moments of Eula LeBel," *Cargoes* 53:4 (1967): 55–62.

away her baton, her sole pleasure. She also remembers how her brother Exodus had once enticed her into skinny-dipping in the local swimming hole and raped her.

Finally, Bennett, Stella, and neighbors gather to watch what they anticipate to be her death throes. While gathered there, they pray over her and then, ironically, share stories of the long-vanished Exodus's pranks as a boy. Their reminiscences agitate her even more and come to a climax when Stella gives her testimonial: "Well one thing about Exodus LeBel, say what you will, is he was devoted to his little sister Eula. Just devoted. I never saw anything like it. And that's more than I can say for some people I know who have no compassion. You remember how nice he was?"[33] A double sense of rape hangs over her now: Eula, the woman who had no capacity to defend herself against incest, has no voice but her spasms to protest the eulogies to her rapist that her neighbors offer at her deathbed. The story closes with Eula's thoughts in a collage of phrases collected during her entire lifetime, ending with a kaleidoscopic remembrance of the rape by Exodus.[34] Smith plays on the meaning of the word *Exodus* to suggest that in death, no longer enslaved by the weight and limitations of her woman's body, Eula makes her own exodus from a wretched earthly life to the heavenly future promised by Stella's Bible. The story never does make clear whether the trauma of the rape triggered Eula's mental and physical collapse or whether Exodus had simply taken advantage of a mentally retarded girl. The story does show, however, that Eula was not only physically raped in her youth but metaphorically and methodically raped of her income and house by her brother Bennett throughout the rest of her life. This addition of the economic rape shows a new maturity in Smith's understanding of the various ways in which women have been oppressed. To write about rape and oppression in such a grotesque context also shows Smith resisting the polite and tacit understanding of southern society that a lady should not discuss—or write about—such matters.

Smith took parts of these apprentice short stories to use as elements in her later novels, but two other stories were expanded into full novels. Both stories are concerned with the issues of "female initiation and *bildung* as they relate to both social and narrative conventions."[35] The earlier of these two stories,

33. Ibid., 61.

34. Smith uses the same technique of a collage of phrases with Brooke Cunningham at the end of "The Red Parts," *Cargoes* 53:3 (1966): 44–55.

35. Virginia Smith, "Conversation with Lee Smith," 237.

"The Wading House," first appeared in *Beanstalks* during Smith's freshman year. Several versions later, the story became her senior creative writing project at Hollins, one of twelve winners in the Book-of-the Month Club writing fellowship contest, and eventually Smith's first novel, *The Last Day the Dogbushes Bloomed.* In its first version, the story is a short vignette about a small girl's first encounter with death. The protagonist, a young girl named Annie, tells how the pleasure she has always associated with the month of August has been compounded by her anticipation that Miss Black the cat is due to deliver kittens at any time. On one morning this August, Annie's mother informs her that her cousin Edward from the city is going to visit them. Annie meets Edward and begins to share her favorite pursuits and places with him, but the pale skinny boy resists her overtures. Quickly and intuitively she perceives that his is a sadistic nature and resolves never to show Edward her wading house. Edward is indeed a petulant young boy who insists on exposing the unpleasantness of life: he declares that his father doesn't love his mother; he grabs the pregnant Miss Black roughly by the scruff of the neck; and he belittles all of the farmyard treasures that Annie has shared with him. One day Annie misses Miss Black and searches everywhere for her. Edward cynically rewards her efforts by leading her to the wading house and telling her, "Look under [the pokeberry bush] . . . and don't ever forget what you see." There she finds Miss Black with six tiny dead kittens. The story quickly concludes with Edward returning to the city and Annie no longer enchanted with August.

"The Wading House" reveals Smith struggling to work out the difficulties of a narrative voice. She has already developed an ear for colloquial idioms, but the narrative voice still proves troublesome. At the beginning of the story, the narrative is briefly burdened with an unnecessary and ill-conceived narrator who, though just a teenager herself, introduces the action as occurring "long years ago." After the first sentence, Smith switches to a younger, first-person point of view that works ineffectively because the older narrator periodically intrudes with authorial commentary that outbalances the younger voice. Aside from this problem with voice, the brief story works well and establishes a pattern that will recur in Smith's professional writing: that of the male interloper. Edward's visit is as disquieting and disruptive as that of the serpent in Eden; and, in this role reversal, the young boy sadistically exposes the girl to the knowledge of mortality that lies beneath the trees in her bower. This pattern of a man bringing knowledge that poisons is repeated in *Something in the Wind,* in which Bentley Turlington IV leads Brooke Cunningham to a confined and limited concept of life and love in the "pit"; in *Oral History,* in which Richard Burlage woos Dory with a romanticized literary worldview and then leaves her; and in *Fair and Tender Ladies,* in which Garnie preaches a hypocritical, deadening religion to Ivy Rowe. Though Smith has sympathetic male characters as well, those who restrict or undermine Smith's female protagonists in the most profoundly deceitful ways are men who bring false knowledge.

In the winter of Smith's sophomore year, "The Wading House" went through another incarnation in *Cargoes* as "Little Arthur," a nine-page story she had revised and expanded for Richard Dillard's course. The story still takes place in August, but the immediate force of the story is shifted by the first sentence to focus on the male interloper: "He happened during that hot green August when I was 8 1/2." [36] In "Little Arthur," the narrator directly and immediately announces a theme that will be suggested only at the end of *The Last Day the Dogbushes Bloomed:* the idea that "Everything was blooming as hard and as fast as it could because maybe it knew that pretty soon it would die." This second version omits the extraneous narrator of the first version; changes Annie from an only child to a girl with a younger sister, Julia, who follows after her through much of the story; and finally, gives Annie and Julia parents, likable people who seem supportive and interested both in the children's club and in their actions. The one respect in which the story strains is in the final lines when Smith evokes the ending of Dylan Thomas's "Fern Hill" as though to ensure that the reader understands the point of the story.

"Little Arthur" begins with a local boy named Bugs Hawthorne suggesting the idea of starting a club. Ironically, all of the children agree to forming a club and immediately vote to exclude Bugs, who then leaves them with the promise that they will be sorry. Bugs does indeed return to the club meeting, but this time brings with him, he claims, an invisible gun-carrying friend whom he calls Little Arthur. This invisible threat intrigues and frightens the children so completely that they allow Bugs and Little Arthur to become club members. Soon Little Arthur, speaking through Bugs, takes over leadership of the club. Little Arthur, claims Bugs, orders the girls to submit to an initiation rite of taking off their panties. At first the girls resist: "Martha Fletcher said it was nasty. 'It's all right,' Bugs said. 'It's all right if Little Arthur says it is.' So we did it and I [Annie] did not feel dirty because then I knew it was all

---

36. Lee Smith, "Little Arthur," *Cargoes* 52:1 (1964): 51.

right. The only thing I felt was a light feeling in the top of my head and my stomach sort of squirming around inside of me while I was doing it."[37] For Annie, moral qualms receive expression not in cognitive recognition of evil, as was true for the Annie of the earlier version, but through physical unease.

Warning the children not to tell their parents of the club's business, Little Arthur thinks of many things for them to do "that we never would have thought of," like bludgeoning a pet rabbit to death. An older playmate, Richard, finally catches the children uprooting the roses in Mrs. Johnson's garden and tells his mother, who in turn calls the other parents. When the children return home to their parents' chastisement, Annie's father concludes with a pronouncement: "There is one more thing," Daddy says. "*Little Arthur* is *dead.* Do you understand that? There is no Little Arthur."[38] This verbal chastisement and decree leave baby Julia happy because she has avoided a spanking. Annie's response is more complex. Her final reactions reveal that she has grown from a child who experiences moral threat as a stomachache into a girl who has acquired a sobering knowledge of evil. A physical spanking would have kept the matter at a physical level; in contrast, her father's words prove ineffectual at killing the mysterious threat she has experienced. Smith portrays Annie's recognition of threat not as an intuition of evil—as it is in the earlier version—but as a knowledge born out of mystery and experience. By the final version of the story, Smith will explicitly mention *The Turn of the Screw,* a story closely parallel to Smith's in its consideration of puberty as a time when good and evil cannot be kept apart. But at this point in the evolution of the story, Smith has primarily added moral weight, first by changing the focus from a misogynist boy to a powerful manipulative force that is mysterious to its victims. That menace, posed as the veiled sexual threat of Little Arthur's gun, becomes literal rape in the final version of the story.

Smith's senior creative writing project was, essentially, the final version of the novel published by Harper & Row in 1968. Like her earlier versions, *The Last Day the Dogbushes Bloomed* remains a story about a young girl's loss of innocence, but new to this rendering is a heightened element of violence against women.[39] The protagonist, Susan Tobey, is a nine-year-old tomboy. In one

37. Ibid., 57.
38. Ibid., 59.
39. Lee Smith, *The Last Day the Dogbushes Bloomed* (New York, 1968). The strange word in the title derived from an incident when Susan found a sick dog underneath some pink bushes near her home; logically, she always referred to them afterward as "dogbushes."

respect, Smith has returned Susan to the state of an only child because, though Susan has family members, they all seem to go their separate ways. Her parents' marriage has deteriorated, and—as Lucinda Hardwick Mac-Kethan has observed—Susan's method for coping with that knowledge is to "[transform] her mother's world into a fantasy land of queen and court." With this version, Smith shows an increased interest in the power of language that will mark her mature work, as Michelle Lodge notes: "[Susan] cannot know consciously how to accommodate her changing world, and it is only in her language, the way she tells her story, that she communicates her own increasing bewilderment." She instinctively turns to story creation as a means for reconstructing the reality that so painfully surrounds her.[40]

Susan's family myth centers on the issue of what it means to be a proper lady. Her mother was the consummate lady, "a real Queen all right. She was everything she should be." Her laughter is like fairy music, her hands perfectly manicured, her manners polite and genteel—she "glittered." And yet, thinks Susan, there are "a lot of rules to know about Queens and how to act," most of which are counter to Susan's natural inclinations: "You have to be quiet when you wait for Queens," she notes. Susan clearly feels herself to be, at best, an observer of the court. A true member in the court of the queen is Susan's sister Betty, newly returned from Europe, the princess who "had long yellow hair to hang out of towers." Betty is "the Queen's daughter" in all the ways Susan realizes that she herself is not. Susan observes, sometimes wistfully, how Betty imitates the ladylike practices of her mother even in details like holding "her finger out like the Queen always does" when she drinks coffee.[41] Yet by the end of the story it becomes clear that the role of princess is painful and ultimately disappointing even to Betty.

Reality does not readily yield to Susan's hopeful fiction. Her father doesn't fit neatly into her family story, partly because he has no clear power to balance that of the queen and partly because he doesn't attempt to play the social role that so attracts the queen. He simply "wasn't the King." The man who more adequately fulfills the queen's expectations is her lover, a stranger known only as "the Baron" to Susan. Susan's brittle family myth is a frail defense against the pain and confusion she witnesses: the princess and the queen argue bit-

40. Lucinda Hardwick MacKethan, "Artists and Beauticians: Balance in Lee Smith's Fiction," *Southern Literary Journal* 15 (1982): 3; Lodge, "Lee Smith," 316.

41. Lee Smith, *Dogbushes*, 5, 4, 3.

terly over Betty's boyfriend; the baron flirts boldly with the queen during a party at the castle. Later, Susan is scarcely surprised when her mother leaves the family to run off with her lover. Blooms withering on the dogbushes seem symbolic records of this dying away of the family relationships. Because of these tensions within her family, Susan spends most of her time in solitary play in an imaginative world far more engaging than the world of her family around her. In her self-created world, she can imagine and name things on her own terms. One of the secret places to which she retreats is what she calls the wading house, not an actual building but a weeping willow tree by the stream. By imagining these games, landscapes, and stories, Susan is finally able to participate in a world that operates on terms that are fair, painless, and comprehensible to her.

In the summer during which the story takes place, Susan's world is invaded by adultery, rape, and death. Smith centers the focal point for this intrusion in the figure of a young boy named Eugene and, more potently, in his imaginary companion, Little Arthur. Returning to her initial concept in "The Wading House," Smith makes the mean-hearted boy an outsider, a city boy who scorns all of the small country delights Susan shows him. When he throws a rock at the small mouse she has befriended, Susan, like the Annie of the first version, recognizes his as a malignant nature. The local children decide to exclude Eugene from their club; but after a time, Eugene finds that he can manipulate Susan and her naive friends by pretending he has an imaginary friend, Little Arthur, who has power to organize and lead them. It is Little Arthur, claims Eugene, who suggests that they torture a small kitten, tear up Mrs. Tate's beloved rose garden, study an anatomy book, and expose their genitals to each other.

Finally, on the night after Susan's mother has run off with her lover, Little Arthur has the children play "iron lung"; the medical game, however, results in Eugene's raping Susan. Some of the parents of the children find out about the iron lung incident and gather the children to tell them to disband the club, but no one will tell Susan's parents, explain to Susan what has happened to her, or attempt to counsel her. As would many more mature rape victims, Susan instinctively feels herself to be somehow evil or the cause of what has happened; and the adults do nothing to explain that she has actually been the victim of another person's evil. She turns to the adults for penance and finds neither punishment nor absolution. That night she dreams the dream of a rape victim, that she is now horribly disfigured. Susan has no one with whom to talk over her confusion. Like Lisa in "Fatback Season," Susan feels her only recourse is to lock away her thoughts. "I had fixed my mind up so it was cut into boxes," Susan states. "That way, if I ever wanted to think about anything I could just pull it out of its box and roll it around in the part of my head that was not boxed in. When I got tired of it I could close it back up in its box, and there were some things that I never took out of their boxes at all."[42] She never cries over the queen's departure, over the iron lung incident, or over the hired man Frank's death. Her response is simply to retreat under the dogbushes like the sick dog she once saw there.

The conclusion of *The Last Day the Dogbushes Bloomed* makes clear that this story has been a small child's account of the evil or strangeness that she sees entering her Eden. Though she never finds the precise words to name them, the interlopers are sex and death. Her mother leaves the family for another man, Betty gets engaged and prepares to leave, and Susan vaguely links the iron lung rape to her own death. Susan may continue to call them "dogbushes," but she realizes even they are now part of a world over which she has little control: "Little Arthur was under the dogbushes now and I was not surprised. I understood then that wherever I went, for maybe the whole rest of my life, Little Arthur would not be very far away. He would be somewhere close outside. I knew that he would always be there, but it didn't scare me."[43] Unlike Annie who, at the end of "Little Arthur," is afraid to sleep without the light on, Susan Tobey clearly understands that she cannot hide from the evil that Little Arthur represents. Susan, however, lacks any clear cognitive understanding of sex, rape, or death.

The Last Day the Dogbushes Bloomed is "redeemed from the ordinary," argues critic Harriette Buchanan, "by Smith's unfailing control of Susan's voice and perspective," but Buchanan then glosses that assessment by suggesting that Susan's perspective is that of a self-centered child: "Susan is unaware of the conflicts within her family, including her mother's adultery, which is revealed obliquely to the reader when Susan throws reference to it in a secondary position to what she sees as the chief event, her personal situation: 'I had been busy with eating a banana and listening to the radio and bending my feet, all at the same time, but then the Baron and the Queen came downstairs and when they made me turn off the radio and told me why didn't I go wash my feet, I thought about the club meeting and left.'" Susan's detailed court

42. Ibid., 173.
43. Ibid., 180.

scenario reveals that, far from being self-centered, she is extremely attuned to her family situation. Her deficiency lies rather in the realistic fact that a young girl simply lacks the adult terminology to label an indifferent and unfaithful mother, a pretentious sister, a milquetoast father, and a mean-spirited boy. Her naïveté and her isolation arise from a family that finds it "impossible to speak about feelings or to utter the least honest word about what is happening to them." That her neighbors will be no more truthful with her makes Susan ultimately a victim of family, Eugene, and community.[44]

The changes Smith made in later versions of the story suggest that she had developed a broader and more complex vision of the ways in which innocence is taken away from young girls. Smith's final revisions make the threats more violent, more immediate to the life situation of the protagonist, and more complex in personal and social implication. In "The Wading House," Edward is a cousin who has come to stay because his father has left his mother; in the novel, Susan must confront the fact that it is her mother who has left the family for another man. In "Little Arthur," Annie's parents are interested and supportive; in *Dogbushes*, Susan must decipher a family code that has been shaped by social and personal expectations beyond her knowledge. In "The Wading House," the threat lies in a boy who embodies—and therefore contains—evil; Little Arthur in the novel version, by contrast, is invisible and all-pervasive evil. Abandonment and incomprehensible rape leave Susan reeling when the final assault on her hopefulness occurs. The hired hand Frank, the one who "was like . . . a tree or a rock" to her, dies and with him goes the last semblance of her control over her world. No longer able to trust anything, Susan comes to see Little Arthur as an intrusive evil that "would always be there" in life.[45]

The second undergraduate story that Smith later converted into a novel began as a project for Richard Dillard's course. She entitled it "The Red Parts," a reference to the practice of Bible publishers of printing in red the words spoken by Jesus.[46] It was first published in the fall 1966 *Cargoes*, edited

---

44. Harriette C. Buchanan, "Lee Smith: The Storyteller's Voice," in *Southern Women Writers: The New Generation*, ed. Tonette Bond Inge (Tuscaloosa, 1990), 324; Jones, "The World of Lee Smith," in *Women Writers of the Contemporary South*, ed. Peggy Whitman Prenshaw (Jackson, Miss., 1981), 255.

45. Lee Smith, *Dogbushes*, 178, 180.

46. Lee Smith, "Red Parts," 44–55. Richard Dillard, personal interview, notes that while at Hollins, Smith also wrote a romance novel, "Children of Cronus," that never progressed beyond manuscript form.

by Annie Doak Dillard and Cindy Hardwick, and later published in novel form by Harper & Row as *Something in the Wind* (1971). "The Red Parts" essentially records the story of Brooke Cunningham and Bentley Turlington IV, two undergraduates living in a basement apartment—"the pit"—while they attend summer school courses. The protagonist of this first-person narrative, Brooke, is a young woman who is witty, observant, and anxious to avoid analysis of the events that occur to her. Because the narrator is nearly compulsive in her willingness to gloss over deeply disturbing issues, that avoidance quickly becomes a central issue of the plot.

The story begins with Brooke and Bentley returning from a morning test in Victorian literature and falling into bed together. They make love, banter with each other, and then fall asleep until late afternoon. Some noise outside the apartment awakens them, and they open the curtains to discover a large crowd of children at a birthday party, a sight that inexplicably sends Brooke into tears: "I cried for 2 hours, for the first time since I was nine years old." Brooke herself never makes the explicit connection established later by the reader that the happy children triggered Brooke's unexpressed grief for her father, who died when Brooke was nine years old. After the crying incident, mysterious phenomena begin happening to the couple, such as noises created by an unseen presence. The next morning, alone in the apartment, Brooke attempts to write to her mother but can only think of her dead father. This looming memory of her father seems counterbalanced in pain by Brooke's ambiguous feelings about her mother. Brooke had come to summer school to please her mother, "the last of the big-time ladies," who wants her daughter there to "meet lots of nice Southern boys for a change." Brooke doesn't resist her mother's plan because she doesn't want to disappoint: "I would rather keep Mother's bubble extant." Ironically, Brooke keeps her own "bubbles" intact by ignoring any self-examination of her own life. When she lost her virginity with Bentley, she "was completely unaffected. I knew I could never understand why I had done what I had done; and I never tried to understand it."[47] Like the protagonists of Smith's other short stories, Brooke essentially attempts to compartmentalize and forget those parts of her life that she finds distressing and uncontrollable. Unwilling to disappoint her mother, too tired to write lies, inexplicably fearful, Brooke picks up a copy of a Bible she finds in Bentley's desk and begins to read "the red parts"—those parts of the gospels wherein Jesus speaks. Bentley returns and quarrels with her so vio-

47. Lee Smith, "Red Parts," 45, 46, 50.

lently for reading the Bible that Brooke fears he will rape her. The under-current of potential violence continues when the two attempt to relieve ten-sions by going to a playground. Bentley keeps pushing Brooke—against her wishes—higher and higher in the swing until she leaps out and nearly hurts herself. That night the noisy presence returns to the apartment; when Bent-ley goes to investigate, he finds nothing and, collapsing from tension, flops onto the couch. Brooke begins massaging his neck and then, they both real-ize, contemplates strangling him. The next morning Brooke moves out of the apartment and gladly accepts her mother's phone invitation for her to come home.

Certainly, one of the complex issues raised by the story concerns the de-structiveness of feelings that pass for love. To express love for her parents, Brooke attempts to be a lady who doesn't disappoint others and in doing so unconsciously imitates the superficiality she dislikes in her mother. When she is drunk and almost shoots Bentley with a rifle, they are both momen-tarily persuaded that they are in love and should move in together. The key to Brooke's self-destructive tendencies seems to lie in the fact that until that summer she had "never had to think about anything at all." She emphatically resists self-analysis, describing herself as living "outside my skin and unbe-lieving."[48] But when the birthday party "gets under her skin" as it were, she is less capable of cynicism and so turns to "the red parts" to discover something in which to believe. Her Bible reading proves an insufficient bulwark against the repression and the destructiveness she and Bentley feel, and so the two lovers part. As Brooke prepares to return home to her mother, her repression becomes expressed in an even more obvious pattern of repeating clichés to herself. The aphorisms are ones that she had once heard her father use, and their use in this context shows that Brooke really is little better off than she was before she met Bentley. She still relies on the aphorisms of a dead father even while she realizes that those sayings cannot stay sufficient to guide her actions.[49] After taking a lover, she is even less able than before to deal with the emotions and memories that shape her, and her easy cynicism has been shaken in the process. Her final invocation of these clichés is an incantation against despair.

Smith expanded the twelve-page story "The Red Parts" into a sixty-page

48. Ibid., 46, 50.
49. Eventually, all words seem comforting and meaningless at the same time, as they do for Susan at the end of *Dogbushes.*

section in the latter half of *Something in the Wind*.[50] The novel's title, from a line in Shakespeare's *Comedy of Errors*—"There is something in the wind, that we cannot get in"—evokes the issues broached in both *Comedy of Errors* and *Something in the Wind:* illusion, concern with appearance, bewilderment, confusion about identity, and madness. Both works end with a marriage, but the novel's relation to comedic convention ends there. For Brooke, there is indeed something in the wind that will not allow her to feel a part of the life she lives. In the novel, the cause for her detachment is linked not to the death of her father but to the death of her twenty-one-year-old boyfriend Charles Hughes in a car accident. Like the father in the earlier version, this young man apparently shaped Brooke's life. "Charles," Brooke thought, "had made my mind and if he was really dead like everybody kept saying, then I didn't know what would go on in my head."[51] Transfixed by his death, Brooke struggles to make any progress in understanding her own motivations and desires.

The novel begins with Brooke, a senior at a private girls' school in Richmond, traveling home for Charles Hughes' funeral. As the story progresses, she realizes that there is something new in the wind that will not allow her to "get in" to conventional life anymore. Upon her return to St. Dominique's, she feels unprepared to deal with solicitous classmates. As was true for Lee Smith at St. Catherine's School, Brooke finds that "We were all alike, everyone, but I was with them and not of them and I had not known it before. Obviously my criteria were wrong. Charles had said one time, 'The thing that is the matter with you is you are not a lady.' But I didn't know what lady meant." Remembering her boyfriend's judgment of her inadequacy, Brooke takes to hiding in a toilet stall at night to have privacy and to work on her "life plan." The only concrete detail about this life plan was that it involved imitation: "I would imitate everybody until everything became second nature, ... I wouldn't have to bother to imitate any more, I would simply *be*." The entire premise of the life plan, she later states, is that "you are what you seem." This imitation seems to coalesce in her life around the idea of what one should do to be *southern,* which actually seems a code word for the term she claims not to understand: southern *lady*. Because she has accepted Charles' assessment

---

50. The Bentley character "comes from a ghost story based on newspaper accounts of a young, unmarried couple's experiences with psychic disturbances." See Katherine Kearns, "Lee Smith," *Dictionary of Literary Biography Yearbook, 1983,* ed. Mary Bruccoli and Jean W. Ross (Detroit, 1984), 324.

51. Lee Smith, *Something in the Wind* (New York, 1971), 5.

of her, Brooke becomes a detached observer of herself. When a new boy-friend, John Howard, unfastens her bra and begins to make love to her, she reflects, "I knew what [a woman] would have done if she was southern. She would have slapped John Howard's hand, not too soon but before he got the bra completely off, and laughed a lot, and then she would have gone to rush [parties with him]." Later, in her freshman year at college, she moves in with Bentley and judges that much of her behavior isn't "southern": she can't cook southern; she yields to Bentley in a way that "wasn't a Southern thing to do"; when she decides to move into the apartment with Bentley, she "knew it wasn't Southern" of her.[52] This story version, then, makes the expectations of a southern lady more clearly one of the images that distances Brooke from her family and from self-definition.

In this heightened atmosphere where Brooke already feels estranged from herself, experiences cascade in her mind like the snowflakes cascading in the snow-dome paperweight she buys at a pawnshop. She fancifully imagines herself as living inside the snow dome, and the addition of this image in the second version emphasizes both the detachment Brooke feels from herself and the isolation she feels from the rest of the world when living in "the pit" with Bentley. When she looks out of the window at the children, it is as though she realizes that she is looking from the inside of the paperweight to the outside world.

One reviewer of the book argues that in Brooke rests a "subconscious wish to play Delilah to all men and symbolically emasculate each in turn, one by one." Nothing could be more false. Robbed of her autonomy, Brooke is a ready and indifferent victim of the men in her life: she is either a "widow" for Charles, the one who "made my mind," or sex object for Houston, Bentley, John Howard, and the other men she dates. She is caught in the age-old di-lemma of being viewed as a virgin or a whore: " 'Girls are different,' Bentley said. 'Guys can do what they want to.' 'But if a girl does it [is promiscuous], she's a whore?' 'That's right,' Bentley said." Her parents want her to be a lady; her boyfriends want to have sex with a perpetual virgin.[53]

Perhaps the most difficult issue to analyze in the story is the metaphysi-cal one. Throughout the novel version, Brooke discounts religion as, at best,

52. Ibid., 25, 117, 41, 153, 175.

53. Review of *Something in the Wind* by Lee Smith, *Virginia Quarterly Review* 47 (1971): xcvi; Lee Smith, *Something in the Wind,* 196.

a joke. Despite this rejection of religion, its presence remains palpable. Brooke's tears—the first she has shed since Charles's death—are soon followed by her reading of "the red parts." Turning to read quote from Jesus in the Bible is not another search for male authority and guidance but a quest for unmediated knowledge. Brooke reads to find out for herself about the weaknesses in her character. The novel version is specific about five particular pieces of scripture, which may all be revelations to Brooke about her life. The first, the invocation "Be ye therefore perfect, even as your father which is in heaven is perfect," continues the theme of imitation or of pleasing male figures. The second passage seems to speak to Brooke's dilemma about her divided self: "No man can serve two masters: for either he will hate the one, and love the other; or else he will hold to the one, and despise the other." The third passage speaks of those who have become eunuchs both voluntarily and involuntarily, an observation that could be construed as a commentary on the status of women rendered sexually and creatively powerless by the constraints of their birth and society. The fourth passage refers to the raising of the dead, a passage, recalls Brooke, that was read at Charles's funeral, yet which might foreshadow a resurrection of Brooke. The final passage is the biblical comment on marriage as the union of two people into one flesh. The reference may apply to Brooke's living with Bentley; but in the context of the entire novel, it seems to suggest the importance of Brooke being united within herself. After reading scripture, Brooke moves out, gives away the paperweight, and returns home.

Such an interpretation of "The Red Parts" makes the novel's final scene—the wedding of Brooke's brother—especially intriguing. This wedding ritual balances the funeral ritual that began the novel; and if, as Anne Goodwyn Jones writes, rituals "presumably integrate public and private worlds," then casting Brooke's own story within this framework "has to do with her coming to terms with her own two worlds, the private, authentic self and the public Southern lady."[54] Brooke, as a bridesmaid in her brother's wedding, observes what has been a recurring pattern in the story, the image of circles: rings of candles, the circular stained glass window, round chocolate candies.[55] In watching the ceremony and considering this cyclical pattern, she decides, "I

54. Jones, "World of Lee Smith," 256.

55. Rosalind B. Reilly suggests that circles have a mystical sense of dream and desire in Smith's *Oral History*. See Reilly, "*Oral History:* The Enchanted Circle of Narrative and Dream," *Southern Literary Journal* 23:1 (1990): 72–92.

could have this too. . . . I could marry John Howard and step into my place like Carter and have all this for the rest of my life. But I didn't think I would. I had come full circle myself, and now there were new directions." Upon realizing that she has closed one cycle in her life, Brooke experiences an unexplained epiphany. She feels a pain in her hand, realizes that she has been clutching her bouquet tightly and sees that a thorn has pricked her: "The blood welled out, one single drop, and then I started crying." If the thorn could be construed to represent a phallic image or the pain of the last year, then the blood—the red part of her—symbolizes her loss of virginity or, metaphorically, the pain of foregoing old and familiar values. The story concludes with the sense that Brooke will hereafter think more deeply about definition by family, society, or men. Her father now seems to her to be an ineffectual cartoon figure "standing open-mouthed and patting air. His mouth was as round as a cartoon mouth and any second I expected a white bubble of words to come ballooning out."[56] Brooke begins laughing, and the mother of the bride jerks Brooke's hand in an attempt to silence her. Brooke's response is to recall the old aphorisms she had learned as a child; but the implication of this recitation is that Brooke will never again be guided by the clichés of her old life.

The expansion from the short story to the novel version naturally produced many additions and refinements in the details of the story. Some changes seem to reflect a change in the Smith's literary tastes: where Brooke reads Emerson in the short story, she reads Eudora Welty in the novel. In the short story version, a girl at a party admires the lovers Bentley and Brooke; in the novel version, the girl looks at Brooke as though she is a whore. The overall weight of the changes is to portray Brooke as more deeply disturbed yet more potentially reflective and rebellious. The Brooke of the short story, though taking a lover, is still a deeply traditional southern woman: she is a good student who is essentially obedient to her mother. In the novel, though her life is marked by more evidence of an aristocratic southern lifestyle, Brooke is far more promiscuous and detached. The new Brooke cares less about grades and calls her mother "Carolyn." The old Brooke was modest about her body. The new Brooke is neither modest nor sexually timid: she has sex with every man she dates; and whereas the short story has Bentley kissing Brooke hard, the novel has Brooke doing the hard kissing. The Brooke of

56. Lee Smith, *Something in the Wind*, 243, 244.

Something in the Wind never achieves a mature thoughtfulness about much of her experience, but the conclusion suggests that she now has some insight into the real danger of fulfilling the social definitions of what a lady should do and be.

As Harriette Buchanan suggests, much of Lee Smith's early fiction is "about women faced with a world for which they are unprepared. These women are not only unprepared but also have little idea of where to look for guidance, because their families and communities provide so little in the way of honest or genuinely nurturing support. The families are usually broken, with key members either physically or mentally absent." Smith's newspaper and fiction writing at Hollins reflected her personal observation and experience that women were oppressed in a variety of subtle ways. It was, in part, because her peers were so supportive of her disruptive behavior and of her writing that Smith understood that an alternative mode of existence was possible for women, one in which she could act and write according to her own lights. In this liminal state at Hollins, she could escape the constraints of her upbringing about who she should be; she saw professors who treated their wives' careers as equal to their own; she experienced a sisterly community that promised to be an enduring and dependable support system. Working from this foundation, Smith continued to explore feminist themes that would become central issues of her professional writing career. By the time her undergraduate stories found their way into novel form, Smith had illuminated the dismal social condition of women with greater fullness. As her friend Lucinda Hardwick MacKethan later observed, Smith had learned to portray female protagonists such as Susan and Brooke as "watchers rather than catalysts, and in each book male friends supplant family ties, setting in motion incidents or delivering challenges that the girl or young woman initially accepts rather passively as a means to balance some lack in the patterns available through her life at home." After leaving Hollins, Smith would work and rework these images of victimized women for more than a decade before she would develop protagonists such as Katie Cocker and Ivy Rowe, who would painfully but successfully eschew the social definitions traditionally imposed upon women.[57]

The initial publication life of Smith's first two novels was short; for a time they were the only two of Smith's novels no longer in print (Louisiana State

57. Buchanan, "Storyteller's Voice," 344; MacKethan, "Artists and Beauticians," 4.

Lee Smith

University Press has since reprinted *Dogbushes*). Houghton Mifflin read and rejected the manuscript of one version of *Dogbushes,* but editor Shannon Ravenel (Hollins '60) advised Smith, who then revised the work, which was published by Harper & Row in 1968. *Dogbushes* sold about 10,000 copies; *Something in the Wind* sold only about 5,000 copies. Critic Mark Scandling has judged that *Dogbushes* "was successful mainly because her former boss James J. Kilpatrick wrote in his nationally syndicated column about it, calling it something like the 'new *To Kill a Mockingbird.*'" Reaction to the novel was certainly unsettling in Grundy. Smith observed, "My mother was furious because all her friends thought she'd had an affair. She got upset. Real upset. I don't think anybody in Grundy has read my other books because my mother called the library and told them not to order them because they had sex in them. She was totally unable to separate the writer from the story." As would many a southern lady, Virginia Marshall Smith still feared what the neighbors would think.[58]

Though Smith rebelled against propriety in many ways, she seemed initially to follow the pattern of countless other women. Only days after graduation she married James Seay, a young poet who had first met her three months earlier when she performed as a go-go dancer at the Black Raincoat poetry reading.[59] She turned down a chance for a writing fellowship at Columbia University and used the $3,000 Book-of-the-Month Club prize to buy, among other things, a refrigerator. She was, she herself noted, "a very traditional Southern wife in all my 20s. I thought you started dinner at 2 in the afternoon and cooked the beans all day." She went to Little League games, PTA meetings, and beauty breakfasts. Despite the demands of conventional married life, Smith continued to write, even while she taught full-time and reared two sons, even when it meant getting up at 5 a.m. While she was pregnant with her first son, she worked as a feature writer, film critic, and editor of the Sunday magazine for the *Tuscaloosa News,* a job that furnished the subject matter for *Fancy Strut. Something in the Wind* was written in a race during the last six weeks of her pregnancy with her second son. She was discovering, as had other women writers before her, the difficulty of writing in brief sections of time sandwiched in between family responsibilities. The result was that her stories sometimes lacked continuity: "In *Fancy Strut,* which I wrote when the children were small, I had whole characters walk behind trees and never reappear. I was writing in fits and spurts. " Still, she seemed to combine writing successfully with the demands of job and family. *Fancy Strut,* dedicated to her friends Susan and Howell Raines, was published in 1973 as Smith was finishing a stint teaching seventh grade in Nashville, Tennessee. She was teaching language arts at the Carolina Friends School in Durham, North Carolina (1974–1977) when Milos Forman and David Susskind took a film option on the book.[60]

58. Scandling, "Profiles," 18.

59. Jo Berson Buckley, telephone interview, July 7, 1992. Seay, who taught at Virginia Military Institute, was a poet from Batesville, Mississippi, and was seven years older than Smith.

60. Lee Smith, personal interview; Scandling, "Profiles," 18–19, 24–25. Forman and Susskind intended to have Warren Beatty star as Buck Fire and Lee Remick as Monica. Artistic differences among the producers canceled the project, and Forman accepted the offer to film *One Flew Over the Cuckoo's Nest.* Alderson, "You Can Go Home Again," 24.

Smith returned to Hollins as a writer-in-residence in 1977, during which time she wrote the short story "Paralyzed," the original version of her 1980 *Black Mountain Breakdown*. In a sense, this novel is the point toward which Smith had been heading in her first two novels: the woman so completely defined by male expectations and social roles that she literally makes herself paralyzed. Smith observes that among her reasons for writing *Black Mountain Breakdown* was to show "that if you're entirely a passive person, you're going to get in big trouble. The way so many women, and I think particularly Southern women, are raised is to make themselves fit the image that other people set out for them." As critic Linda Harris and others have observed, this middle group of novels, *Black Mountain Breakdown, Family Linen,* and *Fair and Tender Ladies,* "trace[s] a progression of women from Crystal Spangler, who passively accepts the roles others define for her, through the various women in *Family Linen,* each of whom is trying to make sense of her life, to Ivy Rowe, who actively defines and participates in her own special place as a woman." In a sense, the title of Smith's 1995 novel, *Saving Grace,* makes explicit an agenda about women exploring possibilities for saving their lives.[61]

From 1977 to 1981, Smith was on the faculty of the University of North Carolina as an instructor in creative writing.[62] Critical articles by Lucinda Hardwick MacKethan and Anne Goodwyn Jones, along with the publication of *Oral History* in 1983, initiated what has become a wide and sustained critical interest in Smith's writing.[63] Winning literary prizes such as the O. Henry Award, the John Dos Passos Award for Literature, the Robert Penn Warren Award for Fiction, and the MacArthur Award have since established Smith's as a significant contribution to contemporary southern literature. *Oral History,* however, was unquestionably Smith's strongest novel until that time and the critical beginning point for most literary scholars. Smith explained that *Oral History* represented "the first time I conceived of a novel in-

61. Arnold, "Interview with Lee Smith," 244; Linda Harris, "Awakening Consciousness: From Crystal Spangler to Ivy Rowe in Lee Smith's Fiction," unpublished paper, University of Richmond, April 1990, p. 2.

62. By this time she had settled comfortably as a part of the Chapel Hill writers' community that included James Seay, Doris Betts, Roy Blount, Jr., Clyde Edgerton, Reynolds Price, and her former teacher Louis D. Rubin, Jr. In 1981 she and Seay were divorced, her short story collection *Cakewalk* was published, and she became a member of the English faculty at North Carolina State University, Raleigh, where she has since continued except for various leaves of absence.

63. PBS even took an option on filming *Oral History* as a five-part miniseries for "American Playhouse." Ringle, "Southern Voice," sec. D, p. 1.

stead of an elongation of a short story. . . . I learned from reading William Faulkner's *The Sound and the Fury* that I could have different segments that would not stand alone by themselves but could combine to make a story." But with this novel Smith also finally discovered a vehicle for using her Appalachian subject matter and her ideas about the cultural expectations of women. Strong mountain women are some of Smith's most moving characters and storytellers in this novel. And Smith was no longer shy about drawing elements from the stuff of ordinary life and employing them as elements of her art, in what Fred Hobson has called "K-Mart Realism, or its even poorer country cousin . . . Grit Lit." In drawing these elements out of context and reworking them in her fiction, Smith sometimes achieves a postmodern sense of revealing "truth" as only a reified form created by a self-serving authority. The multiple narrators and fictive audiences that characterize her mature work evoke multiple perspectives that expose that "truth" as mere subjectivity. In this respect, Smith echoes Annie Dillard's blurring of fact and fiction to the end that both writers reject culturally imposed definitions. Smith's advocacy of women's issues and of Appalachian culture resists the larger culture's dismissal of both.[64]

In 1985, Smith married columnist Hal Crowther. In this year she also published *Family Linen,* the story of a woman who suffers from headaches because she has repressed the memory of her father's murder. The story is, in part, another tale of the victimization of women: Sybill's father had regularly raped his mentally retarded sister-in-law. But ever since *Black Mountain Breakdown,* Smith has created female characters who resist their oppression. In *Family Linen,* when Sybill's mother discovers the continual rape, she ends the situation violently by murdering her husband and hiding his body in an old well. *Saving Grace* (1995) records the struggle of a young Appalachian woman to escape the violence and exploitation of fundamentalist religion. Perhaps Smith's strongest female character was created in her novel *Fair and Tender Ladies* (1988). She discovered the epistolary structure for the story when she went to a yard sale in Greensboro, North Carolina, where she bought "the letters of this old woman who had died—all the letters she had ever written in her life. I took them home and read them and it was just real clear that if she'd had a chance to be educated and not have five children she

64. Tom McKnight, "An Interview with Lee Smith," *Appalachian Heritage* 16:2 (1988): 57; Fred Hobson, *The Southern Writer in the Postmodern World* (Athens, Ga., 1991), 11.

might have really been a writer of some note." The story does echo Smith's experience of having to write in the brief spaces of time between job and family commitments. It also reflects Smith's determination to create strong female characters as role models for her own life. "My mother was dying while I was writing that book," notes Smith, "and we were having some problems with our teenagers and different things. One thing I've always done in my own writing . . . is to write to create a role model for myself. With Ivy Rowe, I really needed to be making up somebody who could just take whatever 'shit hit the fan.' Sort of assimilate it and go on." Ivy Rowe is, indeed, a woman who weathers every physical obstacle, who successfully resists social censure, and who ends life happily because she has, as Smith once advocated at Hollins, had the "chance to mess up, or clean up" her own life. Or, in the metaphor of the novel, Ivy Rowe realizes that she can climb Blue Star Mountain by herself whenever she chooses.[65]

In 1989, Smith published her second collection of short stories, *Me and My Baby View the Eclipse,* and in 1992 published *The Devil's Dream,* a cycle of stories linking an Appalachian family's growth to the development of the country and western music industry. The novel is a natural extension of Smith's work to date. Structurally, the novel is presented as an "album," with each chapter as a song on that album. Eschewing the single first-person narrator, the structure embodies the feminist assertion that all voices must be heard in a society. In Smith's early novels, a common metaphor for women's paralysis and repression is silence or restricted communication. With each successive novel, Smith's protagonists have progressively discovered their own voices: Ivy Rowe pours out her thoughts in private letters; Katie Cocker takes to the stages of Nashville and sings her own songs publicly. On the occasion of receiving the 1988 North Carolina Distinguished Service Award for Women, Smith echoed Katie Cocker's thoughts at the opening to *The Devil's Dream,* and I quote Smith here at length:

> Speaking strictly as a writer, I frankly don't know whether I have been of any service to anybody at all; but in my work, this is what I have tried to do—I have tried to write honestly about average women and their lives. I have tried to write about the dangers of passivity. I have tried to write about the kind of

65. Ringle, "Southern Voice," sec. D, p. 1; Virginia Smith, "Conversation with Lee Smith," 785. In 1989, *Fair and Tender Ladies* was made into the off-Broadway production *Ivy Rowe,* starring Barbara Bates Smith and directed by Mark Hunter.

woman whose life is not usually recorded, the kind of woman whose life is marked mostly by those great rites of passage common to us all: births, deaths, illnesses, loss—things like Christmas, putting in the garden, and canning the beans. . . .

It took me years to understand that our first responsibility is to *ourselves*. In the South that I grew up in, this notion was—of course—heresy. There was a pattern that well-brought-up girls were expected to fall right into, there were roles already laid out for us by our parents, by the men we would marry, by the schools we would attend, by society itself. It was a canvas like a paint-by-number set; all we had to do was fill ourselves in. We were to be of service, sure, but to our children, to our husbands, to our parents, to those less fortunate than ourselves . . . in fact, we would be so busy, all our lives long, that we would almost never have time to stop and remember ourselves as the young women we were at 20, the young women you are now, or see ourselves again as full to bursting with potential, with hope, with idealism, with possibility—as you are now. . . .

Anyway, this whole idea of *women* and *service* is a minefield, as you see. . . .

I have fallen into every pitfall in that minefield; have spent years there. I am covered with battle scars.

Smith's reflections here seem not simply an echo of Katie Cocker's School of Hard Knocks, but a rehearsal of the cultural restrictions that have historically faced all women. Smith's work has demonstrated how damaging cultural definitions have persisted for southern women who, despite often enlightened educational rhetoric, have become "fair and tender ladies" cramped and confined by cultural forces that stripped them of professional futures and left them with only the memory of personal aspirations.

Carol Gilligan argues that a woman's "different voice" involves "not only the silence of women but the difficulty in hearing what they say when they speak."[66] The protagonists in her early stories portray the damaging social roles that are still forced upon women in our culture, but the fact that the undergraduate Smith could identify and write about that problem was a sign that she, like Ivy Rowe, was beginning to realize that she could climb her own literary Blue Star Mountain—and do so without the permission of oth-

66. Acceptance speech for the North Carolina Distinguished Service Award for Women, 1988, in North Carolina Collection, Wilson Library, University of North Carolina at Chapel Hill; Carol Gilligan, *In a Different Voice: Psychological Theory and Women's Development* (Cambridge, Mass., 1982), 173.

ers. And in her writing she has listened not only to people's words but to their silences as well. In accepting her Appalachian roots and coming to terms with her own self-definition as a woman and writer, Smith has been persuaded to move beyond definitions of problems to the establishment of alternative, resisting role models.

Afterword

$\mathcal{W}$hat creates a productive writing community for women? In the case of the Hollins Group, not all of the influences are mysterious. As deceptive as statistics can sometimes be, they still provide some intriguing clues to cultural change. In 1870, women constituted 21 percent of all students enrolled in institutions of higher learning in this country; a century later, that number had risen to 41.9 percent. By 1962, more than 53 percent of all female college graduates held jobs. These numbers alone could have predicted some of the social and political upheaval on the campuses, in the workplaces, and in the homes of Americans during the 1960s. The greatest number of American women *ever* were attending college and then entering the work force and creating new patterns of home life for their families. Books such as Betty Friedan's *Feminine Mystique* transformed into national issues the grievances of women who felt that their education was not solely a preparation for the roles of wife and mother. Women also took instruction from the civil rights movement, seeing in the goals of African Americans a desire for opportunity and freedom from cultural stereotypes with which they too could identify. Undeniably, the effect of higher education for women in the country has always been to expand women's allotted sphere and, in doing so, to consistently jar cultural conventions.[1]

Statistics also suggest—almost against all logic—that women's colleges

1. Solomon, *Company of Educated Women*, 63; Chafe, *American Woman*, 219.

have remained in the vanguard of these changes. The number of women's colleges fell from its high point in 1890 of approximately 216 colleges to just over half that number by the end of the 1960s. Yet despite dwindling numbers attending these colleges during that decade, their alumnae constituted 35.1 percent of high-achieving women in this country. These numbers suggest that women's colleges have remained highly successful at attracting talented young women and at educating and supporting their students' aspirations. The case of Hollins is representative of that point. What becomes even more intriguing about Hollins is how an outward peacefulness on the campus co-existed with great internal change within the student body. No radical protests interrupted classes or cotillions; disagreements were civil and negotiated. Yet this small southern women's college still came—by mannerly indirection—to a point that the Seven Sisters reached far more directly and with greater fiscal support. This phenomenon was what Lee Smith was trying to label by describing Hollins as a womb: a dynamic, creative, and safe place for young southern women to discover their identities and their voices.[2]

One hazard of studying the foreground of successful careers is to overly romanticize the effect of college experiences as being central to development. There was nothing inevitable about the success of women's colleges. Such institutions have always faced difficult cultural reservations about whether they should exist at all. As we have seen, the tenuous cultural status of women's institutions often made fundraising and grant approvals even more difficult, and regionalism in the South exacerbated that problem even further. In the case of Hollins, even the leaders most supportive of rigorous academic standards for women could still question whether this quest for an intellectual life was entirely prudent, whether it could go too far and ultimately be a disservice to both student and community. Advocates for the spiritual survival of women's colleges had to adapt strategies calculated to reassure a broad and uneasy society, as had President Randolph, that the higher education of women was at least an enhancement of a lady's social polish and most certainly would undergird the civil government. Far from being inevitable, it remains a small wonder that women's colleges gained the financial and popular support that has allowed them, for more than a century, to provide a space in which women could venture their own ideas.

Little, too, was inevitable about the establishment or success of the writing

2. Solomon, *Company of Educated Women,* 44; Oates and Williamson, "Women's Colleges," 797.

program at Hollins. Women's colleges had, for years, encouraged student writing and yet had seldom seen the success that Hollins' program achieved in the single graduating class of 1967. Undeniably, the Hollins Group benefited from the instruction of Louis Rubin; but they also benefited from his ties to the New Critical publishing establishment. Because Rubin liked his students and respected their work, he chose to use his influence to draw them along with him as he progressed to become a central figure in the southern literary establishment. Having gained this entrée, Hollins students could—and have—followed their own lights. Dillard's writing is highly meditative, piercingly attentive of nature, and bears almost no mark of the southern nostalgia that Jefferson Humphries associates with Rubin. MacKethan and Jones have become strongly feminist in their critical studies of southern literature. Smith, a profoundly feminist novelist, has ventured into postmodern

Hollins College creative writing program reunion, November 1986; left to right, Richard Dillard, Louis Rubin, William Jay Smith, and George Garrett.
Photo by Richard Braaten

writing which, again, Humphries declares to be outside the realm of Rubin's interests. A Hollins network of writers would not have succeeded, even with Rubin's influence, had the writers themselves not been charged with high ambitions and strong personal visions. In *Daughters of Time*, MacKethan's garden metaphor almost exactly states this relationship in noting that she was studying "daughters of time who have turned the father's house of fiction into mothers' gardens of lifegiving, freedom-singing song," women who "found ways to name themselves and their experience in a South that promoted men's versions of culture more radically and for a longer time than other regions."[3]

I do not believe I have either overromanticized or overemphasized the influence of four or five collegiate years in the formation of these women's careers. Certainly, one of the effects of college life has always been to help a young person make that cultural passage from a young person dependent upon the opinion of others into an adult who has a clearer vision of whom she wants to be; and historically, women's colleges have been exceptionally helpful to women in this regard. Instruction and publishing ties were helpful to the Hollins Group, but by their own judgment, their association with each other at Hollins was the most significant influence on their progress as writers. These young women came to college with the high hopes shared by many college freshmen. Like many students, each carried with her the yet-undiscovered subject of her interest—nature, Appalachia, feminism, or cultural history. In *An American Childhood*, Dillard recalls that she had early been drawn to wonder at the awe-inspiring design of nature, a wonder that would lead her to write about her reflections about Hollins' Tinker Creek. Smith, who had determined to abandon Appalachia as a subject for her writing, finally turned to it as the very center point of her literary interests. In *Daughters of Time*, MacKethan would observe that she conceived her idea of a study of the voices of southern women storytellers by recalling the letters that her mother began writing to her the year she left to go to college. *Tomorrow Is Another Day* arose from Jones's discovery that the restrictions on the lives of nineteenth-century southern women writers bore disturbing similarity to her own. Women's colleges of the 1960s did not inspire these interests so much as they provided the "womb" of which Smith wrote: a sanctuary in which women could recognize the issues that concerned them. Women's col-

3. MacKethan, *Daughters of Time*, 13, 14.

leges provided women with a forum in which their interests would be taken seriously and in which they could explore with other women the questions that seemed to cluster about them especially because of the fact that they were women.

In assessing the Hollins Group, it is crucial to remember that these women were sent to Hollins to be molded into a genteel feminine ideal. Paradoxically, the school may have provided some cultural polish, but the spirit of the women and the intellectual climate of the writing program overcame the conventional images so that instead of emulating a feminine ideal, they discovered new, satisfying identities as *writers*. As writers, they learned to challenge the literary establishment of their college. As writers, they could imaginatively experience other lives and decide the ones they would ultimately choose to follow. Sharing many of the same courses, they encountered many of the same intellectual issues and, through their discussions and disagreements, shared the exploration of those ideas. They learned the politics of publishing and the habit of working to place themselves in positions in which they could support their friends by accepting their writing for publication. In the 1960s, Smith laughingly wrote of Hollins women leading themselves into a Promised Land. In 1990, MacKethan used the wording of a scholar in saying that women must become their own storytellers. Such women "went against cultural and familial expectations in risking the changes that their roles as storytellers demanded" and in doing so "have successfully brought themselves and a woman's world into creative presence."[4] Becoming writers was crucial to these women because their autobiographical, critical, and fictional writings have been their means of telling their stories, of describing the unique perspective from which each woman sees the world.

The very nature of writing itself explains why the study of the Hollins Group's collegiate writing is vital for us to examine. In it we see the tentative experimentation, the false starts, and the glimmering insights that mark the work of inquiring women and maturing writers. As MacKethan suggests, the inquiring woman can scarcely be separated from the maturing writer. In her own collegiate writing, we can see how her concerns turned from romantic fancy to literary and cultural analysis; and in Jones's writing, from the broad realm of politics to the more focused issues of feminism. In Smith's collegiate writing, we see how her humor is intertwined with a deep concern about a

4. Ibid.

woman's precarious role in society. Dillard's writing shows her struggles with religion and with the metaphor that can best contain her own budding philosophies. The apprentice writing shows not just the evolution of thought but the writer's skill of pushing beyond self as audience. We see ways in which the writer finally connects personal experience to the issues shared more broadly in her society. In another context years later, Dillard would muse about the relationship between writer and writing, wondering, "How many books do we read from which the writer lacked courage to tie off the umbilical cord?" The apprentice work shows us young writers trying to discover that moment.[5]

In *One Writer's Beginnings*, Eudora Welty identifies three skills essential to her craft: listening, learning to see, and finding a voice. "Writing a story or a novel," she observes, "is one way of discovering sequence in experience, of stumbling upon cause and effect in the happenings of a writer's own life."[6] The writing community at Hollins offers us one paradigm for aiding women in their search to find a voice, to make sense of their lives, and to articulate that vision to the world. And thirty years later, the world of ideas and literature finds itself all the richer for the writing, editing, and publishing of these fair and tender ladies from Tinker Creek.

5. Annie Dillard, *Writing Life*, 7.
6. Although Eudora Welty was of a different generation from the Hollins Group, she shared at least two touch points with them. Before transferring to the University of Wisconsin, Welty attended the Mississippi State College for Women, a two-year women's college in Columbus that was, in her parents' opinion, not "too far from home." At MSCW, Welty later wrote, "I was lucky enough to have found for myself, at the very beginning, an outside shell, that of freshman reporter on our college newspaper," the *Spectator*, where she was able to test some of her early writing. Welty, *One Writer's Beginnings* (Cambridge, Mass., 1984), 77, 79.

SELECTED BIBLIOGRAPHY

Abbott, Jill. "Flannery O'Connor Discusses Writing." *Hollins Columns,* October 24, 1963, p. 3.

"An Act to Amend the Charter of the Valley Union Education Society." December 19, 1855. In Fishburn Archives, Hollins College.

"An Act to Incorporate Hollins Institute." February 2, 1901. In Fishburn Archives, Hollins College.

"An Act to Incorporate the Valley Union Education Society." January 13, 1844. In Fishburn Archives, Hollins College.

Alderson, Laura. "You Can Go Home Again." *Hollins* (April 1981): 23–24.

Alexander, Maxine, ed. *Speaking For Ourselves: Women of the South.* New York, 1977.

Allen, John. Personal interview, January 17, 1991.

Ammons, Elizabeth. *Conflicting Stories: American Women Writers at the Turn into the Twentieth Century.* New York, 1991.

Annual of Hollins Institute. In Fishburn Archives, Hollins College. Roanoke, Va., 1888–91.

Armistead, Mary Bland. "Privacy 'Up the Creek' on Girls' River Jaunt." *Roanoke World-News,* June 24, 1966, p. 10.

Arnold, Edwin T. "An Interview with Lee Smith." *Appalachian Journal* 11 (1984): 240–54.

Ashley, Kathleen M., ed. *Victor Turner and the Construction of Cultural Criticism: Between Literature and Anthropology.* Bloomington, Ind., 1990.

Auerbach, Nina. *Communities of Women: An Idea in Fiction.* Cambridge, Mass., 1978.

Baker, John F. "Story Behind the Book: 'Pilgrim at Tinker Creek.'" *Publisher's Weekly,* March 18, 1974.

"Banged Hair." *Album,* 1878. In Fishburn Archives, Hollins College.

Bawer, Bruce. "Poetry and the University." In *Poetry after Modernism,* edited by Robert McDowell. Brownsville, Ore., 1991.

Baym, Nina. "Melodramas of Beset Manhood: How Theories of American Fiction Exclude Women Authors." *American Quarterly* 33 (1981): 123–39.

Beagle, Ben. "Pulitzer Author Prizes Privacy." *Roanoke Times,* May 6, 1975, p. 1.

Beckham, Nancy. Letter to Mrs. Carter, June 1966. In Fishburn Archives, Hollins College.

———. "The Remarkable Voyage of the Rosebud Hobson." *Hollins College Bulletin* (November 1966): 41–45.

———. Telephone interview with author, June 2, 1992.

Belenky, Mary Field, et al. *Women's Ways of Knowing: The Development of Self, Voice, and Mind.* New York, 1986.

Bennett, John. *Strictures on Female Education.* Worcester, Mass., 1795; reprint, New York, 1971.

Benstock, Shari, ed. *The Private Self: Theory and Practice of Women's Autobiographical Writings.* Chapel Hill, 1988.

Berson, Jo, et al., eds. *Beanstalks.* Roanoke, Va., 1964.

Bledstein, Burton J. *The Culture of Professionalism: The Middle Class and the Development of Higher Education in America.* New York, 1976.

Book-of-the-Month Club News (April 1974): n.p.

Buchanan, Harriette C. "Lee Smith: The Storyteller's Voice." In *Southern Women Writers—The New Generation,* edited by Tonette Bond Inge. Tuscaloosa, Ala., 1990.

Buckley, Jo Berson. Telephone interview, July 7, 1992.

Calliope's Comments (Hollins English Department's former newsletter), 1963–67. In Fishburn Archives, Hollins College.

Cantwell, Mary. "A Pilgrim's Progress." *New York Times Magazine,* April 26, 1992, sec. 6, p. 34ff.

Catalogue of the Female Seminary at Botetourt Springs, Virginia, Session 1852–53. Richmond, 1853.

Centennial Celebration of Hollins. Roanoke, Va., 1949.

Chafe, William. *The American Woman: Her Changing Social, Economic, and Political Roles, 1920–1970.* New York, 1972.

Chenetier, Marc. "Tinkering, Extravagance: Thoreau, Melville, and Annie Dillard." *Critique: Studies in Contemporary Fiction* 31 (1990): 157–72.

Clark, Suzanne. "Annie Dillard: The Woman in Nature and the Subject of Nonfiction." In *Literary Nonfiction: Theory, Criticism, Pedagogy,* edited by Chris Anderson. Carbondale, Ill., 1989.

Clifford, James, and George E. Marcus, eds. *Writing Culture: The Poetics and Politics of Ethnography.* Berkeley, 1986.

Cocke, Charles Lewis. "Fifty-second Address to Graduating Class." *Semi-Annual.* 1858. In Fishburn Archives, Hollins College.

———. Personal papers. N.d. In Fishburn Archives, Hollins College.

Conrad, Susan Phinney. *Perish the Thought: Intellectual Women in Romantic America, 1830–1860.* New York, 1976.

Conway, Jill. *The Female Experience in Eighteenth- and Nineteenth-Century America: A Guide to the History of American Women.* New York, 1982.

———. "Perspectives on the History of Women's Education in the U.S." *History of Education Quarterly* 14 (1974).

Cornelius, Roberta D. *The History of Randolph-Macon Woman's College: From the Founding in 1891 through the Year of 1949–1950.* Chapel Hill, 1951.

Cott, Nancy F. *The Bonds of Womanhood: 'Woman's Sphere' in New England, 1780–1835.* New York, 1977.

Coultrap-McQuin, Susan. *Doing Literary Business: American Women Writers in the Nineteenth Century.* Chapel Hill, 1990.

Crist, Renee. "Writers' Reunion." *Hollins* (January 1987): 9.

Delamont, Sara. "Domestic Ideology and Women's Education." In *The Nineteenth-Century Woman: Her Cultural and Physical World,* edited by Sara Delamont and Lorna Duffin. New York, 1978.

Dickinson, Emily. *The Letters of Emily Dickinson.* Edited by Thomas H. Johnson and Theodora Ward. 2 vols. Cambridge, Mass., 1958.

Dillard, Annie Doak. "The Affluent Beatnik." In *The Girl in the Black Raincoat,* edited by George Garrett. New York, 1966.

———. "After Noon." *Cargoes* 53:3 (1966): 32.

———. "Alice." *Cargoes* 51:1 (1963): 12.

———. *An American Childhood.* New York, 1987; paperback reprint, 1988.

———. "Baltimore Oriole." *Cargoes* 53:1 (1965): 15–17.

———. "The Boston Poems of Ho Chi Minh." *Cargoes* 53:4 (1967): 13–14.

———. "Dream Birds, Bird Skins, and Birds." *Cargoes* 53:2 (1966): 6.

———. "The Clearing." *Cargoes* 53:3 (1966): 32.

———. "Education be D——d!" *Hollins Columns,* October 11, 1966, p. 2.

———. *Encounters with Chinese Writers.* New York, 1984; paperback reprint, 1985.

———. "For PLD." *Cargoes* 52:2 (1965): 24.

———. "The Hollins Dateline of Social Progress." *Hollins Columns,* November 19, 1964, p. 4.

———. *Holy the Firm.* New York, 1977; paperback reprints, 1984, 1988.

———. "I Think Continually of Those Who Went Truly Ape." *Cargoes* 53:2 (1966): 7.

———. "John Moore: A Sense of Proportion, a Gracious Heart." *Hollins Magazine* (October 1985): 8–9.

———. "The Last Thing I Saw Before I Closed My Eyes." *Cargoes* 53:2 (1966): 8.

———. "Lee Smith." Brochure for 13th Annual Literary Festival, Old Dominion University. Norfolk, Va., 1990.

———. Letter to author, December 14, 1991.

———. Letter to Tony Thompson, July 17, 1987. In Fishburn Archives, Hollins College.

———. "The Living." *Harper's* (November 1978): 45–64.

———. *The Living.* New York, 1992.

———. *Living by Fiction.* New York, 1982; paperback reprint, 1988.

———. "The Merchant of the Picturesque: One Pattern in Emily Dickinson's Poetry." *Hollins Symposium* 3:1 (1967): 33–42.

———. "Monica at the Window." *Cargoes* 52:2 (1965): 21–22.

———. "New Quiz Tests 'Camp' Insanity." *Hollins Columns,* September 20, 1966, p. 2.

———. "Northern Quebec—August." *Cargoes* 51:1 (1963): 12.

———. Notes to author, September 3, 1996.

———. "On George Gordh's Retirement: An Unsolicited Testimonial." *Hollins* 27:6 (1977): 14–16.

———. "Overlooking Glastonbury." *Cargoes* 52:1 (1964): 22.

———. *Pilgrim at Tinker Creek.* New York, 1974; paperback reprint, 1988.

———. "Rimbaud." *Cargoes* 51:2 (1964): 13.

———. "SGA Lacks Real Powers." *Hollins Columns,* September 29, 1966, p. 2.

———. "Sojourner." *Living Wilderness* (summer 1974): 2–3.

———. "Song for Myself." *Cargoes* 53:1 (1965): 17.

———. *Teaching a Stone to Talk: Expeditions and Encounters.* New York, 1982; paperback reprint, 1988.

———. *Tickets for a Prayer Wheel.* New York, 1974; paperback reprint, 1986.

———. "Walden Pond and Thoreau." M. A. thesis, Hollins College, 1968.

———. "Weekend." In *Beanstalks,* edited by Jo Berson et al. (Roanoke, Va., 1964), 14.

———. "Wilson Discusses His Works." *Hollins Columns,* September 20, 1966, p. 1.

———. *The Writing Life.* New York, 1989; paperback reprint, 1990.

Dillard, Annie Doak, and Anne Bradford. "Hollins Inn Greet with Song." *Hollins Columns,* September 29, 1966, p. 3.

Dillard, Richard, personal interview, March 5, 1991.

———. *News of the Nile.* Chapel Hill, 1971.

Donaldson, Susan. "Gender and the Profession of Letters in the South." In *Rewriting the South: History and Fiction,* edited by Lothar Honnighausen and Valeria Gennaro Lerda. Tubingen, Germany, 1993.

Duke, Paul. "A Southern Literary Giant." *University of Richmond Magazine* 52:3 (1990): 18–20.

Edwards, Allan D., and Dorothy G. Jones. *Community and Community Development.* The Hague, 1976.

Egan, John M. "Golding's View of Man." *America* (January 26, 1963): 140–41.

Epps, Garrett. "Learning to Write Can Be Fun." *New York Times Book Review,* August 7, 1988, p. 1.

Evans, Sara M. *Born for Liberty: A History of Women in America.* New York, 1989.

Everett, John R. "Nation Cannot Flourish with Uneducated Women." *Hollins Herald* (July 1957): 1ff.

———. "Neglecting the Wife Can Prove Dangerous." *Hollins Herald* (October 1951): 1ff.

Faderman, Lillian. *Surpassing the Love of Men: Romantic Friendship and Love between Women from the Renaissance to the Present.* New York, 1981.

Fekete, John. *The Critical Twilight: Explorations in the Ideology of Anglo-American Literary Theory from Eliot to McLuhan.* London, 1977.

Fetterman, John. "16 Girls on a Raft." *Louisville Courier-Journal Magazine* (July 24, 1966): 17–22.

Fox-Genovese, Elizabeth. *Feminism Without Illusions: A Critique of Individualism.* Chapel Hill, 1991.

———. "Scarlett O'Hara: The Southern Lady as New Woman." *American Quarterly* 33:4 (1981): 391–411.

———. *Within the Plantation Household: Black and White Women of the Old South.* Chapel Hill, 1988.

Freedman, Estelle. "Separatism as Strategy: Female Institution Building and American Feminism, 1870–1930." *Feminist Studies* 5 (1979): 512–29.

Friedlander, Amy. "A More Perfect Christian Womanhood: Higher Learning for a New South." In *Education and the Rise of the New South,* edited by Ronald K. Goodenow and Arthur O. White. Boston, 1981.

Friedman, Jean E., and William G. Shade, eds. *Our American Sisters: Women in American Life and Thought.* Boston, 1973.

Geertz, Clifford. *The Interpretation of Cultures.* New York, 1973.

Genovese, Eugene D. *Roll, Jordan, Roll: The World the Slaves Made.* New York, 1972.

Gilbert, Sandra M., and Susan Gubar. *The Madwoman in the Attic: The Woman Writer and the Nineteenth-Century Literary Imagination.* New Haven, Conn., 1979.

———. *No Man's Land: The Place of the Woman Writer in the Twentieth Century.* New Haven, Conn., 1988, 1989.

Gilligan, Carol. *In a Different Voice: Psychological Theory and Women's Development.* Cambridge, Mass., 1982.

Golding, William. *The Hot Gates and Other Occasional Pieces.* London, 1966.

Gottschalk, Earl G., Jr. "Huck Finn Revisited: Youthful Adventure on Old Man River." *National Observer,* September 25, 1967, p. 1ff.

Graham, Patricia Albjerg. "Expansion and Exclusion: A History of Women in American Higher Education." *Signs* 3 (1978): 759–73.

Grande, Luke M. "The Appeal of Golding." *Commonweal* (January 25, 1963): 457–59.

Hall, Jacquelyn Dowd, and Anne Firor Scott. "Women in the South." In *Interpreting Southern History: Historiographical Essays in Honor of Sanford W. Higginbotham,* edited by John B. Boles and Evelyn Thomas Nolen. Baton Rouge, 1987.

Harris, Linda A. "Awakening Consciousness: From Crystal Spangler to Ivy Rowe in Lee Smith's Fiction." Unpublished paper, University of Richmond, 1990.

Harrison, Elizabeth Jane. *Female Pastoral: Women Writers Re-Visioning the American South.* Knoxville, 1991.

Hearsey, Marguerite Capen. "Hollins College: Unleveling Education." *Junior League Magazine* (March 1930): 39–40.

Heilbrun, Carolyn G. *Writing a Woman's Life.* New York, 1988.

Hershey, Katharine Corbin. *Virginian-Pilot* (July 10, 1966): sec. C, p. 4.

Hill, Dorothy Combs. *Lee Smith.* New York, 1992.

Hobson, Fred. *The Southern Writer in the Postmodern World.* Athens, Ga., 1991.

Hohner, Robert A. "Southern Education in Transition: William Waugh Smith, the Carnegie Foundation, and the Methodist Church." *History of Education Quarterly* 27 (1987): 181–203.

Hollins Columns, 1944–67. In Fishburn Archives, Hollins College.

Hollins Herald, 1951–59. In Fishburn Archives, Hollins College.

Horowitz, Helen Lefkowitz. *Alma Mater: Design and Experience in the Women's Colleges from Their Nineteenth-Century Beginnings to the 1930s.* New York, 1984.

———. "The 1960s and the Transformation of Campus Cultures." *History of Education Quarterly* 26:1 (1986): 1–38.

Howe, Florence, ed. *Women and the Power to Change.* New York, 1975.

Humphries, Jefferson, ed. *Southern Literature and Literary Theory.* Athens, Ga., 1990.

Hurt, Henry. "Hollins Girls on 'Rosebud' See Vicksburg, Resume Trip." *Roanoke World-News,* June 17, 1966.

Janeway, Elizabeth. *Man's World, Woman's Place: A Study in Social Mythology.* New York, 1971.

Johnston, Eliza. Letters to John P. Johnston, 1839–40. In Fishburn Archives, Hollins College.

Jones, Anne Goodwyn. "A Landscape of Her Own." *American Quarterly* 37 (1985): 619–26.

———. Telephone interview, January 6, 1993.

———. *Tomorrow Is Another Day: The Woman Writer in the South, 1859–1936.* Baton Rouge, 1981.

———. "The World of Lee Smith." In *Women Writers of the Contemporary South,* edited by Peggy Whitman Prenshaw. Jackson, Miss., 1984.

Kearns, Francis E. "Salinger and Golding: Conflict on the Campus." *America* (January 26, 1963): 136–39.

Kearns, Katherine. "Lee Smith." In *Dictionary of Literary Biography Yearbook, 1983,* edited by Mary Bruccoli and Jean W. Ross. Detroit, 1984.

Keller, Evelyn Fox, and Helene Moglen. "Competition and Feminism: Conflicts for Academic Women." *Signs* 12 (1987): 493–511.

Kelley, Mary. *Woman's Being, Woman's Place: Female Identity and Vocation in American History.* Boston, 1979.

———. *Private Woman, Public Stage: Literary Domesticity in Nineteenth-Century America.* New York, 1984.

Kerber, Linda K. "Separate Spheres, Female Worlds, Woman's Place: The Rhetoric of Women's History." *Journal of American History* 75 (1988): 9–39.

———. "Women and Individualism in American History." *Massachusetts Review* 30 (1989): 589–609.

Kerber, Linda K., and Jane De Hart-Mathews, eds. *Women's America: Refocusing the Past.* New York, 1987.

Kronik, John W. "On Men Mentoring Women: Then and Now." *Profession* 90 (1990): 52–57.

Lawson, Anna Logan. "Thinker, Poet, Pilgrim." *Hollins* (May 1974): 12.

"Lee Smith." *Contemporary Authors* 114 (1983): 422.

"Lee Smith." *Contemporary Authors* 119 (1987): 345–47.

Lerner, Gerda. *The Creation of Patriarchy.* New York, 1986.

Levine, David O. *The American College and the Culture of Aspiration, 1915–1940.* Ithaca, N.Y., 1986.

"Locals." *Euzelian Album,* 1878. In Fishburn Archives, Hollins College.

Lodge, Michelle. "Lee Smith." *Publishers Weekly,* September 20, 1985, pp. 110–11.

Logan, John A., Jr. *Hollins: An Act of Faith for 125 Years.* New York, 1968.

"Lord of the Campus." *Time,* June 22, 1962, p. 64.

Lucas, Nancy. "Annie Dillard." In *Dictionary of Literary Biography Yearbook: 1980,* edited by Karen L. Rood, Jean W. Ross, and Richard Ziegfeld. Detroit, 1981.

McBryde, John M., Jr. "Womanly Education for Women." *Sewanee Review* 14 (1907): 467–84.

McCain, James Ross. "The Growth of Agnes Scott College, 1889–1955." *Agnes Scott College Bulletin* (April 1956): 1–4.

McConahay, Mary Davidson. "'Into the Bladelike Arms of God': The Quest for Meaning Through Symbolic Language in Thoreau and Dillard." *Denver Quarterly* 20 (1985): 103–16.

McCorkle, Jill. "Achievement, Tradition, Vision, 1842–1992." *Hollins* (October 1991): 54.

McGehee, Overton. "'Voice of Poor White Trash' Isn't How Smith Would Say It." *Richmond Times-Dispatch,* May 4, 1989, sec. D, pp. 1–2.

McIlroy, Gary. "Pilgrim at Tinker Creek and the Burden of Science." *American Literature* 59 (1987): 71–84.

———. *"Pilgrim at Tinker Creek* and the Social Legacy of *Walden." South Atlantic Quarterly* 85 (1986): 111–22.

MacKethan, Lucinda Hardwick. "Artists and Beauticians: Balance in Lee Smith's Fiction." *Southern Literary Journal* 14 (1982): 3–14.

———. *Daughters of Time: Creating Woman's Voice in Southern Story.* Athens, Ga., 1990.

———. *The Dream of Arcady: Place and Time in Southern Literature.* Baton Rouge, 1980.

———. Telephone interview, September 16, 1991.

McKnight, Tom. "An Interview with Lee Smith." *Appalachian Heritage* 16:2 (1988): 57–60.

McPherson, William. "A Conversation with Annie Dillard." *Book-of-the-Month Club News* (April 1974): 1–4, 25.

Manning, Carol S., ed. *The Female Tradition in Southern Literature.* Urbana, Ill., 1993.

Martenstein, Lynn. "Author Localizes Book Setting, Recalls Undergraduate Years." *Quadrangle* (March 7, 1974): 5–6.

Mayo, A. D. *Southern Women in the Recent Educational Movement in the South.* Washington, 1892; reprint, Baton Rouge, 1978.

Meese, Elizabeth A. *Crossing the Double-Cross: The Practice of Feminist Criticism.* Chapel Hill, 1986.

Merriam, Sharon. "Mentors and Proteges: A Critical Review of the Literature." *Adult Education Quarterly* 30 (1983): 161–73.

Merritt, Robert. "Gibbons Miles Away from 'Ellen Foster.'" *Richmond Times-Dispatch,* May 7, 1991, sec. B, p. 5.

Montgomery, Anne N. "Hollins College: A School with More Than a Century of Tradition." *Iron Worker* (winter 1954–55): 1–12.

Morgan, Robin, ed. *Sisterhood Is Powerful: An Anthology of Writings from the Women's Liberation Movement.* New York, 1970.

Newcomer, Mabel. *A Century of Higher Education for American Women.* New York, 1959.

Niederer, Frances J. *Hollins College: An Illustrated History.* Charlottesville, Va., 1973.

Oates, Mary J., and Susan Williamson, "Women's Colleges and Women Achievers," *Signs* 3 (1978): 795–806.

O'Barr, Jean F. *Women and a New Academy: Gender and Cultural Contexts.* Madison, Wisc., 1989.

O'Brien, Michael, ed. *All Clever Men, Who Make Their Way: Critical Discourse in the Old South.* Fayetteville, Ark., 1982.

———. *The Idea of the American South, 1920–1941.* Baltimore, 1979.

———. *Rethinking the South: Essays in Intellectual History.* Baltimore, 1988.

Packard, Donna Marie. "Conservative Progress in the Higher Education of Southern Women: Hollins Institute, 1855–1901." B. A. thesis, Princeton University, 1979.

Palmer, Paulina. *Contemporary Women's Fiction: Narrative Practice and Feminist Theory.* New York, 1989.

Pieschel, Bridget Smith, and Stephen Robert Pieschel. *Loyal Daughters: One Hundred Years at Mississippi University for Women, 1884–1984.* Jackson, Miss., 1984.

Pryor, Judith. "What Goes On in the Ladies Room? Sarah Orne Jewett, Annie Fields, and Their Community of Women." *Massachusetts Review* 30 (1989): 610–28.

Randall, Julia. *The Puritan Carpenter.* Chapel Hill, 1965.

Ravenel, Shannon. "Achievement, Tradition, Vision, 1842–1992." *Hollins* (October 1991): 13.

Reilly, Rosalind. "*Oral History:* The Enchanted Circle of Narrative and Dream." *Southern Literary Journal* 23:1 (1990): 72–92.

Review of *Something in the Wind* by Lee Smith. *Virginia Quarterly Review* 47 (1971): xcvi.

Richardson, Eudora Ramsay. "The Case of the Women's College in the South." *South Atlantic Quarterly* 29 (1930): 126–39.

Ringle, Ken. "A Southern Voice in Her Own Write." *Raleigh News and Observer,* December 9, 1988, sec. B, p. 1ff.

Rosenbaum, Claire Millhiser. *A Gem of a College: The History of Westhampton College, 1914–1989.* Richmond, Va., 1989.

Rosenberg, Rosalind. *Beyond Separate Spheres: Intellectual Roots of Modern Feminism.* New Haven, Conn., 1982.

Rubin, Louis D., Jr. *The American South: Portrait of a Culture.* Baton Rouge, 1980.

———. *An Apple for My Teacher: Twelve Authors Tell About Teachers Who Made the Difference.* Chapel Hill, 1987.

———. *The Curious Death of the Novel: Essays in American Literature.* Baton Rouge, 1967.

———. "The Difficulties of Being a Southern Writer Today; or, Getting Out from Under Faulkner." *Journal of Southern History* 29 (1963): 486–94.

———. *The Faraway Country: Writers of the Modern South.* Seattle, 1963.

———. "Hollins College: An Account of 25 Years in the Life of a School." 1967. In Fishburn Archives, Hollins College.

———. "The Justice Behind Women's Lib." *Chapel Hill Weekly,* January 23, 1972.

———, ed. *The Literary South.* Baton Rouge, 1979.

———. "My Say on Southern Literature." *Publishers Weekly,* May 23, 1986, p. 102.

———. *No Place on Earth: James Branch Cabell, Ellen Glasgow, and Richmond-in-Virginia.* Austin, Tex., 1959.

————. Personal interview, May 7, 1991.

————. "Southern Letters and the State of the Art." *Southern Literary Journal* 14:2 (1982): 3–7.

————. *Teach the Freeman: The Correspondence of R. B. Hayes and the Slater Fund for Negro Education, 1881–1893.* Baton Rouge, 1959.

————. *The Teller in the Tale.* Seattle, 1967.

————. "Thomas Wolfe: Homage Renewed." *Sewanee Review* 97 (1989): 261–76.

————. *The Wary Fugitives: Four Poets and the South.* Baton Rouge, 1977.

————. "The Way It Was with Southern Literary Study: A Reminiscence." *Mississippi Quarterly* 43 (1990): 147–62.

————. *The Writer in the South: Studies in a Literary Community.* Athens, Ga., 1972.

Rubin, Louis D., Jr., and Blyden Jackson. *Black Poetry in America: Two Essays in Historical Interpretation.* Baton Rouge, 1974.

Rubin, Louis D., Jr., and Robert D. Jacobs, eds. *Southern Renascence: The Literature of the Modern South.* Baltimore, 1953; paperback reprint, 1966.

Rubin, Louis D., Jr., and James J. Kilpatrick. *The Lasting South.* Chicago, 1957.

Rudolph, Frederick. *The American College and University: A History.* New York, 1962.

Scandling, Mark W. "Profiles of Three North Carolina Writers." M. A. thesis, University of North Carolina at Chapel Hill, 1979.

Scheick, William J. "Annie Dillard: Narrative Fringe." In *Contemporary American Women Writers,* edited by Catherine Rainwater and William J. Scheick. Lexington, Ky., 1985.

Scott, Ann Firor. *The Southern Lady from Pedestal to Politics, 1830–1930.* Chicago, 1970.

Seller, Maxine S. "The United States." In *International Handbook of Women's Education,* edited by Gail P. Kelly. New York, 1989.

Semi-Annual, 1892–93. In Fishburn Archives, Hollins College.

Sipchen, Bob. "Down-to-Earth Writer Inspires Awestruck Devotion." *Richmond Times-Dispatch,* July 3, 1992, sec. D, p. 7.

Smith, Lee Marshall. Acceptance speech for the North Carolina Distinguished Service Award for Women, 1988. North Carolina Collection, Wilson Library, University of North Carolina at Chapel Hill.

————. Appalachian State University commencement address, Boone, N. C., May 19, 1991.

————. "Arlan's a Must for Fashions." *Hollins Columns,* April 26, 1966, p. 5.

————. "Beanstalks to Be Published May 1." *Hollins Columns,* April 16, 1964, p. 1.

————. *Black Mountain Breakdown.* New York, 1980.

————. "The Bubba Stories." *Southern Review* 27 (1991): 115–35.

————. *Cakewalk.* New York, 1981.

————. "Collective Psyche Is Probed." *Hollins Columns,* January 10, 1967, p. 2ff.

———. "Columnist Fixes Navel Site." *Hollins Columns,* November 1, 1966, p. 2.

———. *The Devil's Dream.* New York, 1992.

———. "85 for Candida in Best of All Possible Dorms." *Hollins Columns,* April 23, 1964, p. 2.

———. "Eudora Welty's Beginnings." *Southern Literary Journal* 17:2 (1985): 120–26.

———. "Exams Made Easy by System." *Hollins Columns,* January 17, 1967, p. 2.

———. *Fair and Tender Ladies.* New York, 1988.

———. *Family Linen.* New York, 1985.

———. *Fancy Strut.* New York, 1973.

———. "Fatback Season." *Cargoes* 52:1 (1964): 41–49.

———. "Genesis." In *Beanstalks,* edited by Jo Berson et al. Roanoke, Va., 1964.

———. "H. A. Finds Paris Is 'Tres Formidable!'" *Hollins Columns,* February 25, 1965, p. 3.

———. "H. A. Learns Art of Gorging in France and How to Be French Tom Joneses." *Hollins Columns,* March 18, 1965, p. 3.

———. "Ha, Ha, Ha, Ha Cry, Jane, Cry Ha, Ha, Ha, Ha." *Hollins Columns,* May 14, 1964, p. 2.

———. "Hollins Four Go-Goes to Beatnik Folk Tune." *Hollins Columns,* October 25, 1966, pp. 4–5.

———. "Hollins' Myths Are Explained." *Hollins Columns,* November 15, 1966, p. 2.

———. "In Her Own Write." Lecture at Virginia Museum, Richmond, March 7, 1990.

———. "Is the U.S. a WAST Eland?" *Hollins Columns,* November 22, 1966, p. 2.

———. "Interview: Lee Smith." Edited by Nancy C. Parrish. *Appalachian Journal* 19 (1992): 394–401.

———. Personal interview, July 25–26, 1991.

———. "Jumping Juniors Flatten Faculty." *Hollins Columns,* March 15, 1966, p. 3.

———. *The Last Day the Dogbushes Bloomed.* New York, 1968.

———. "Little Arthur." *Cargoes* 52:1 (1964): 51–59.

———. "Lex and the College Girl." *Hollins Columns,* October 18, 1966, p. 2.

———. *Me and My Baby View the Eclipse.* New York, 1990.

———. "Miss Hawthorne and the Beautiful Song." *Cargoes* 52:2 (1965): 37–47.

———. "Moral Conformity: Poor Conception." *Hollins Columns,* October 4, 1966, p. 2.

———. "Olson Finds Your Friend and Mine Good for One Term Only." *Hollins Columns,* December 3, 1964, p. 3.

———. *Oral History.* New York, 1983.

———. "Nemerov Speaks About Metaphors." *Hollins Columns,* February 22, 1966, p. 3ff.

———. "The Red Parts." *Cargoes* 53:3 (1966): 44–55.

———. "Rejoyce." *Hollins Columns,* May 3, 1966, p. 2.

———. *Saving Grace.* New York, 1995.

———. *Something in the Wind.* New York, 1971.

———. "Sun Psalm." *Hollins Columns,* April 30, 1964, p. 3.

———. "Thought Might Negate Life." *Hollins Columns,* November 8, 1966, p. 2.

———. "'Twiggy' Is Mod Bod." *Hollins Columns,* December 6, 1966, p. 2.

———. "The Voice Behind the Story." In *Voicelust,* edited by Allen Wier and Don Hendrie, Jr. Lincoln, Nebr., 1985.

———. "The Wading House." In *Beanstalks,* typescript. Personal library of Richard H. W. Dillard. Roanoke, Va.

———. "What, Me Worry?" *Hollins Columns,* February 15, 1966, p. 3.

———. "White Parts; or, The Last Moments of Eula LeBel." *Cargoes* 53:4 (1967): 55–62.

Smith, Lee Marshall, and Jo Berson. "Spinster Blasts Off for '67." *Hollins Columns,* September 29, 1966, p. 4.

Smith, Lee Marshall, and Karen Long. "How to Fox Your Freshman Faux-Pas." *Hollins Columns,* October 8, 1964, p. 4.

———. "Macke Is Nabbed in Snack Bar Assault." *Hollins Columns,* October 15, 1964, p. 3.

———. "The Night That Goodheart Passed: A Parable of Social Pressure; or, On Selfseeking." *Hollins Columns,* November 12, 1964, p. 2ff.

Smith, Linda L. *Annie Dillard.* New York, 1991.

Smith, Virginia A. "On Regionalism, Women's Writing, and Writing as a Woman: A Conversation with Lee Smith." *Southern Review* 26 (1990): 784–95.

Smith, William R. L. *Charles Lewis Cocke: Founder of Hollins College.* Boston, 1921.

Smith-Rosenberg, Carroll. *Disorderly Conduct: Visions of Gender in Victorian America.* New York, 1985.

"Smith Wins Hollins Straw Vote." *Hollins Student Life* (October 20, 1928): 1.

Smyth, Jeannette. "Annie Dillard: Southern Sibyl." *Washington Post,* May 19, 1974, sec. G, p. 1ff.

Solomon, Barbara Miller. *In the Company of Educated Women: A History of Women and Higher Education in America.* New Haven, Conn., 1985.

Spinster, 1898–1967. In Fishburn Archives, Hollins College.

Stafford, William. *Writing the Australian Crawl: Views on the Writer's Vocation.* Ann Arbor, Mich., 1978.

Stanton, Elizabeth Cady, Susan B. Anthony, and Matilda Joslyn Gage. *History of Woman Suffrage.* 6 vols. Vol. 4. Rochester, N.Y., 1902.

Stetar, Joseph. "In Search of a Direction: Southern Higher Education after the Civil War." *History of Education Quarterly* 25 (1985): 341–67.

Stohlman, Martha Lou Lemmon. *The Story of Sweet Briar College.* Sweet Briar, Va., 1956.

Stringer, Patricia A., and Irene Thompson, eds. *Stepping Off the Pedestal: Academic Women in the South.* New York, 1982.

Summer, Bob. "Battles and Campaigns at Algonquin." *Publishers Weekly,* August 18, 1989, p. 31.

Turner, Victor W. *Dramas, Fields, and Metaphors: Symbolic Action in Human Society.* Ithaca, N.Y., 1974.

———. *The Forest of Symbols: Aspects of Ndembu Ritual.* Ithaca, N.Y., 1967.

———. *On the Edge of the Bush: Anthropology as Experience.* Edited by Edith L. B. Turner. Tucson, Ariz., 1985.

———. *The Ritual Process: Structure and Anti-Structure.* Chicago, 1969.

van Gennep, Arnold. *The Rites of Passage.* Chicago, 1960.

Vickery, Dorothy Scovil. *Hollins College, 1842–1942: An Historical Sketch.* Roanoke, Va., 1942.

Waage, Frederick G. "Alther and Dillard: The Appalachian Universe." *Appalachia/ America: Proceedings of the 1980 Appalachian Studies Conference.* Johnson City, Tenn., 1981.

Waddell, Joseph A. *History of Mary Baldwin Seminary from 1842 to 1905.* Staunton, Va., 1905.

Wagner-Martin, Linda. "'Just the Doing of It': Southern Women Writers and the Idea of Community." *Southern Literary Journal* 22:2 (1990): 19–32.

Walker, Nancy A. *A Very Serious Thing: Women's Humor and American Culture.* Minneapolis, 1988.

Watters, Mary. *The History of Mary Baldwin College, 1842–1942.* Staunton, Va., 1942.

Weber, Katherine. "PW Interviews Annie Dillard." *Publishers Weekly,* September 1, 1989, p. 67.

Welter, Barbara. "The Cult of True Womanhood: 1820–1860." *American Quarterly* 18 (1966): 151–74.

Welty, Eudora. "Meditation on Seeing." *New York Times Book Review,* March 24, 1974, pp. 4–5.

———. *One Writer's Beginnings.* Cambridge, Mass., 1984.

Wiggins, S. P. *Higher Education in the South.* Berkeley, 1966.

"Woman." *Album.* 1879. In Fishburn Archives, Hollins College.

Woodward, C. Vann. *Origins of the New South, 1877–1913.* Baton Rouge, 1951.

Woody, Thomas. *A History of Women's Education in the United States.* 2 vols. New York, 1929.

Wyatt-Brown, Bertram. *Southern Honor: Ethics and Behavior in the Old South.* New York, 1982.

INDEX